S0-CPS-112

INTEGRATION OF THE SOCIAL SCIENCES
THROUGH POLICY ANALYSIS

This monograph is the fourteenth in a series published by The American Academy of Political and Social Science. Monographs previously issued in this series are:

Monograph 1: October 1962	THE LIMITS OF BEHAVIORALISM IN POLITICAL SCIENCE
Monograph 2: June 1963	MATHEMATICS AND THE SOCIAL SCIENCES: THE UTILITY AND INUTILITY OF MATHEMATICS IN THE STUDY OF ECONOMICS, POLITICAL SCIENCE, AND SOCIOLOGY
Monograph 3: August 1963	ACHIEVING EXCELLENCE IN PUBLIC SERVICE
Monograph 4: April 1964	LEISURE IN AMERICA: BLESSING OR CURSE?
Monograph 5: February 1965	FUNCTIONALISM IN THE SOCIAL SCIENCES: THE STRENGTH AND LIMITS OF FUNCTIONALISM IN ANTHROPOLOGY, ECONOMICS, POLITICAL SCIENCE, AND SOCIOLOGY
Monograph 6: December 1966	A DESIGN FOR POLITICAL SCIENCE: SCOPE, OBJECTIVES, AND METHODS
Monograph 7: May 1967	GOVERNING URBAN SOCIETY: NEW SCIENTIFIC APPROACHES
Monograph 8: October 1968	THEORY AND PRACTICE OF PUBLIC ADMINISTRATION: SCOPE, OBJECTIVES, AND METHODS
Monograph 9: April 1969	A DESIGN FOR SOCIOLOGY: SCOPE, OBJECTIVES, AND METHODS
Monograph 10: October 1970	A DESIGN FOR INTERNATIONAL RELATIONS RESEARCH: SCOPE, THEORY, METHODS, AND RELEVANCE
Monograph 11: December 1970	HARMONIZING TECHNOLOGICAL DEVELOPMENTS AND SOCIAL POLICY IN AMERICA
Monograph 12: October 1971	INTERNATIONAL STUDIES: PRESENT STATUS AND FUTURE PROSPECTS
Monograph 13: March 1972	INSTRUCTION IN DIPLOMACY: THE LIBERAL ARTS APPROACH

INTEGRATION OF THE SOCIAL SCIENCES THROUGH POLICY ANALYSIS

Monograph 14 in a series sponsored by
The American Academy of Political and Social Science

Editor: James C. Charlesworth

© 1972, by
THE AMERICAN ACADEMY OF POLITICAL AND SOCIAL SCIENCE
All rights reserved
Library of Congress Catalog Card Number 72-87188

PHILADELPHIA
October 1972

Issued by The American Academy of Political and Social Science at Prince and Lemon Sts., Lancaster, Pennsylvania.

Editorial and Business Offices, 3937 Chestnut Street, Philadelphia, Pennsylvania 19104.

H
61
.I57

CONTENTS

198759

PREFATORY NOTE ON CONSULTANTS

This monograph grew out of informal conversations with several of my colleagues at the University of Pennsylvania:

Richard D. Lambert, at that time Professor of Sociology, Chairman of South Asia Regional Studies, Editor of *The Annals*, and later also the President of the Academy,
Alan W. Heston, Associate Professor of South Asia Economics and the International Comparison Project, also Assistant Editor of *The Annals*,
Henry J. Teune, Professor of Political Science,
Karl von Vorys, Associate Professor of Political Science,
William M. Evan, Professor of Sociology and Industry, and
Ralph B. Ginsberg, Assistant Professor of Sociology.

In addition, there was a limited correspondence with Harold D. Lasswell, Albert Lepawsky, Yeheskel Dror, Richard A. Easterlin, and Lee Benson. These contacts were very valuable, but this listing does not indicate that any of these persons is to be held responsible for the scope and objectives of the conference and monograph.
The conference was held in Philadelphia, June 16 and 17, 1971. All of those listed as contributors were present except Professors Coleman and Easton, who were detained on imperative business in Europe.

JAMES C. CHARLESWORTH

H
61
.I57

FOREWORD

It has been said that Leibniz (1646–1716) was the last man to attempt to assemble in one mind the entire body of Western knowledge. Since his time, the academic and scientific disciplines have become more and more highly fissiparated and fragmented, which can be defended in the case of the "hard" sciences on the ground that greater expertise comes with greater specialization.

Most of us will doubtless agree that the hard sciences are more readily separable than the social, or "soft," sciences. All of the social sciences deal with the behavior of man, and the behavior of man is essentially a unified concept. A strong argument can be made, for example, to support the statement that "political economy" was more meaningful than the separate fields of "political science" and "economics."

A trend toward reunification, or at least reconciliation, of the social sciences can be observed in the recent creation of a number of professorships which bridge two or more disciplines, as sociology and politics, or social psychology and sociology, or international relations and area studies. The professors of economics have made the least noticeable response to this trend, being still heavily involved in mathematics.

If one considers that it is desirable to explore the possibility of integrating the social sciences, there are a number of ways to attempt it. One way is to create a basic model of man, amenable to analysis according to the predilections of all kinds of social scientists. Thus, instead of examining the nature of the old-fashioned "economic man," we can hypothesize a single "man," who makes observable responses to all the questions put by all types of social scientists.

Another approach is to study the impingement areas among the social sciences to see if at their various points of contact they exhibit a common set of principles.

Yet another is to select a single, presently well-developed discipline, like mathematics, and use it to analyze and enrich all of the social sciences. According to this method, all of the social sciences will be mutually translatable if they are pushed through a common process. Mathematics need not be the only matrix. Metaphysics, once it is released from the bonds of tradition and classicism, could serve as well.

Still another method is to study the history of each discipline to see how and why it broke off from the mother body of philosophy and whether a return is feasible or desirable.

And still another approach is to apply the methodology of behaviorism to the various disciplines to see if man's motivations and responses are essentially the same in the different parts of his life.

Finally, we may use each discipline to analyze public policy—that is, policy which affects the public, whether it is governmental or not. Why have we selected policy analysis as the key to this particular monograph and passed over the others identified above? Let us give some reasons, substantive and procedural, for rejecting the others, and let the rest of this volume elucidate the reasons for selecting policy analysis.

Many efforts have been made to create models of man, but they have all fallen short in the area of specificity and concreteness. There is no reason to believe that another effort in that direction will be any more successful.

As to impingement areas, who is to say where one discipline impinges on another? Where, for example, is the interior of political science, and where is its periphery? If all parts of each discipline are pertinent to some parts of man's activity, then the total activity is a behavioral unity, and there are no subdivisions and boundaries.

With respect to mathematics, it must be stressed that mathematics is not a substantive discipline but a way of expressing something which is adduced in other ways. Also, as a practical matter, it should be noted that this Academy previously published a monograph on *Mathematics and the Social Sciences.*

Metaphysics would be more fruitful than mathematics as a pervasive methodology, but presently there is not enough skill available to exploit this method successfully. And, just as there is insufficient skill in elucidating this approach, there is insuffi-

cient interest and competence in examining what would be eluci-
dated.

As to the history of the several disciplines, it may be said
that historians and other backward-lookers rarely become activ-
ists. What we should be interested in here is where the social
science disciplines—or a consolidated social science discipline—
are going, and not where they have been.

Behaviorism has different meanings for practitioners in different disciplines, and, indeed, as a recent monograph published
by this Academy demonstrates, it does not have an exchangeable
meaning to members of the same disciplines—in this case, political science. An instrument of Protean shapes cannot be used to
reconcile or integrate.

Nor can we integrate the social sciences through the training
of Ph.D.'s or the reshaping of undergraduate curricula. This is
a procedural, not a substantive, approach; it begs the question.
What are the methods and objectives of this synoptic training?
The methods and objectives are what we are seeking.

And now, it seems to me, this recital leaves us with policy
analysis as the most likely approach.

JAMES C. CHARLESWORTH

Integration of Economics and the Other Social Sciences through Policy Analysis

By Charles E. Lindblom

FOR FIVE reasons, I doubt the wisdom of giving policy analysis the assignment of integrating the social sciences, although the last of the five reasons is simultaneously an argument for giving it a distinctive integrating role for a certain kind of study now part of the social sciences.

The Conservative and Superficial Bias of Policy Analysis

Consider some representative policy questions. When an economist studies policies to reduce unemployment, he takes as given an institutional structure which can itself be questioned. When he asks how to improve social security and welfare programs, he takes as given a wages system. When he asks how to facilitate international trade, he takes for granted the existence of a multiplicity of sovereign nations. When he asks how to curb pollution, he takes—in the United States or western Europe—private enterprise as a given. He is correct to take the main structures of society as given. Otherwise his analysis would be irrelevant to the circumstances in which policies are actually made.

The consequence, however, is that as a policy analyst he has to practice a conservative and superficial kind of social science. It is conservative because it does not ask radical questions about fundamental features of the social structure. (Whatever answers a less conservative kind of social science might reach, at least it would ask radical questions.) It is superficial not because it is badly done, for in fact it may be assiduously pursued with first-rate intellectual sophistication, but because it considers only those ways of dealing with policy that are close cousins to existing practices. In this context, I do not make much of

1

the distinction between conservatism and superficiality. Both terms refer to one and the same set of characteristics of policy analysis, but where conservatism emphasizes the political direction of policy analysis, superficiality emphasizes its intellectual direction.

The radical and fundamental kind of analysis from which policy analysis diverts the social sciences is, for example, Plato's question: "What is justice?" Plato's pursuit of that question in *The Republic* leads him into an examination of the fundamentals of social organization, even if his way of posing his question, on one hand, and the authoritarian implications of his analysis, on the other, lead some men to attack him both as superficial and conservative. *The Republic* is a monument to the kind of analysis that advanced by calling into question, step by step, increasingly fundamental aspects of society.

Another example is Hobbes's question: "How can social order be maintained?" Compare it with the Kerner Commission Report, not in pure intellectual distinction, for that would be unfair, but in method. Or compare it with any contemporary analysis addressed to maintaining order on the campus, in the city, or in the ghetto. Hobbes takes as little as he can as given. He keeps pushing back, back, and back to fundamental questions about social organization and human behavior. His answers to his own radical questions were themselves sufficiently radical to give to the world a continuing intellectual tradition that persists, for example, in contemporary political science and that far overshadows the conservative implications of his defense of monarchy.

Adam Smith is another excellent example—there are very few from economics—of fundamental and radical analysis. If, as may have been the case, he began his investigation of economics as an attempt to deal with a practical policy question, specifically, mercantilist constraints on trade, he quickly threw off the conservative and superficial constraints of ordinary policy analysis and went after bigger game. The title of his work describes an intellectual ambition that runs far beyond policy analysis: *An Inquiry Into The Nature and Causes of the Wealth of Nations*.

The discipline of economics is the most successful policy science of all the social sciences, with the possible exception of psychology, and at the same time the most conservative and superficial. Since Smith and then the marginalists, one does not often find in economics scholars who pursue radical and fundamental questions to compare with those who do so in other social sciences: for example, Weber, Durkheim, Parsons, Homans, and Merton in sociology; MacIver, Friedrich, Key, Lasswell, Almond, and Dahl in political science; or Radcliffe-Brown, Malinowski, Linton, and Kluckhohn in anthropology. These lists no more than sample the variety of scholars in the social sciences who, quite aside from the great political philosophers of the past, can qualify as asking fundamental and radical questions.

To be sure, the same kind of work is not wholly absent from economics. It is, for example, represented by a stream of work on preference aggregation that has its source in Kenneth Arrow's *Social Choice and Individual Values*. For the most part, however, the most fertile minds in economics have been meticulously and skillfully engaged in refining—that is, making more precise—earlier, rougher insights into processes in the market system for allocating resources, distributing income, improving productive capacity, and regulating the volume of production and employment. It is excellent work, not to be deprecated. But while it pays off handsomely in policy applications, for which it has largely come to be designed, it offers little new fundamental insight into economic or social organization. One evidence of this is that while in the twentieth century the brightest, best educated, and most thoughtful minds are finding exciting new discoveries about the natural world, man, and society in physics, biochemistry, biology, anthropology, psychology, sociology, and political science there has emerged from economics almost nothing to engage these minds. Who reads economics for a new view of the world?

Am I forgetting Keynes? His theoretical innovations took the form of conceptual improvements and a theoretical reconstruction, both of which substantially increased the skill with which economists approached policy analysis. But they did not provide any great new insights into man or social organization. The greatest significance of Keynes is that he provided a set of concepts and a theoretical model that were operational in the specific sense that policy-makers could manipulate the variables of his model. For the first time, man had a set of concepts and a theoretical model that could immediately and directly guide policy. Keynesian analysis, taken together with national income accounting, made possible a kind of rational or scientific policy-making new to the world.

The impressive accomplishments of economics in tool-making, theory-building, and in policy analysis are now recognized in the three Nobel prizes that have been awarded to economists. To none of these distinguished economists do we owe much for new answers or hypotheses on fundamental or radical questions about man and society. To each of them we owe an enormous debt in analytical tools and skill in policy analysis and refinements of earlier findings.

I do not wish to criticize economics for its relative inattention to fundamental or radical questions. As a discipline, it developed from strength to strength, that is, along lines that promised fruitful results. It became, therefore, a discipline marked less by its attention to fundamental and radical questions than by its analytical rigor, its inventiveness in methods of analysis, and its skill in handling the narrow range of questions for which its tools and skills gave it a marked advantage. The kinds of questions about economic life that can be called fundamental or radical lie, for the most part, outside the recognized boundaries of the discipline, given its intellectual traditions.

I am not even suggesting that people who call themselves economists should undertake the analysis of these questions. My only point is that a policy orientation for social science as a whole would preclude anyone's picking them up. Someone ought to be asking such questions as what the effect of life in a milieu of exchange relationships is on personality and culture; how defects in popular control (through the market system) over corporate leadership compare with those of popular control (through political processes) over political leadership; what necessary connections there are—logically and empirically, existing and possible—between market systems and governmental systems; whether a Cuban-style moral incentives system can be reconciled with a market system; and whether the economists' traditional identification of market relationships with voluntary or free relationships is, in fact, valid in societies in which necessity compels people to enter into market relationships. There is a weak tradition in economics that accounts for occasional speculative writing on such topics as these, but neither in economics nor in any other social science are they systematically studied. Nor would a policy orientation for social science improve the prospects.

Under some circumstances, of course, policy analysis drives toward fundamental and radical questions. For example, the policy question of whether a developing country should or should not use import controls, industrial licensing, and other administrative substitutes for market forces does push economics toward a more fundamental clarification of the differences between market systems and administrative systems.

A more striking example is the field of psychology where "policy" analysis in the form of practice of individual therapy is a major avenue to fundamental discoveries about the human psyche. Why does the study of "therapy" in public affairs not work the same way? Because, it seems, psychiatric therapy can consider, even experiment with, alternatives entirely unlike those open in public policy-making. In therapy, individuals can be asked to make, or at least experiment with, fundamental changes in behavior. They can also be subjected to traumas, as in shock therapy. In short, therapy strikes at fundamentals in ways not permitted to policy-makers because of the rigidities of the social order, the limited manipulative ability of the policy-maker, and the fragility of the social order. For the society, consequently, even if not for the individual in therapy, the inverse relationship between policy analysis, on one hand, and fundamental or radical analysis, on the other, seems to hold.

In my own work on incremental analysis, I have wanted from time to time to defend it from the charge that it is a conservative form of policy analysis. Incremental analysis is no more conservative than any other form of policy analysis. There is no contradiction between that position and the one I am taking here. Here I am saying that all policy analysis tends to be conservative—and not in the trivial sense that it is more Tory than Liberal, more Republican than Democratic, but in a sense that it does not ask radical and fundamental questions which are troublesome and irrelevant to policy analysis, however important they may be to man's understanding of himself and his world.

MODES OF INTEGRATION ALTERNATIVE TO A
POLICY ORIENTATION

Since about the end of World War II, the social sciences have been integrating in a number of fertile ways. The number and richness of these integrations suggest, first, that integration is now proceeding more successfully than it did for many decades; secondly, that the route to integration through policy analysis is only one of a fairly large number of possible alternatives; and, thirdly, that some of the other methods of integration look superior to integration through policy analysis.

Some of the points, areas, or methods of integration are:

Decision theory

Economists have brought to the analysis of decision-making their experience in the study of rational choice. They have been joined by mathematicians and statisticians in applying probability theory and game theory to cope with problems of risk and uncertainty in rational choice. Psychologists have converged on the field with their studies of perception, cognition, and problem-solving. Anthropologists and sociologists have added the study of decision-making in observed small groups in the laboratory, and students of public administration and political science have incorporated into decision-making studies the analysis of decision-making in administrative organizations and in more complex political structures. This summary hardly does justice to all the contributors to the study of decision-making, philosophers as well as social scientists, but it suggests how thoroughgoing an integration of the social sciences has been achieved around one fundamental phenomenon.

Organization theory

A related and overlapping point of convergence is organizational theory, which has drawn on all the literature of decision-making but has added to it a convergence of anthropological, sociological, social psychological, administrative, and political studies of formal organizations including, from economics, the study of the business enterprise.

Collective choice

Within these common areas, there has been a specialized theoretical cultivation of the phenomena of collective as against individual choice. It owes much to Arrow's work on social choice; some to a critique, traditional in economics, of defects in market choice; and some to a growing interest among political scientists in the peculiar characteristics of voting as a method of making collective choices.

Exchange theory

The success of economists in explaining a great deal about social organization by reference to acts of exchange among individuals has led both economists and other social scientists to try to explain aspects of society beyond those usually embraced in economics. The earlier work of John R. Commons is now largely forgotten; but Homans and Blau have attempted general explanations of this kind, and the attempt to explain political phenomena by reference to exchange relationships is now attractive to some political scientists including, for example, Curry and Wade in their *Exchange Theory of Politics*. Homans' work, I would guess, owes something to earlier anthropological work on reciprocal and exchange relationships among primitive people. In any case, every social science is represented in this area or focus of integration.

Structural-functional analysis

In postulating economic functions to be performed, like resource allocation and income distribution, and then examining the market system as a structure for discharging the functions, economists have always practiced an unsophisticated kind of structural-functional analysis. But the more explicit theorists and practitioners of structural-functionalism have been anthropologists, like Malinowski and Radcliffe-Brown; sociologists, like Parsons and many of his followers; and political scientists, like Gabriel Almond. Many more names could be added, of course, and one could also incorporate philosophers like Hempel, who has written a now classic critique of the method.

Talcott Parsons

The work of Parsons has itself been a kind of integration of social science in which many followers have joined him; some, like Levy and Smelser, following the Parsons integrations very closely and others, like Almond or Holt and Turner (*The Political Aspects of Economic Development*), less closely.

Political culture and political socialization

Some political scientists, like Almond and the authors of the Social Science Research Council's series on development, have turned much of the study of political phenomena away from legal forms to aspects of human behavior on which the political scientists acknowledge a heavy indebtedness to sociology. Others, like Lasswell and Lane, have brought psychology and psychoanalysis to bear on political culture and behavior; and sometimes the mining of psychology by political science is very specific, as in Greenstein's work on political socialization of children.

Political development

Taken as a whole, the field of political development is a point of considerable integration in the social sciences, drawing as it does on materials in the study of economic development. Both political scientists and economists are busy these days trying to understand, for example, the relationship between government and market in modernization. The study of political development, however, also draws on the integrations of social science achieved above in the study of political culture and socialization.

Economic development

Similarly, the study of economic development in the hands of economists has drawn on political studies of the role of government and administration in developmental tasks. In a few conspicuous cases it has also drawn on psychology, as in Hagen's *Theory of Social Change,* which builds on McClelland's psychological studies of motivation.

It becomes tedious to list all the important integrations that are now occurring in the social sciences. Some lesser but still significant ones spring quickly to mind: role theory, studies of the prerequisites of democracy, attempts to analyze and make power measureable, and studies of authority. In each of these cases, every social science is represented with the possible exception of economics. Not to be forgotten are attempts to anticipate or plan a social science built around cybernetics or communications.

The older tradition of attempting a major integration in order to answer a single fundamental question also ought not to be forgotten, even if it has, perhaps, gone out of style. Plato's "What is justice?" took him through psychology, political science, economics, sociology, and anthropology. So also did Hobbes's "How to maintain social order" or Rousseau's attempt to explain why "man was born free, but is everywhere in bondage."

It seems quite clear that successful integration is a monopoly of no particular mode of integration. In the examples listed, we find cases of integration through common analytical tools, as is true for much of decision theory, in which scholars of various disciplines try to work out the logic of choice under conditions of risk and uncertainty. We also see integration organized around the study of a root phenomenon, as in studies of authority or exchange, or around concepts, where it is not even clear that a common phenomenon is at issue, as in the example of the study of power. Sometimes integration is explicitly itself a major objective, as in the work of Parsons, and sometimes it grows out of a diversified interest in explaining various aspects of very complex empirical trends or developments like modernization. Only some of it develops around policy questions, as has conspicuously been the case for some integration in the study of economic development. Finally, there are some of the greatest integrations, which have been the product of a fruitful question, such as those of the political philosophers.

INTEGRATION THROUGH GRADUATE ACADEMIC TRAINING

To the extent that the various modes of integration now being practiced are inadequate so that we might consequently seek a way to give an additional impetus to integration, there is no apparent reason for choosing policy analysis over the other methods; and, in fact, one can think of at least one alternative method that might well be superior to policy analysis if one is looking for a feasible, practical program.   It is simply to alter the character of the Ph.D. program in the social sciences.

Using training in economics as an example, while it is true that many graduate economics students are content to cultivate economics to the exclusion of other social sciences, a significant and perhaps growing number of others find that such convergences as have just been listed greatly attract them.   There is today, among graduate students in economics and the other social sciences, a powerful incentive toward integration as well as enough examples of successful integration to leave them untroubled as to its feasibility.

But graduate training throws obstacles in their paths.   By the testimony of a number of graduate students, it seems clear that many Ph.D. programs compel a student to pursue a finely honed, technical competence in formal economic theory at the expense of fruitful ventures into neighboring disciplines.   To be sure, some graduate departments have moved a great deal toward incorporating training in related social sciences, but in this respect I believe that economic departments are well behind departments of political science, psychology, sociology, and anthropology.   For many graduate students in economics, whatever training they obtain around existing integrations comes, as in the example of decision theory, from instruction by faculty in their own departments much more than from courses permitted them in other departments.

Some decades ago one would have hesitated to propose changes in the structure of graduate education to achieve integration, for graduate instruction was then more informally organized than it is now.   One could be reasonably confident that a sufficiently enterprising student would find his way to whatever faculty he needed.   But graduate education has had to accommodate larger numbers and has, for this and other reasons, become bureaucratized.   Its requirements and its options have come to be somewhat more rigidly defined than earlier.   At Yale, for example, as at many other universities, the last decade has seen a growing pressure for completing course work in two years and the dissertation in two more.   In Yale's case, pressure was stimulated by a desire to economize on the new large funds invested in graduate fellowships.   That source of pressure is symptomatic of the kind of force that has routinized graduate education.

In short, a sufficient number of young scholars want to do integrative work. There is no dearth of fruitful modes. To accelerate integration, then, one ought simply to break the bottleneck of graduate education. It is not necessary, if this argument is correct, to be much concerned about which of the various modes of integration is the most fruitful.

ARCHITECTONIC INTEGRATION?

One might argue that the kinds of integration now to be found in the social sciences are, with an occasional exception, too fragmentary or incomplete. One might hope for some method of integration, like policy analysis, that would bring together *all* of social science.

The objection to such an argument is that an architectonic integration of social science, an all-embracing structure of social science knowledge, is a premature aspiration. Premature at least, and possibly forever impossible of achievement. The social sciences are still in a state—they may forever be—in which the disciplines taken together do not embrace the whole of the social world and in which each one taken singly by no means encompasses, in the range of its accomplishments, all that is by intellectual tradition assigned to it.

Take economics again as an example. Its highly skilled preoccupation with resource allocation in the market system leaves economics still underdeveloped on the economics of nonmarket economies. More than that, it has left unattended such questions as some of those mentioned above, like the question concerning the effect of life in a market milieu on personality and culture. To be sure, that illustrative question happens to be one that calls for some integration of social science. But a particular integration is required to answer it. It will be a long time before work on that and other questions now neglected can be seen as part of an architectonic whole.

But perhaps, one might reply, the way to complete the unfinished work of each of the disciplines is to map the whole of social science, divide up assignments, and encourage each scholar to work at his own specialized assignment in the cooperative construction of a great structure. If this were to have the effect of turning scholars away from such effective foci of integration as they have already found, it might turn them from fruitful work into jejune system-building. Aside from that, it is to be doubted that social science yet has captured enough pieces of a grand structure to infer from them what the design of the grand structure should look like. There have been impressive intellectual achievements in architectonic integration—much of Lasswell's work in the last two decades, for example, or Kuhn's *Study of Society*. But they remain, so far, more idiosyncratic than syncretic.

On several specific counts, social science seems a long way from an achitectonic integration. First, most of the social sciences—including those closest to public policy—have so far produced few nomothetic propositions. Instead their propositions are true or valid only for particular times, particular places, particular cultures, particular nations. Even the maxims of rational choice in economics that give rise to such propositions as that entrepreneurs maximize profits assume certain culture patterns, specifically certain choice patterns between money, on one hand, and leisure and other kinds of satisfaction, on the other. Empirical propositions about corporate behavior are very much the product of observation of twentieth-century institutional development. The same is true for propositions on unions and wage determination, and so on.

In political science, to take another example, what the discipline has to tell us about the behavior of parties, interest groups, or even about voting, which is the most splendidly cultivated area of empirical research in political science, gives us propositions that are true for only limited domains.

Secondly, social science faces a problem that, for the most part, does not plague natural scientists. Societies learn. They change their ways. A society's experience with forms of economic behavior and economic organization teaches it to change those forms, as also for parties, interest groups, and other political institutions. So far, social science has done very little more than to try to analyze systematically a contemporary cross-section picture of behavior rather than the learning process itself. An architectonic social science is an impossibility until social science turns to the learning process and develops the capacity to say something about sequences of social behavior and institutional organization, in addition to describing correctly a series of cross-sections.

Obviously social science has not even begun such a task, except for an occasional Marx whose very ambitions on this score tend to disqualify him as a social *scientist* in the eyes of less ambitious scholars. It is, of course, possible that what I call social learning is a dynamic process that will always—forever and inevitably—leave emerging patterns of behavior beyond the competence of an always-lagging social science. In that case, the architectonic social science will always elude us.

Finally, it is certainly of some significance to our plans for integration that the physical and biological sciences, which are much less ambitious in scope than the social sciences and which are not plagued by a counterpart process to social learning, are themselves not integrated, despite their greater degree of maturity or comprehensiveness when compared to the social sciences.

The Need for Policy Analysis

But if policy analysis is not the way to integrate social science, perhaps it is a way of integrating pieces of social science and other studies which, though useful for the guidance of policy, may fall short of what we call social *scientific*.

Presumably, enormously larger informational and analytical input into policy-making would be desirable. I do not propose an unlimited new input, since at some point the cost of the input is worth more than the benefits produced. Still, a much larger input would seem almost certainly to promise benefits. Much of the required new input, however, takes the form of information on particular configurations of events and the analysis of relationships there displayed. It is not the kind of information collection and analysis that contributes greatly to a cumulating body of knowledge, even though there is, of course, a good deal of spillover from policy analysis to a cumulating body of knowledge. For example, to develop better policy on irrigation in India, which is a good example of a major policy problem, the policy-maker needs to know a great deal more than he does about the state of the arts in the practice of irrigation by Indian peasants. He also needs to know more than he does about the way in which present seed strains respond to water and how seed strains to be developed in the foreseeable future will respond to water. He also needs to know—I am choosing only a few examples—about the costs of different irrigation technologies. It is information that will quickly become obsolete and which has only limited fruitfulness for cumulating science.

It looks as though we do, indeed, need an enriched policy analysis and one that is integrated in that it does not much respect disciplinary boundaries. But it ought not to be confused with social science. Should it not bear something of the same relationship to the social sciences that medicine bears to the natural and biological sciences? And should we not systematically train people in it as former President Harry Rowan of The Rand Corporation proposed to do at Rand? Should we not dignify an integrated, analytically sophisticated, continuing, professionalized study of policy with some such status as the study of medicine enjoys?

If factoring out of contemporary social science a recognized integrated profession of social "medicine" or social "engineering" might greatly improve society's skill in policy-making, a subsidiary advantage might be a great improvement in social *science* itself. For it would make clear, as it is now not clear, that there is a difference between social science and the highly professional study of policy problems. It would give social scientists, or young men who want to be social scientists, a clear conscience about what their scholarly responsibilities might best be. It might turn the social sciences toward more ambitious attempts at nomothetic propositions. In the case of economics, it might arrest what seems to be an increasingly rapid flight of that discipline from the pursuit of significant scientific aspiration. For, thanks to its elegance, its tools, and its analytic inventiveness, economics has itself become the core of policy analysis—a point of integration in the analysis of policy. Recognizing this accomplishment and giving it an institutional status might free other economists to pursue the relatively neglected *science* of economics, which remains a worthy aspiration, now too timidly pursued.

Commentary on Lindblom's Paper

BY THOMAS C. SCHELLING

I AGREE with most of Lindblom's answer, but remain puzzled about what the question is, or what the questions are.

One question is whether policy analysis, or anything else, will ever articulate the several social sciences as a coherent discipline of "social behavior." Will the basic patterns of behavior cut across the several disciplines as they are now arbitrarily defined? Will people stop specializing in economics, social psychology, political science, or anthropology? Lindblom says that would be a premature aspiration. But I don't see why we should aspire to it.

The disciplines may be differently defined a couple of generations from now; there may occur some fusions and some schisms and even some new disciplines. But I don't see why a synthesis would be in the interest of science, or of the people who practice it, or of policy analysis. Policy analysis has surely done little or nothing in that direction where it has already been most widely practiced—for the most part, in the federal government—nor in the other place where it has been much practiced—in the universities. I do not believe that a new set of schools or departments or journals or organizations or curricula will have disproportionate influence.

Another question is whether particular social scientists will master several different disciplines and do work that draws necessarily on several of the social sciences, synthesizing the social sciences in their own work, perhaps stimulating others to follow the example, but without performing the intellectual feat of unifying once and for all the several disciplines. The answer must be yes. Some have done it. The teaching of policy analysis in schools and departments set up for the purpose may encourage more of it. A lot will depend on what kinds of people get drawn into policy analysis and what kinds of students get drawn in. I doubt whether a great social scientist is going to be spoiled, along the lines of superficiality described by Lindblom, just because he

15

spends part or all of his teaching time on something called "policy analysis" or designing new curricula within his own discipline for that purpose. I should expect a mild and salutary influence to the contrary. It remains to be seen whether creative young people are more constricted in policy-analysis curricula than they used to be in the separate social sciences, or instead find greater freedom with no reduction in rigor. A lot depends on things like office arrangements, lunch dates, journal subscriptions, and book borrowing. If a policy-analysis program brings people fruitfully together who might otherwise not have known each other, some integration may occur. But whether that qualifies under the title of this symposium, I don't know.

A third question is whether new fields of inquiry will develop that appear to be within the social sciences but not belonging to any social science in particular. Lindblom's list of nine "points, areas, or methods of integration" includes at least two or three that I would call nondisciplinary, although some of them occasionally bid to become disciplines. "Collective choice," for example, or "decision theory" seem to me of this sort. I know of no reason why these studies would do any integrating except with respect to collective choice or decision theory. In fact, it does not really seem to me that they integrate anything; rather, they abstract from the content of a particular discipline and may be relevant to two or more disciplines. I find it interesting, though objectionable, that game theory is often described, even by social scientists, as a branch of mathematics, not as a highly mathematical branch of the social sciences. Somebody could as well refer to Arrow's work and other work in collective choice as a branch of mathematics; doing so would imply that it is nondisciplinary rather than multidisciplinary. The only integration is the discovery that several of the social sciences are customers in common for a particular line of inquiry.

Still another question is whether a burning interest in policy, and efforts by social scientists to analyze policy systematically, can powerfully stimulate the development of the social sciences along the lines that Lindblom favors, namely, profundity, generalization, and reduced disciplinary parochialism. I think the answer is yes, and I take my evidence from Lindblom, who put economic development at the end of his list of "points, areas, or methods of integration." What has distinguished the study of economic development, at least within economics, has been its comprehensive policy orientation during the past two decades. Most economists everywhere are oriented toward policy, but most economists everywhere want to do the part of policy that is economics. They assume or pretend that the noneconomic parts will be taken care of by somebody else, and their incremental suggestions are usually intended to be independent of noneconomic considerations. But when Everett Hagen (cited by Lindblom) went to work on development policy in Burma, either he didn't trust the anthropologists or there weren't any working on institutional change in Burma. And there was no audience for a purely economic study of Burmese development that its own author could not draw policy conclusions from. So Hagen had to look at family, village, religion, and the things we call the culture of the country and had to think about political, legal, and social aspects of economic change. The study of poverty in the last few years and the study of the economic status of the disadvantaged are requiring many economists to stop doing the neatly economic work that they were trained for and that they enjoy and to start studying, on their own responsibility, a larger phenomenon. Whether they bother to learn another discipline or merely somewhat abandon their own, I'm not sure. They may yet stimulate some multidisciplinary science. Some of them may yet become multidisciplinary scientists themselves. My *ad hominem* impression is that Lindblom himself became multidisciplinary by studying the policy process and that James Coleman became multidisciplinary by studying policy, but I may be jumping to unwarranted conclusions.

Let me come now to the question that I originally thought we were addressing. Can we, for purposes of policy analysis, integrate in a person's training, or in a curriculum, or in an institute or a department, enough social science that is pertinent to policy analysis to make this limited and focused effort at integration worthwhile? I realize, rereading the preposition "through" in the title of this symposium, that the question was not whether policy analysis could become an integrated bit of social science, but whether it would provide a fulcrum or a "leading salient" or an excuse for some grander integration of all the social sciences, this grander integration being desired for its own sake and not to facilitate policy analysis. Since I am presently quite busy with a group of people in a program entitled "Public Policy," I am interested even in this smaller question. I do not yet know the answer.

I am not even sure whether this integration is something that occurs in the mind of a student years after he gets his training, or in the mind of the student while he is studying, or in the curriculum of his school, or in the minds of the faculty that teaches him, or in the organization of the faculty. It may even be that only people with a high propensity toward integration will get drawn into the business; and while it might then look as though policy analysis causes people to synthesize and to organize and to integrate, the truth may be that the people who would have done it anyway do it in programs labeled policy analysis.

All of this is only indirectly a comment on Lindblom's paper, a paper with which I am in substantial agreement. We differ on particulars, but I do attach high value to successful multidisciplinary efforts and to nondisciplinary lines of development. Where we may differ is in our belief that somehow the social sciences constitute a proper domain for integration.

First, can one really expect great works in the social sciences and the men who produce them to be multidisciplinary and eventually to unify theory and method in several disciplines? Second, if so, is it likely to be the social sciences that become thus integrated? This may be as much a question of fruitfulness as of logical compatibility. Economists can learn a lot about the economy by studying engineering, not because the economy is full of engineering, but because physical systems provide analogies and illustrations of phenomena that are easier to perceive once one has worked with a physical model. I believe many sociologists and political scientists, even economists, could learn much by studying animal systems, especially ecological systems; again, it may just be that basic principles are easier to recognize in an unfamiliar field because an unfamiliar field precludes indulgence of one's preconceptions in the familiar and habitual way. I should not like to see psychology mistakenly elect to join economics if it meant abandoning physiology; it is not out of the question that mathematicians and biologists could learn a lot by integrating occasionally with economics or sociology or political science. (Game theory may have done more for mathematics than for the social sciences, at least during its first decade or so.)

This is only partly a matter of the underlying structure of the sciences. Science is made by people, and is largely dependent upon whether the methods and the contents of the different social sciences are temperamentally compatible within most people. It has to do with the problems and puzzles that intrigue a person, where he gets his ideas, how he takes his recreation, where the competition and criticism will be most constructive, and even what makes a man's science a source of fun.

I should guess that policy analysis is about as good as any other method for rubbing social scientists together to see whether any benefit comes of it. It may equally rub together political scientists and engineers, or sociologists and meteorologists, or economists and biologists. I expect just as much good to come from these liaisons outside the social sciences—good in the Lindblom, scientific sense as well as in the policy sense.

Commentary on Lindblom's Paper

By Duncan MacRae, Jr.

BECAUSE I agree with so much of Lindblom's paper, I wish to use some of these agreements as a basis for extending his argument.

When Lindblom points out the possible conservatism and superficiality of policy analysis, he mentions Plato and Hobbes in contrast. In effect he is saying that a concern with fundamental questions of the ordering of societies, rather than simply with minor policy questions within a given order, might furnish a better basis of connection among various sciences. This basis can be found by extending our concern from policy to these broader questions, whether they be considered questions of public choice; of authorities, regime, and political community; [1] or simply of ethics in its philosophical sense. There is, indeed, a framework within which particular policies are made. But in considering policy analysis, we have taken a first important step away from the purely factual notion of "social science" patterned after a particular image of natural science. Further steps can be taken in the same direction, and Plato, Hobbes, and other such thinkers can serve as guides. But economics can play an important part as well.

Lindblom also correctly points out that there are multiple modes of integration of the social sciences, some of which do not derive from policy or valuative considerations. These can evolve around empirical findings, like interdisciplinary combinations in the natural sciences. Perhaps all we need to do to encourage this sort of integration is to recognize cross-disciplinary contributions when they are made, rather than viewing them through the sometimes myopic perspective of particular disciplines.

But more important for our present topic are the multiple modes of interdisciplinary combination that center about policy

1. David Easton, *A Systems Analysis of Political Life* (New York: Wiley, 1965), chaps. 11–13.

or valuative questions.   These combinations are by no means restricted to the social sciences; problems of public health, atmo-
spheric pollution, and nuclear strategy are examples of urgent
policy questions that require combined contributions from natural and social science.   These problems, if profoundly explored
and not limited to the particular requests of existing authorities,
might also lead to reconsideration of questions concerning regimes
or human needs.

These possible combinations illustrate one of Lindblom's final
points—that particular integrations or combinations of sciences
are called forth by particular valuative problems.   In this perspective, the integration of the social sciences is no longer an end
to be attained through consideration of policy or valuative problems; rather, policy, values, and ethics define prior ends to which
particular combinations of scientific and other knowledge are
means.

We may be led, therefore, to reverse the sequence of topics in
the title of our symposium and to reformulate it as "Policy (or
valuative) Analysis through Integration of the Social Sciences."
In this formulation we would interchange means and end, and
depart from the prevalent view that science is somehow superior
to valuation as a subject of discourse.   The rest of my comments
will center about those elements of Lindblom's paper that suggest how this might be done.

Lindblom notes that economics—like most other social sciences [2]—contains a weak tradition that includes speculative writing on major valuative problems.   In addition, it contains a
stream of work on preference aggregation that has its source in
Kenneth Arrow's *Social Choice and Individual Values*.   And at
the end of his paper he suggests that economics has itself become
a point of integration in the analysis of policy, thanks to its elegance, its tools, and its analytic inventiveness.   A careful consideration of these aspects of economics can aid us in combining
the social science disciplines for consideration of valuative problems ranging from particular policy choices to the more fundamental questions that Lindblom mentions.

2. See Duncan MacRae, Jr., "Scientific Communication, Ethical Argument, and Public Policy," *American Political Science Review*, vol. 65, no. 1
(March, 1971), pp. 38–50.

In recent decades, the social sciences have emulated natural science, and economics has perhaps been the most successful among them.   Institutional economics has been replaced by powerful mathematical techniques; the apparently unwarranted assumptions of welfare economics in the time of Pigou have been replaced by the careful and weak inference of the "new" welfare economics, which includes Arrow's work.   Sociology has moved from concern with particular social problems to general theory and away from valuative concerns.[3]   Political science has become more behavioral, even though the tradition of political philosophy remains.   Many psychologists seem concerned as persons with modern society and international relations, although their central disciplinary literature does not reflect this concern.

Thus every social science discipline, like economics, has a weak and secondary current of concern with valuative problems. In books more than articles, in auxiliary fringe associations rather than the central and official periodicals, it persists.   New recruits to the social sciences are taught to work on problems of disciplinary significance and to discipline their valuative or reformist impulses.   To some extent this restriction of scope must be required in the disciplines of a university, but in another sense we may be carrying it farther than necessary.

The valuative discourse conducted on the fringes of each discipline is seen, as it were, in the periphery of our field of vision. We thus regard it less rationally and less critically than our central, factual discourse.   We manage to incorporate it because the same terms carry factual and valuative meanings.   We can thus verify propositions about human behavior, but still feel that we are studying problems that have valuative importance.

But we pay a price for this compromise.   We cannot place our main focus on systematic statement and criticism of valuative assertions.   And, as Lindblom has implied, we cannot include in one discipline the semi-valuative terms of another.   Arrow's restriction of his concern to ordered preferences results from the place that these preferences occupy in the conceptual scheme of positive economics.   The failure of economists, which Lindblom

3. Duncan MacRae, Jr., "Science Versus Policy: A Dilemma of Sociology," *American Sociologist*, vol. 6 (supplementary issue, June, 1971), pp. 2–7.

criticizes, to deal with major problems of power, regimes, personality, and culture results simply from restrictions of their valuative vocabulary so that it will match the empirical concerns of their discipline.

Economists are not alone in this respect.   Political scientists see the alternatives for choice and the values to be realized as largely political; sociologists, as residing in social structure; psychologists, as residing more in the individual.   A broad view of the disciplines reveals the parochialism of the valuative concerns of each.

The primary task in discussing valuative questions—including those of policy—is, therefore, to integrate the *valuative* discourse of the various disciplines.   Scarcely any real choices allow us to stay within the confines of a particular discipline's values.   Economic development involves social and psychological changes.   Political regimes and government have implications for economics.   Any effort to judge policies or regimes by the narrow standards of a single discipline is likely to be short-sighted.

It is here that the formal sophistication of economics, combined with the substantive concerns of the other social sciences, can contribute to a basis for integrated valuative discourse. I shall try in the space available to sketch out a form that such discourse might take.   Insofar as this proposal is intelligible and open to criticism, that criticism itself can further the valuative integration of the discourse of the social sciences.

We can approach this task by returning to what is now called the "old" welfare economics, but basing some of its assumptions on philosophical foundations rather than the pseudo-scientific foundations from which it was later toppled.   The work of Pigou made use of a cardinal notion of welfare, distinct from desire or preference.   Later writers assumed a cardinal "utility" and related it to both economic behavior and valuative questions.   Subsequent critics, however, correctly noted that cardinal utility and interpersonal comparison were unnecessary to account for economic choice—indifference surfaces were sufficient—and violated the scientific canon of parsimony.[4]

4. A. C. Pigou, *The Economics of Welfare* (London: Macmillan, 1920), p. 23; J. R. Hicks, *Value and Capital* (Oxford: Clarendon Press, 1939);

But if we approach policy with a deliberate concern for rational valuative discourse, not alleged to rest on scientific observation alone, then the quest for an ethical system applying to all the choices we must make leads us away from indifference surfaces immediately.[5] We are forced, moreover, to compare individuals—at least in a wide range of prevalent ethical systems—and this interpersonal comparison also increases the convenience of a cardinal utility function. The conclusion is not a certain one, either empirically—for this criterion is irrelevant—or logically—since other "ethical hypotheses" are admissible; but a burden of proof may be placed on the critic to propose and employ a consistent, alternative ethical system. In the meantime, while awaiting the critic's alternative, we may usefully explore the implications of an extensive class of ethical systems that satisfy these requirements.[6] And with suitable generalization, this approach can provide a certain integration of contributions from sociology, psychology, and political science. Thus a deliberate stress on the valuative discourse latent in all these disciplines can provide the basis of a social philosophy that penetrates into the organization of all the social sciences—seen as systems of reasoned communication but not exclusively as empirical sciences. Such discourse may combine these disciplines in a way that is appropriate to the general discussion of practical judgments, ranging from choice of policy to choice of regime.

When we casually assume the possibility of interpersonal comparison and cardinal utility, the reader may well ask not only the basis of our assertion but also its precise implications. As regards the basis, I have suggested that it lies in a procedure for ethical argument, of which I have attempted a systematic justifi-

---

Lionel Robbins, *An Essay on the Nature and Significance of Economic Science* (London: Macmillan, 1937); Paul A. Samuelson, *Foundations of Economic Analysis* (Cambridge, Mass.: Harvard University Press, 1947), p. 91.

5. See John R. Harsanyi, "Cardinal Welfare, Individualistic Ethics, and Interpersonal Comparisons of Utility," *Journal of Political Economy,* vol. 63, no. 4 (August, 1955), pp. 309–321.

6. This seems to have been the approach of the Cambridge welfare economists, as cited in Abram Bergson, "A Reformulation of Certain Aspects of Welfare Economics," *Quarterly Journal of Economics,* vol. 52, no. 2 (February, 1938), p. 324. Presumably much of their work can be reinterpreted as systematic ethics.

cation elsewhere.[7]   As for its substance, we are dealing with a
class of ethical systems or social welfare functions rather than a
particular one and thus need not specify an individual member of
this class in detail.   A similar strategy of argumentation has been
followed in the philosophical discussion of types of utilitarianism
where "rule" and "act" utilitarianism have been compared extensively without precise specification of the summum bonum.   In
welfare economics, a parallel strategy was followed in Bergson's
classic paper.[8]

A very useful step at this point is to define two separate functions for each individual: *welfare* and *preference*.   The welfare
function may well be cardinal and interpersonally comparable,
for the reasons stated above; it is explicitly normative and does
not derive exclusively from observation.   The preference function, on the other hand, would have the familiar properties recognized by economists in their treatment of consumer behavior.   It
could be simply ordinal and characterized by indifference surfaces as its isoquants.   It is—at least in principle—empirically
ascertainable for a choosing individual at a given time.

This distinction between welfare and preference cuts through
two parallel, semantic confusions that have plagued economics
and political science.   Each of these disciplines has made use of
a term that combines both of the above meanings.   In economics
the term in question is "utility"; in political science, "interest."
Numerous debates about the proper use of these terms have re-
volved about whether the empirical or the normative meaning, or
both, are being used.   The combination of the two meanings in a
single term implies a sort of psychological hedonism—or more
generally, the notion that what humans seek is also valuable—
which prejudges an empirical question on grounds of terminology.
If we had made such a prejudgment by superposing two empirical
meanings, we should recognize it more easily and separate the two,
but the combination of separable empirical and normative meanings creates a problem for which we are less well prepared by our
half-articulated philosophy of science.

By separating individual welfare from preferences, we can
deal more clearly with both uninformed preference and informed

7. MacRae, "Scientific Communication," op. cit.
8. Bergson, op. cit.

preferences that run counter to the chooser's welfare, such as drug addiction and, perhaps, masochism.   We are also able to say—as we could not so easily before—that altruistic acts, such as the sacrifice of one's life or endurance of torture, may not promote the welfare of the actor.[9]   This separation is even more important for political preferences than for economic because of the remoteness of the entities that are preferred by the voter.

The separation of these two concepts will permit economics to participate in a broad discussion of questions of social philosophy together with the other social sciences.   It will reveal more clearly, however, that the central concepts of economics are not ipso facto policy desiderata; the conditions for disparity between the two will have to be explored.   The introduction of a distinct welfare concept into the discourse of economics might, it is true, lead to imprecise, controversial, valuative considerations in a discipline that had largely succeeded in escaping them.   It might even demote some of the discourse of economics to the status of that of sociology.[10]   In compensation there might be potential gains for society and even for the other social sciences, but the discipline of economics, enjoying both scientific status and the confidence of statesmen, might find it harder than other disciplines to make this change.

We may proceed in this direction toward a further integration of the normative components of the social sciences by asking what individuals' preference and welfare functions *should* be.   In this inquiry, we go beneath the characteristic assumption of economics that preferences constitute the ultimate criterion of social decisions and ask how these preferences should be shaped and changed. We can ask, within the same conceptual scheme, what modes of education, mass communication, political campaigning, advertising, or propaganda are desirable.   The question is not an easy one and, indeed, is not answerable within the narrow framework

9. See also Richard B. Brandt, "Personal Values and the Justification of Institutions," in Sidney Hook, ed., *Human Values and Economic Policy* (New York: New York University Press, 1967).

10. The prestige of economics in relation to more speculative social science is discussed in an interchange between J. K. Galbraith and Robert M. Solow, which the latter concludes with the quip, "Après moi, la sociologie." Solow, "A Rejoinder," *The Public Interest,* vol. 9 (Fall, 1967), p. 119.

that takes preferences both as a standard and as given.[11]   But it does involve the linking of the disciplines, as some economists have recognized in their study of related empirical questions.[12]

The problems we have used so far as illustrations relate mainly to normative choice among preference functions.   But we can equally well ask what an individual's welfare function should be.   How should we educate children as regards the satisfaction, a possible synonym for welfare, that they derive from the welfare of others?   How should the tastes of the public, or parts of it, be cultivated as regards their possible appreciation of new experiences—whether from consumption of goods and services, from nonmarket transactions, or simply from utilization of their own personal resources?   The possibility that people should want less, or should learn to derive their satisfactions more cheaply, is sometimes suggested by a narrow-minded elite, but it also arises from the current quest of some of our youth for a simpler life.   Again, central valuative questions can be attacked through a modest enlargement of the conceptual armory of economics.

Some of the questions that we would approach in this way are precisely the fundamental ones that Lindblom fears we would ignore through a narrowly conceived policy analysis.   The effect of life in a milieu of exchange relationships on personality and culture might well be regarded as an effect on individuals' preference and welfare functions.   This problem is profound enough to embrace the communist quest for a "new Soviet man" and John Stuart Mill's expectation that participation in representative government would develop the citizen's character.   Lindblom's mention of therapy as an example also involves a process of change in individuals' preference and welfare functions.   The reorganization of preferences and the reduction of their mutual conflict is often an aim of therapy, and changes in welfare may be produced not only for the patient but also for others affected by his actions.

In these comments I have digressed somewhat from my assignment to comment on Lindblom's paper as a political scientist.

11. See Talcott Parsons, *The Structure of Social Action* (New York: McGraw-Hill, 1937), chap. 2.

12. For example, Gary Becker, "A Theory of Social Interactions," 1969, unpublished; Kenneth Boulding, "The Network of Interdependence" (Paper presented to the Public Choice Society, Chicago, February 19, 1970).

But in a symposium on the integration of the social sciences, perhaps we must bravely discard our limiting identities as members of particular disciplines and attempt this integration within each of our own minds as well as within the covers of this volume. Nevertheless, it is important to return to the political implications of the type of integration I have proposed.

In the first place, I am simply proposing a terminology—a set of concepts—that will link theories of behavior with ethical systems of an individualistic type.   Any behavioral theory as to how preferences develop can be related to a preference function.   We need only get on with the job on which economists, for example, have long asked for the help of psychologists—although perhaps some economists could aid in this endeavor themselves.   The corresponding class of ethical systems may be termed "individualistic" because it assumes that social welfare functions are to be derived from individual welfare functions, perhaps by simple addition.

This approach does set aside certain types of value systems that are well known to political scientists.   Values, such as those of human rights, justice, freedom, and equality, might well be less than ultimate criteria if we made use of a notion of welfare akin to that of the earlier welfare economists.   But if the proponents of such other values can formulate the problem in their terms, they may propose alternative ways to integrate the social sciences in valuative discourse.[13]

The task of evaluating regimes and policies, then, becomes one that has been stated by Buchanan:

A normative theory of politics should . . . array the alternative sets of rules in accordance with their predicted efficacy in producing certain ends or goals which should be, if possible, made quite explicit.[14]

The task with which he is concerned is the reform of political institutions rather than of human behavior; but in the interdisciplinary perspective that we must take here, the alteration of individuals' preference and welfare functions is an alternative means to these same goals.   Education, communication, and psy-

13. See John Rawls, *A Theory of Justice* (Cambridge, Mass.: Harvard University Press, 1971).

14. James M. Buchanan and Gordon Tullock, *The Calculus of Consent* (Ann Arbor: University of Michigan Press, 1962), p. 308.

chology take their place beside the reform of institutions. Moreover, as Lindblom notes, the alteration of personality through the
effects of political and economic systems is not to be neglected.

I hope, therefore, that it will not be necessary to document
in detail the relevance of my proposal for politics. The question
of the criteria in terms of which regimes are to be judged is one
of the oldest in our discipline. The effort to deal with particular
policy problems, such as the reform of the seniority system in Congress, may well require us to posit intermediate goals, such as the
recruitment of able and public-spirited persons into positions of
leadership. But even these intermediate goals can also be discussed and justified in terms of the preferences of leaders as they
relate to the welfare of the public. Let me simply reiterate, then,
my hope that a consideration of general ethical questions may provide a useful and lasting link among the social sciences, and perhaps other disciplines as well.

Commentary on Lindblom's Paper

By Harold Guetzkow

COULD it be that Professor Charles E. Lindblom, in conceiving the social sciences in the sophisticated terms held by an intellectual aristocracy for centuries, finds by definition little wisdom in "giving policy analysis the assignment of integrating the social sciences"? Could it be that this perspective inhibited Professor Lindblom in carrying forward seminal hints in the last section of his essay to the end that perhaps the social sciences will become integrated inadvertently by development of an "enriched policy analysis"?

Let me hope it is constructive to proceed as follows: Examine whether my guess that Lindblom's conclusions follow mainly from a traditional definition of social science is correct, then, shifting gear, formulate an alternative query, "How might integrations of the social sciences *with* policy analyses be realized?"

SOCIAL SCIENCES DEFINED AS TRADITIONAL STUDIES

Does Professor Lindblom's pessimism regarding the potential integrating value of policy analysis for the social sciences derive from his implicit definition of the social sciences in terms of a scholarly ideal held now by an intellectual aristocracy? Perhaps such is the case.

The essay argues that the "conservative and superficial" proclivity of policy analysis is a "bias," tending to integrate but weakly the social sciences in ways which "fail to ask radical and fundamental questions. . . ." But such opinion depends upon an acceptance of Lindblom's judgments as to how the social sciences need moving, should they become integrated. The esteem he renders Plato and Hobbes, for example, is not shared by all. Can you rest easy with the "authoritarian implications" of Plato's *Republic*? One may argue that the "continuing intellectual tradition" of Hobbes in which politics centers in conflict has disastrously inhibited serious analysis of cooperative phases of the political life of mankind.   It is difficult to believe that study in contemporary forms of "individual therapy is a major avenue to fundamental discovery. . . ." In addition to being clinical rather than scientific, most psychiatry is quite culture-bound, almost always working at a remote distance from its neurophysiological base.   Its goals in aiding patients to adapt to an immediate environment seem superficial and conservative to many.

When less was known in the social sciences, one might seek new discoveries in a new way.   But developments in the disciplines have not been without some substance over the decades past; perhaps today's search for the radical and fundamental will take forms other than sheer innovation.   Creative people seek relief from boredom.   Given scholarly leisure it is not surprising they find satisfactions in the novel.   Today the social sciences seem to have become more encompassing and more cumulative as we develop models less dependent upon polemics and jargon.

Unless I misunderstand Lindblom's discussion of "Modes of Integration Alternative to a Policy Orientation," I have trouble in using his evidence to conclude with him that "only some" of the integration "develops around policy questions" inasmuch as more than half of his list (decision theory, organization theory, political culture and political socialization, political development, and economic development), along with cybernetics or communications, represents important integrations deriving from policy work.   The essay seems permeated by a nostalgia for social science as it was idealized in the past.   Given the paucity—despite the tenacity— of findings political science has gained from Plato, Hobbes, and Rousseau, is it not time now that an orientation aiming "to answer a *single* fundamental question" (italics mine) should rightly go out of style?

In the essay's discussion concerning graduate academic training, the retrospective viewpoint reveals treasuring of "informally organized" study.   With the flamboyance of a master of broad-gauged verbal theory, Lindblom hopes that a clear differentiation between "social science and the highly professional study of policy problems" will give all, including the "young men who want to be social scientists, a clear conscience about what their scholarly responsibilities might best be."   But is such a separation in intellectual activity appropriate for more than a minority, an intellectual elite?

Despite the many hints Lindblom gives in his essay as to nexuses for integrations which might be formed between social science and policy, especially in his final section on "The Need for Policy Analysis," the implicit idealization of anthropology, economics, political science, psychology, and sociology as *the* disciplines chains his speculation to the past.   He seems to be carried away, thinking that only disciplines in their more pristine forms can be fundamental and radical—let alone innovative.   He then writes as though "new" disciplines are hardly conceivable, relegating such fundamental and radical fields as "communications" to the biased domain of policy.   He seems to want elites to join the disciplines defined as of yore eschewing scholars, young and old, with proclivity toward policy.

Yet Lindblom's stimulating paper encourages one to examine another alternative in which knowledge for fun and for use is thought of as integrable, so interwoven that an attempt to separate these modes of endeavor is perhaps fruitless, as those who have attempted to unravel the knotting of basic and applied research know.

AN ALTERNATIVE INTERRELATION OF THE SOCIAL SCIENCES WITH POLICY ANALYSES IN TERMS OF INTEGRATION

Men of knowledge need integrations within their disciplines. The integration which develops around policy questions seems to be often but a casual by-product of multidisciplinary effort.   If we are concerned with integrations within the social sciences, what would be the result were concerted efforts made to reap benefits from policy analyses, combining outputs for usable components? Could it be that a new active posture is necessary to gain integrations with the social sciences from policy analyses?   Is it useful to restructure the question of our conference: Can we gain integrations of the social sciences *with* policy analyses?

Such a query permits at least one alternative.   Conceive of knowledge developed for fun in the social sciences in continuum with knowledge developed for use in policy analysis.   In each domain one needs to delineate entities; these entities in both cases are then described quantitatively in terms of variables, dimensions, or factors.   The variables, in turn, are posited as being related across the population of entities in various ways, sometimes simply, other times with complexity.   There is, then, no need for continuation of the boundaries marked among the disciplines decades ago on the basis of inadequate understanding.

Further, there is then no need for artificially distinguishing between the highly general, nomothetic and the quite specific, idiosyncratic, as one may work alternatively at very abstract or quite particularistic levels.   By denigrating precision in a social science conceived as consisting of broadly painted, encompassing inquiries, the essay seems to neglect the need for relatively fine-grained measurement in which the contribution of many factors determines variance in complex ways in a large number of dependent variables, as is illustrated in the collaboration of personality scientists with personnel psychologists.   Are not these important, nitty-gritty determinations of as much importance in the designing of a structure of the intellect, as is being done by Guilford, as the loosely formulated theories of freedom developed by Rousseau?   With aid from computers, so that one's data may be aggregated and disaggregated with some ease, perhaps we gradually can learn to move from quasi-idiographic studies which have been traditionally thought of as involved in policy analysis to the propositional analysis engaged by those working in nomothetic styles.   No longer must we endure the seemingly perpetual stress on generalizations made in the vernacular.   By mounting one's verbal theory in simulation formats, it may not be impossible to interface pieces of theory in syncretic efforts.   One then may slowly surmount, perhaps, the limitations faced by a Lasswell or Kuhn, dependent upon human memory for synthesizing a multitude of disparate components.   By working at abstract levels, it may be possible to exploit policy studies, thereby gaining nomothetic "patterns" from analyzers programmed to exhibit general propositions.   Theory banks, derived from a cross-cultural array of policy studies, may enable one to become less culture-bound. Perhaps one can develop an empirical base for nomothetic propositions by relying upon fact-gatherers, as their efforts are organized the world over through policy-developing organizations.   Perhaps the difference between policy and science, as such is conceived today, is the level of generality and inclusiveness each seeks.   But with some effort cannot those concerned with the elegance of science as an abstract, all-encompassing study utilize the incremental, more idiosyncratic materials developed by the pragmatic professions?

It may possibly be that the policy professionals will use the knowledge of the scientists to tremendous advantage; likewise, the scientists will free themselves from vacuous speculation by a new ability to handle massive amounts of data as marshalled by the empirically oriented practitioners, once the latter tame the abilities of their computers. Were there sufficient resources, the longitudinal materials needed to probe learning and change might also be included in these architectonic constructions, thereby lengthening the perspective of the scientist and increasing the ability of the policy analyst to handle long-term effects. Given knowledge formated as data and theory banks, with a capability of performing at various levels of aggregation and generality, one almost inadvertently moves toward integrations of social science within policy analysis simultaneously. As one works ahead, building theory banks and data banks, could it just be that the needs for knowledge of both the elitist social scientist and the professional policy analyst will be satisfied simultaneously? Each benefits from the other; each contributes to the other.

As the older definitions of the social sciences and policy analyses are dropped, faculty and graduate students can work with fewer invidious comparisons. Neither policy nor science should be "conservative and superficial." One is "engaged in refining" such as seems required for one's purposes. "Exciting new discoveries" are open to all. How can one do policy analysis of quality, especially as such involves alternative futures, unless one asks radical questions of a fundamental nature within a multidisciplinary context? "Radical and fundamental questions" are just as "troublesome and relevant" to the policy analyst concerned with alternative futures as to the social scientist attempting to enrich "man's understanding of himself and his world." The scholars and professionals concerned with knowledge about social processes will instead gradually place themselves in activity in terms of their personal styles and resources at hand without definitional preconception.

Are more than ten to twenty percent of the scholars now in the social sciences sufficiently gifted and consummatively motivated for work as scientists per se? Given the burgeoning of the disciplines within the last half-century, how can one expect untalented recruits, pressured for publication by their academic institutions, to develop fundamental clarifications and discoveries? It may well be that the proclivity of the younger scholars to move toward policy work is in response to a quiet, self-acknowledged assessment of their capabilities and interests. In my judgment, a society need support only a few in situations which encourage serendipitous pay-offs. We now need to attract wonderfully bright men to serve as bridge-builders between a few endowed disciplinarians and organizations involved in knowledge-based policy analysis. To obtain bases for vigorous integrations between the social sciences and policy analyses, it would seem much upgrading is needed in policy work, and a drastic reduction in force is demanded within the disciplines. One should not sell short the societal benefits to be obtained from incremental, cumulative work in the social sciences through policy activity. In the future, the bulk of our world resources devoted to knowledge may no longer be allocated to disciplinary pursuits in the social sciences; instead such may be channeled to policy analysis. Are there too many in the disciplines with pretentions to originality and encyclopedic vision? Do we need to tighten the bottlenecks of admission so that within the disciplines we have only the outstandingly gifted? Should not the social scientists give the bulk of the resources of their disciplines to the professions so that scientific study may benefit from policy analyses?

Is it the case that Lindblom's implicit definition of social science reinforces barriers to the integrations of knowledge, be such developed for science or for policy? Yes, "an enriched policy analysis" is needed. But fruitful differences between policy and science in social arenas are perhaps not defined in terms of the traditional relation between the sciences and the professions. It seems to me that we may develop integrated knowledge for science and use by articulating our knowledge at varying levels of generality, both in terms of theory and in terms of data, so that such may be generated by all and then shared by all in an interacting way. Would it not be well to reduce the confusion by nurturing aspirations commensurate with contemporary potentials for the integration of multidisciplinary work in the social sciences *with* rather than *through* analyses for policy?

In addition to regretting the hidden contradictions which may permeate my remarks, I am abject concerning my inability to do more than question and speculate about Lindblom's fascinating ideas. Should my queries, however, lead to rigorous research on these important matters, founded empirically and developing more than the one alternative future I've nurtured, the comments may be worth print. We need a social science of the social sciences as well as a philosophy of social science. As the successive studies of the various commissions mounted by the National Science Foundation, the National Academy of Science, and the private foundations continue to become less free-flowing in their modes, perhaps there's some chance of developing a systematic basis for iterative judgment on the ever recurring probblems involved in the integrations of the social sciences *with* policy analyses.

Conference Discussion I

CHARLESWORTH: Gentlemen, we have with us here Richard D. Lambert. He is a professor of sociology at the University of Pennsylvania. He is chairman of the South Asia Program there. He is editor of THE ANNALS, and he is president of the Academy. From about twelve at night to five in the morning he doesn't have much to do, but he is kept busy the rest of the time.

I think it would be nice for him to give you a word of greeting here before we start.

LAMBERT: I want to welcome you all here on behalf of the Academy. If I may, since the topic of this conference, I hope, marks a direction the Academy is going to play in the future increasingly, I would like to set up my four don'ts for the morning session for you, interfering a little bit with Jim Charlesworth's role. What I think the Academy is going to try to do is to play a bridge function among the social sciences in order to bring together people across the social sciences to talk to one other on various topics and to encourage cross-fertilization.

Now, I just counted about two months ago the number of scholarly conferences I have attended and came up with sixty-three and a half, but I think that you gentlemen must far outdo me in this. Because I am in area studies, most of them have been interdisciplinary of one kind or another, and so for your amusement I want to set up out of that long scar tissue my four don'ts for the next two sessions.

Let's not spend the time, as my colleagues in my center used to do, saying that everybody else's discipline is better than our own. Let's not spend the time with the political scientists patronizing the anthropologists, or the sociologists patronizing the political scientists, or the psychologists patronizing the sociologists, and with the economists feeling superior to everybody, largely on the grounds of hard versus soft science.

Let's not play the game of general debates about the methodology of science for a day and a half, which is always a very tempting way to waste time.

Let's not spend the time on symbolic warfare, examining the justification for the title of the conference word by word as we go through the days.

And let's not spend the time in examining each other's disciplines, doing what I have seen many conference anthropologists representing different village studies do, and that is to let each representative of a village be a plenipotentiary representative of his village, being able to speak for it without anybody else knowing about it. Let's all assume we have visited one another's villages.

Now if that doesn't put the calm on any fruitful discussion, I don't know what, if anything, will. So with that, I think I will just turn you over to Jim Charlesworth who is your chairman here and whom, I assume, you all already know.

CHARLESWORTH: Thank you, Richard. We're glad the essays are all here, meaning by "we" the people who will make written contributions to the forthcoming monograph. I heard just recently from Coleman, who is in England, that he expected to be here, but something came up at the last minute and he couldn't make it, although he made every effort to try to rearrange his schedule. Easton talked to me on the phone. He is president of an organization in Europe, and he couldn't very well get out of attending its meeting. He said that if I beat him over the head he would appear here, but I thought no; if he is president of whatever that is over there, he'd better go there.

I am a kind of secretary and general factotum at these conferences. I don't do much presiding, so my introductory remarks here will not be substantive but will relate to small matters of management. It has been our custom—and we don't adhere to it because it is a custom but because we think it has worked pretty well—to call on the author of the theme paper first and let him say what he thinks of the people who said what they thought about his paper. Then we call on the people who said what they thought about his paper to see if there can be a reconciliation or a further deviation. After that, the conference is thrown wide open, and we have discovered in the past that wide open really means wide open. These conferences are not tightly structured. Whatever occurs to you to talk about, that is what we want to hear.

This whole conference will be taped—you can see our functionary down at the end—and all participants will be allowed to polish their syntax before the publication of the monograph. Now, I don't need to tell a group of sophisticated scholars like this that the speed of the convoy is the speed of the slowest ship. So if you don't get your editing of the tape in at a reasonable time, I will edit it, and God help you.   Usually, however, we don't have much trouble.

I don't believe that I have anything further to say about my management role, so suppose we call on Professor Lindblom to comment on the comments on his paper.   I take it that we all understand that there will be no reading of papers at this conference.

LINDBLOM: Thank you.   In my experience with conferences that run a day or more, I have found that it doesn't matter what the first speaker says; it is quickly forgotten in the subsequent useful drive of the discussion.   But I am required to speak first. Let me comment on each of the papers that comment on my paper, beginning with Guetzkow's.

In his opening paragraph he sees me practicing a perversion of elitism.   I am indebted to him for pointing that out.   I want to say explicitly that social scientists, scientists, scholars—people who pursue knowledge—are indeed an elite, and I don't think we should be frightened of that.   We ought to think of their functions and their most useful methods as though they were frankly engaged in a very elitist enterprise.

But more than that, Guetzkow's comment puts me in mind to say that I believe we ought to consider the possibility that there is within the social sciences—or many sciences—inevitably a super-elite, an elite of very powerful performers, an elite of which I am not a member, an elite whose membership is restricted to those who have significantly moved the science or the social science in ways that will be recorded in history written long after they are gone.

I see, therefore, a first issue that I would like to interject into the discussion.   It is this.   I would like to suggest to us that we consider the possibilities of integration and the possibilities of using policy analysis as a method of integration, not only in the light of the needs, prospects, and probable fruitfulness of ordinary social scientists, but also in the light of the needs, prospects, and fruitfulness of the most distinguished social scientists.

Secondly, I am indebted to Mr. Guetzkow for pointing out that a great deal of social science, more than I seem to acknowledge in my paper, is already policy oriented. Knowledge is power, and almost all science and social science is distantly related to an interest in manipulation and control, and at least distantly related, therefore, to policy. But what a distance sometimes! The systems analyst trying to find out, for example, whether we should establish a desalinization operation for the development of agriculture on the arid coasts of the southern Mediterranean is a long, long way from a Hobbes, who also has a policy orientation but who has the patience and the sense of perspective to permit his policy orientation to carry his analysis through the most extraordinarily ambitious inquiries into the fundamentals of social organization.

I would say, therefore, that Guetzkow's point reminds us that we are not so much interested in whether a policy orientation is useful for the integration of social sciences, but in whether a relatively immediate and direct policy orientation is. And it may be that by drawing a distinction between those two possibilities we can clarify some of the points of difference between us. For example, Mr. Lane is interested, it is quite clear, in a more immediate policy orientation than Mr. Guetzkow is.

Thirdly, I am inclined to amend Guetzkow's second section. There he proposes to move from the verbal to the quantitative, from the ambitious generalism—sometimes, he says, a flamboyant kind of scholarship—to a more particularistic and specific scholarship. He wants to move to what he calls quasi-idiographic studies. He is suspicious of generalizations, verbalism, and speculation. Somehow, however, he slides into an identification of the quantitative, the quasi-idiographic, the specific, and the particularistic with policy orientation. And that, it seems to me, either is a flaw in the logic or a point in which I misunderstand him and on which I would therefore hope to have some further clarification. Grant him his distinctions in style between two forms of social science, I don't understand how the particular, the quantitative, the hard-headed, the data-oriented studies, to all of which I am quite sympathetic, are equivalent to policy oriented.

MacRae and Schelling say, on the whole, that they agree with me here. I will comment more briefly on their papers. I find in each of them, just as I found in Guetzkow's comments, an interesting issue that we might want to talk about.

What I see in Mr. MacRae's suggestion to us—I will change his message a little bit—is that evaluative and normative discussion cannot be left to philosophers. Social science must plunge in deeply, take it seriously, and set up some sort of guidelines as to how to go about it. If you look at the character of evaluative discussion about social policy—or even an evaluative discussion about how to lead the good life—you will note that it consists almost wholly of factual statements. If you look at evaluative discussion you will see that what we are ordinarily alleging are empirical connections as well as, of course, logical connections. Overwhelmingly, so-called philosophical discussion pertinent to social science and individual affairs is factual. That means that those people who have a specialized claim to competence in certain factual material—say, economists in discussions of economic affairs—have an obvious specialized virtuosity in handling evaluative discussion which philosophers don't have.

Now, if we were to agree with MacRae that the social sciences ought to take normative analysis more seriously, then a question for this group to discuss is whether that normative analysis could be, as I believe MacRae suggests, a more suitable focus for integrative work than policy analysis.

Mr. Schelling raises a number of questions. The one that I want to single out is: "Why bother to integrate at all?" He bridles in the opening paragraphs of his paper at the notion that we have to take for granted that there is a general case for integration.

A possible way of attacking his question is by indirection. We might in these discussions first ask ourselves, in a cooperative, nondisputatious way, what it is that we really want to know about the social world that we don't know. What knowledge do we hunger for? Then, with an illustrative, specific, concrete list of the questions for which we want answers, we could ask the question whether their answers would, in fact, call for integration or whether their answers lie in advances in social sciences along particular lines that have nothing to do with integration. I suspect that if we were to develop a list of such questions—the most significant questions in social science—we would find that they were questions that back away from policy analysis.   They would not have any immediate bearing on policy in most cases.   The exercise would, therefore, possibly suggest that policy analysis was not the way toward integration, even if we concluded that integration were required.   But we might conclude that integration, itself, is not required, which is what Schelling suggests.

When I look at the questions that scholars and scientists have historically asked, it seems to me that their important questions, the answers to which turned out to be fruitful and world-shaking, can generally be characterized as those that have backed off from immediate policy questions as chemistry backed off from alchemy.

SCHELLING: The question raised by both Lindblom and Lane was whether policy analysis is a superficial thing—taking for granted what the client takes for granted on a time schedule that would have embarrassed Hobbes.   There is a tendency for policy analysis to be superficial, to be the application by the analysts of what they already know.   But I have observed that applied and fundamental research are not opposite ends of a single scale. There are two dimensions.   Much basic work is instantly applicable because it opens up something that was closed, and a lot of the most applied research isn't applicable because the researcher didn't understand what the problem was, or there was a new problem by the time his work was done, or he alone knew what his results were and couldn't communicate them.

Often the most basic research is the most instantly usable. What policy analysis often requires is a fundamental breakthrough.   Sometimes an effort to do policy analysis can stimulate a person to make that breakthrough.   I notice in the history of economics something that may be true in other disciplines.   Once in a while a policy or program leads to the acquisition of data, and possession of data leads people to work with it and to develop theory.   In the history of economic theory, one striking thing is how well advanced international trade theory was by the middle of the nineteenth century compared with theories that American economists cope with now.   The reason is simple.   About the only place the government ever got statistics was at its boundaries. So people who wanted to look at data looked at international trade data and speculated on it. They discovered things that weren't obvious, including things that didn't depend on data.

In the same way it was the generation of national income data in the early 1930s that stimulated national income theory. This means that one of the roles of policy in the development of science is that it provides free, or at least available, data for people who have nothing better to do than to look at it. And it sometimes leads them to think.

There is a positive side of what Lindblom referred to as my negative question—whether we really want to integrate the social sciences. If I were asked what integration I would most like to see among the sciences, social and other, low on my answering list of valuable clusters would be the cluster that pulls together the disciplines represented here at this conference—the cluster that calls itself the social sciences. I don't mean I wouldn't want to sit with you, but that I might want to add other disciplines to this group and might be willing to dispense with one or two disciplines or subdisciplines represented here.

I find it useful, for example, to deal with legal scholars. They tend to be interested in what I am interested in. I find it very useful to deal with people who are at the science-fiction avant garde of bio-medical advances and who lead me to speculate what would happen to institutions like the family if everybody lived to be two hundred or if you couldn't identify paternity in a legal or biological way. I sometimes find that there are things so common to external communications systems and internal communications systems that I may want to team up with a neurologist, an organization theorist, and a psychologist to think about systems.

I wouldn't attempt to sell you any particular grouping that I find interesting because it depends upon my interests—and I may not have the same interests as you. It depends, too, on what kind of people, what kind of problems, and what kind of ideas stimulate a person. Where do I get intrigued? Do I, by the sheer strangeness of somebody else's subject, suddenly see something I missed before? With whom can I engage in two hours' useful conversation because we have similar ways of composing questions and thinking about them?

So the farthest I will go, considering the object of this conference, is to agree that integration is interesting, but on condition that it be opportunistic, not permanent, and that it be multi-centered or a variety of different clusters that are found useful together for particular purposes. Integrate may be too strong a term, especially if it means "unify." If it means to try to make into one, then I want instead a word that suggests severalty. Marriage of convenience, with divorce allowed and made easy, is the kind of integration I can support. And, as I started out saying, for my purpose, although maybe not for yours, I would not begin with the presumption that I want to integrate with other *social* scientists. My integration would include some, but no more than it would include people who deal with evolutionary biology, sanitary engineering, criminal law, or ancient history.

UNIDENTIFIED VOICE: Schelling is a scholar-for-fun. I have always felt this about his work even though at times he has taken a very serious set of problems that he has been concerned with in terms of his interests, and this is part of the modern way of saying he is a scholar-for-leisure. He mentioned this throughout his remarks. Yet I find myself having quite a bit in common with him even though I am a scholar for utilization.

I agree with his remarks that you have to ask the right kind of fundamental questions. It may have been that if they had originally started asking the stock questions, policy questions, they would have gotten just as battered as they did in terms of asking the other questions. You see, part of the innovation comes from asking the fresh question, I think, and getting away from the customary ways of looking at problems.

The problem of data, yes. One is stimulated to have fun with data, but if you are interested in utilization, you are also interested in the problems of validity—of conflicting kinds of speculations which persons verbally gifted tend to be able to speculate about. Schelling and I have had two hours of conversation in which about one hundred hypotheses have been developed, mostly by him, but in terms of the fun of the conversation. However, when you are interested in utilizing, and when you take seriously the kinds of concerns that, say, McCord worries about in the excruciatingly difficult confrontations you have with those people with whom you have had an opportunity to participate—confrontations indirect as well as direct in your social systems—then the data aspects become very important. For instance, I was quite fascinated with your recording of a finding in which there was no statistically significant difference, and yet you took it as if there were a significant difference in terms of which way you would operate in utilizing that kind of data.

So, Ed (Lindblom), in terms of our pushing ahead with my conceptions here concerning data, I think you are right. I was too narrow there. That is, certainly the scholar-for-fun can have highly idiographic data. I think historians tend in that direction sometimes where their interest is in arranging their particularistic materials in a chronological way. They don't want to have any generalizations about that data. It just has to be strung out and that's it.

Now as one looks at the problems we have in international trade of trying to understand what is happening in the balance-of-payments problems and so forth, it seems to me that, as I understand the controversies, there just aren't enough data to be able to decide which kinds of factors are having more impact in this complicated system, and that the reason for the polemic in this last year or two since we have been running into money problems is that we don't have a validated set of theories that we can work with. They don't seem to come clean, so we are in a very messy situation as so often happens in the development of the social sciences.

It isn't just quantitative because I think that one can look at qualitative kinds of idiosyncratic data too, and I guess I overstated that and am in error there as you suggest. But if we are able to use the data for testing, then for my kind of purposes, the utilization interests, one has, I think, possibilities of distinguishing among rival theories.

The coming now of the quasi-experiment in the field situation is, I think, a very important kind of step in enabling us to do a better job in the utilization of that, as is implicit in your remarks about how data are no longer being gathered. Rather, it seems as though more and more people are becoming aware of our ability to gather data in ways that give us dirty experiments, but experiments that perhaps will approximate a small step for asking the question among these three or four different kinds of questions we have asked; that is, which one is going to give us the more useful kind of answer, depending upon the norms that one is willing to set around this whole discourse.

MacRAE: I would like to throw out several main lines of reasoning, which you may or may not agree with, that will organize the discussion—questions that have come out in all of the remarks so far as well as in some of the papers. There are three general kinds of questions that have been raised. First, what are we trying to do in this conference? What are the goals? Second, what would an integrated social science look like if it were possible or desirable? Third, how does this enterprise relate to the contemporary situation in the United States?

Now, to turn to the first of these questions, it seems to me that there are within it three types of goals that various members of our group want to pursue. We seem to be a little bit at odds about this. One is integration of the social sciences. Some people see this as a desirable goal, and I think this was one reason why the conference was called. The second thing that we may be after is policy advice or, depending upon what we mean by policy, super-policy advice like the question of what political regime to choose—or even super-super-policy advice on the question of what ethical standards we should use for choosing regimes or policies. The third goal which some of us set ourselves might appear to be the goal of leaving things in our disciplines the way they are, assuming that our disciplines are going to follow or ought to follow a kind of natural science model. According to this model, pure science and validated propositions are at the center of it all, although one can argue that pure science has spillovers for integration and for policy.

The second general set of questions that I think we are asking ourselves is: What might a set of integrated, interrelated social sciences or other sciences look like? This also has three aspects. The first aspect about which we ask is: What would its intellectual content be? Here I strongly agree with Schelling and others who suggested that this ought not to be limited to the social sciences. Having gone through chemistry, physics, and electronic engineering myself before coming into social science, I don't feel that social science is the only world in which one can

exist, and I think we could all proliferate examples of cooperation with the natural sciences. Philosophy has also been mentioned as regards the question of where our goal-setting relates
to the humanities. This question also needs to be discussed,
whether from the point of view of systematic ethics or from the
point of view of the humanistic protest movement against scien-
tism in social science. So the intellectual content and the type
of integrations that individuals might make are among our subjects of debate.

But even if we had agreement on the intellectual content of
our integration of disciplines, there would remain a much longer-
run question of what would be the social structure, the interrelations of persons, in these disciplines or groups. Here I am talking about down-to-earth questions that relate to the survival of
departments and disciplines, such as the Harvard Social Relations Department in which McCord and I got our degrees, which
has now largely disappeared. We must think seriously about
what sorts of arrangements are made for degrees in departments,
professional associations, and journals. In interdisciplinary work
one can have a great deal of playing around for fun, but if it is
not institutionalized in these ways, the playing may not last beyond the interests of a particular group of people.

Thirdly, with regard to what the integrated social sciences
would look like, I think we have to be concerned with the external politics of the university. The more deeply you get into
fundamental, controversial, political issues the more you have to
deal with the question of whether the university itself will be
politicized. One of the virtues of fundamental science as it is
practiced is its detachment from the real world. The more we
connect ourselves with the real world, the more the real world
connects itself with us; so we have to be concerned, as Easton
was in his paper, with what happens if the policy school gets too
deeply involved and gets attacked from Washington or gets investigated by a House committee. Dave's suggestion is that
such an institution, an Academy for Action, would just be dis-
owned by the university and thrown to the wolves. But that is
only the beginning of asking the question, not the end of it.

The third major question, which I wasn't concerned with in
my prepared comments but was reminded of by the papers of

Henry Kariel and Harold Guetzkow, had to do with contemporary social diagnosis. Why are we here? Is it because funds are available for certain things and not for others? Do our proposals have something to do with the contemporary power structure in the United States? Should they be made in the Soviet Union, or France, or some other country? So although it is nice to deal with questions which have answers in an abstract, universal, timeless frame of reference, I think some of our members are going to force us to ask whether these questions have particular answers here and now.

BIERSTEDT: I was delighted to observe that Lindblom defended himself against the charge of Guetzkow about being a member of an elite. Unfortunately, the term elite, in a political context at least, has a pejorative connotation. But certainly it musn't have that connotation in an intellectual context. All of us would like, after all, to be able to say a new word. This is why we exist. I think it was Nietzsche who said something to that effect. So here we have a situation in which the first point that was made was, I think, an excellent point.

So also was the second point, that a lot of social science is already policy oriented. Sociologists tend to be a little bit sensitive about the relationship between pure and applied science, the reason being that in the history of our discipline, especially in the United States, many early sociologists came into sociology from the ministry. They were Protestant preachers and missionaries. This was a period in the earlier history of our discipline when sociology was confused with social reform, and efforts to ameliorate the situation of the poor, and even sometimes with socialism.

We have, therefore, been sensitive to this issue. We have tried, I think, very often, although not always successfully, to maintain a distinction between pure and applied science. We have tried to suggest that the criterion that we should respect in our research is not that of an immediate utility but rather that of an ultimate utility. I don't think anyone of us would go as far as the mathematician who, when asked what he was doing, gave his reply saying, "And I hope it will never be of any use to anybody." I think that the ultimate use and consequence of our knowledge must always play some role.

On the other hand, I know that some of us would not go as far as the late Robert S. Lynd when he objected to what he called lecturing on navigation while the ship was going down. This is something that used to aggravate Bob Lynd a great deal. I like also the notion of Lindblom's, therefore, that we have to back off from policy questions on occasion and, as a matter of fact, quite frequently. I am reminded of Disraeli's observation that the practical man is the one who practices the blunders of his predecessors.

Somehow, as a sociologist, I'd like to be an occupant of the ivory tower. I think it makes some sense. The most cogent observation on this subject that I know of was made by Morris Raphael Cohen who said that purely theoretical contributions to mathematics and astronomy, by increasing the precision of navigation, have saved more lives at sea than any possible tinkering with the carpentry of lifeboats. The lesson is quite plain. The practical man wants to build a better life boat, whereas the theoretical man wants to climb the stairs in his observatory and examine the stars.

I am reminded on the other hand, however, of the very cogent point made by Mr. Schelling that pure research is sometimes instantly useable whereas applied research may not be. Also, I am impressed by Schelling's low priority on questions of integrated concepts or integrated knowledge among the social sciences themselves and think that perhaps there are other questions that one should emphasize. I think among these is the one of seeing the relationship between biology and sociology. We have lived in a century when environmentalism has had the field pretty much to itself. I think there are basic biological conditions which have something to do with the structure of society and that we should examine these more than we have been inclined to do.

Of course I am a little appalled, as you are, by the notion that there might be only 100,000 fathers in the world and all the rest mothers. I think that society is what it is, to some extent at least, because we have a binocular parallax and are able to have a three dimensional perception, because our thumbs are opposable, and because there are two sexes rather than a number. Who was it— Samuel Hoffenstein I think—who said, "Breathes there a man with hide so tough who says two sexes aren't enough?" (Laughter) Well, the fact that there are two sexes is a basic biological fact that does have something to do with the structure of the family. Just suppose there were two species of human beings, one of whom was twice as tall or twice as strong as the other.   Then we would certainly have a biological basis for social stratification.

All these things, I think, are important and interesting.   I am delighted to see the current interest in biology in sociology, in work in animal ecology, to which Schelling made reference.   It is easy to criticize the popularizers in this field, but I think that we are beginning to ask some important questions.

I am not so sure that I can agree with MacRae on the components of normative judgments in social science, whether we have as much right to employ them as philosophers do.   I don't know enough about recent contributions to ethical theory to be able to answer this question, but I do appreciate very much his observation on the danger of politicization if we go too far in the policy direction.

MacRae: I would like to respond to one point that Lindblom made about Schelling's observation, "Why bother to integrate?" He pointed out that we can back off from immediate policy analysis and deal with important questions.   The question I would like to ask is: In what direction should we go back?   Is it back toward pure science?   That is the way I think we are all familiar with because the ideal of pure natural science has been held before us constantly.   But we can also back off into fundamental, philosophical questions, and that is where an argument might arise.

Lindblom: I agree that an argument might arise, and I would be willing to deal with it if this is the direction the discussion should take at this point.

Lane: Well, I will engage in that argument very briefly.   A method of philosophy is the British Analytical School.   That may be the method, aside from historical methods.   This is quite different, somewhat different at least, from what social scientists do. That is, this is a clarification of terms by fission, in part, letting off different meanings.   What do we mean by blame?   What do we mean by moral responsibility?   I have seen the Oxford people go at each other in these kinds of ways.   It is edifying in the vulgar sense as well as in another sense.

I think that we have a lot to learn, that it is a way in which we might back or even turn around and enter, and that the way in which those concepts get clearer boundaries, more clarified and more inter-personally observable reference, is extremely valuable; and I think that we could use that device in reference to empirical variables and especially with reference to the normative ones. Doing that, I think, is an intellectual operation which has some parallels with policy analysis, although some differences. But I think that moral clarity, which is a good word, seems to me to be a useful and perhaps a necessary ingredient for the kinds of things that Kariel, Hacker, and Bierstedt were talking about and should be a recognized arm of our social science analysis.

Now, beyond that, I don't think that philosophy really has a method, and I suspect that much of it is semantic confusion. I think that what they are talking about substantially, aside from that, is preference. So I would limit it to that and say it is terribly useful and desirous to go further in that method.

LINDBLOM: I have a comment on that. It seems to me that contemporary philosophy is, if it is interested in moral discourse at all, overwhelmingly interested in how to do it. Philosophical articles and books are about how to undertake evaluative discussion. They don't do it. They talk about how to do it.

On our part, we social scientists have allowed our own practices to be guided by what Mr. Schelling ten years ago referred to as the doctrine of the fictitious colleague. We have postulated that there is a somebody else who does the evaluative work. The result is that no discipline or branch of learning does the job.

HACKER: I agree very strongly with Lane. Our colleagues in philosophy were probably the first of us to cop out years ago. People who talked about philosophy here were not talking about what our philosophical colleagues are doing, which is totally useless and a total perversion. It is not philosophy.

Now, if one wants philosophy of the sort you have in mind, one has got to go to the amateurs. Some of them are sociologists, like Philip Slater. But I would be very wary about calling philosophy professors to join us. I am sorry to be so intolerant about this, but with the budget cuts at the universities, that department could go first. (Laughter)

McCORD: Are you suggesting then that social science——

HACKER: They go second. (Laughter)

McCORD: I mean, should we take out what philosophers have contributed?

HACKER: I would say that philosophers can come off the San Francisco docks. They can come out of the fundamentalist Baptist colleges. After awhile some people begin to say, "There's a man with a mind." But they don't say that about professors of philosophy.

KARIEL: Let me follow up on what you have said. I think we might be well advised not to argue for normative discourse as such—as a kind of an independent discipline that might be carried on then with more or less sophistication or in a more or less opinionated way. We should argue instead for an integration, not in the sense that we have been using the word integration here, but integration of normative discourse and empirical work, and seeing those as so meshed that there is not some second-dated discipline that we can then later refer to or that we might, in Lindblom's phrase, back off from or back into, but that would be a component of whatever empirical work we would be doing.

We would then be continuously involved in putting whatever values we entertain to the test, in practice, in actual operations. And if we follow up our operations in a public fashion or in a conspicuous way, which is to say, if we communicate the entire process as we are engaged in doing this, I think we would be protected against the charge of elitism.

We would do this with any special skills and in a way that displays to others that we enjoy this kind of thing, and we would then frankly accept what Guetzkow pointed to, namely, about scholars having fun, and say, "It is all right for scholars to have fun or to play at serious games," because we do this in such a conspicuous and dramatic and open way—perhaps not in an ivory tower, but in some type of a glass tower where we can be observed and welcome the observation of others until others, this tower being out of glass, will want to crash in and participate in playing this kind of a game.

GUETZKOW: As this conference proceeds, I find myself at prickly edges. I so often feel that I agree, but then almost immediately I find myself adding, "But . . ."

My "but" in the present situation is the importance of utilizing sophisticated amateurs in value analysis inasmuch as they work in areas in which they are well versed. They often are capable of developing value judgments of merit. Yet, it seems to me, they also must obtain the scrutiny of professional philosophers so that the depths of their insights may be plumbed. They would be well advised to utilize the services of social scientists in assessing the empirical firmness of their appraisals of the moral contexts in which they operate.

The observations of the philosophers and the anthropologists may be checked through by empirical studies of value, as was done by the Kluckholms and their associates. Monitoring devices may help policy analysts in maintaining their awareness of change. Philosophers can utilize the findings from empirical studies in ferreting out dilemmas and contradictions in value structures. Sometimes philosophers become policy analysts, as is illustrated by the activities of Wes Churchman. Then my "buts" seem less important inasmuch as one has expertise consolidated within one person, allowing philosophic formulations to serve as the seedbed within which change in values may be assessed professionally as social science knowledge is utilized in policy work.

May I argue with an analogy—our use of statistics in the social sciences? Our mathematical colleagues have built important structures of knowledge in their work in statistics. They often realize they cannot work effectively in specific substantive areas inasmuch as they possess only the competence of the amateur. Yet, as substantive specialists, we often cannot get along without statistical consultants—even though at times we refuse to concur in their formulations of our problems inasmuch as we have more confidence in our intuitive judgments than their analytical ruminations. We work in tandem with them. So in the case of normative activity we should insure ourselves of access to the knowledge of those who specialize in the formulation and assessment of value structures and their change.

LAMBERT: I want to call something to your attention. One of the reasons for this conference, one of the hidden agendas, was a previous title we had assigned to it, "Models of Man: Problems of the Integration of the Social Sciences." To bring it down to earth, we chose policy applications as one domain in which integration might become possible.

As I sat here and listened, it became clear to me that it didn't really matter which discipline any of us was from because we were having a sophisticated discussion about applied and research roles for all disciplines.   I wonder if somewhere in the course of this conference the original purpose reflected in the format can also be served, which is the pulling together of people distinguished in their own disciplines to consider the interface of their disciplines with other disciplines.   Can we take our eyes off the question of whether a policy orientation is or isn't worthwhile and ask ourselves the other question: If each of us reached across the border into the disciplines which represent the other man's domain, would there be something that we would like to put right?   Are there kinds of concepts that have the same form but different meaning? I noticed that Guetzkow as a political scientist began to assault the economists' "economic man," and that is only the beginning of the game.   Are there other similar differences we can flush out? Conversely, do we have the beginnings of convergences among the disciplines?

I agree that this is a much more diffuse kind of a target, and maybe you don't want to address yourselves to it.   I merely want to call your attention to the fact that you are not doing it yet.

HUGHES: Could I just follow up on that?   I don't really mean to violate one of your earlier commandments, but as I listen to a lot of the comments I am concerned, very concerned, with the purpose that you just enunciated insofar as it relates to the use of the term "social sciences," for example.

I prefer, far prefer, to think of what we are doing as relating to a framework to be called the behavioral sciences.   There are several reasons.   One of them is that, implicit in social science—and I didn't want to get into this kind of nit-picking—are a lot of social species that are not human, and we should be dealing with them.   What we are talking about are human kinds of social behavior, but if that is the case, why have we excluded from representation here vast fields of psychology, for example, which certainly relate to human interaction or social kinds of behavior? I don't mean to just be semantic about this, but I think—if we are really going to begin to address ourselves to integration or to the development of complementarity among several diverse pieces of this total picture, which is, I believe, a better way of looking at integration—that we have to very specifically and with a rough and ready approach enlarge our fields of the disciplines.

I don't like the term "discipline." It is already too constrictive. But we certainly need, as has been suggested, some of the ecological work. Here I am much more drawn toward the biological base which underlies all our behavior and which is the empirical root of our data and our abstractions. We need to begin to put a large framework or bracket around what we are concerned with and then, within that, see where there are overlaps that emerge in terms of the dialectics of knowledge about life and our conceptualization of these elements in life. But I don't know if this was an explicit decision. I know it comes from the title of the Academy itself, but how constrictive must we be in terms of that kind of an outlook?

I, as an anthropologist, am perhaps not so concerned as Bierstedt was about having rediscovered biology lately, as I tried to suggest in my paper. We go all over the map and with a good deal of immodesty, but with a lot of fun in the process. But more than that, we accept as a basic dictum of our discipline or our lack of discipline the fact that man is an animal. And we've got to bring these basic kinds of considerations and all the data that pertain to them into our attempt at conceptualization—that conceptualization itself being a contributing portion to the total evolving knowledge of human social behavior. Am I wrong here in trying to enlarge the conceptual framework, implicit and rough though it may be, that we are working in?

SCHELLING: I'll give a quick answer to your last question. You're not wrong as long as you equally encourage other people to go off in other directions. I'll argue in a minute that man is an animal, but it is also useful to think of man as a machine.

In talking about these things—how you should combine normative and non-normative analysis and so forth—I am reminded of a very strong principle that General George Marshall had, which was that he would never trust a general who made a decision after twelve o'clock noon. I think what Marshall didn't know was that he had a morning temperature peak. A lot of people have late afternoon temperature peaks, and he should never trust a late afternoon type with a judgment before noon. But he assumed that everybody worked best on the same daily schedule that he did and prescribed accordingly for officers under his command.

I have even heard that our former President Pusey alleged—I don't know whether he believes it—but alleged that a man can't do proper research unless he teaches, just as he can't be a proper teacher unless he does research.   To me it is equally plausible to say a man can't be a good teacher if he does research and a man can't do good research if he spends his time teaching.   I am inclined to think that, like the principle of George Marshall, one principle applies to people like Pusey, and maybe another principle applies to people like me.

Even on the question of whether we were really being a little bit deadly or merely friendly when we talked about having fun, I think it is probably the case that some people do their best work when it is hard work to them, and some people only achieve anything useful or creative when it is fun.   I think this is true in business.   I think it is true in fighting.   I think it is true in baseball.   I think it is true in journalism.   I think it is true in biological science.   I think it is true in political science.   I think it is true everywhere.

Some people do it one way, some another.   Some people can't work by themselves.   They've got to have somebody to be stimulated by, maybe to talk to or just to be with.   Other people can't work with somebody present.   Some people can never complete work; some people can never start work.

And my guess is, on questions of how fruitful it is to dirty your hands with very applied policy questions or how useful it is to mix up your notions of societies' values with efforts to learn about traffic flows, that it is a case of some people getting stimulation one place and some getting stimulation another place.   Some do better when they abstract from all but the little thing that they know, and some people get lost when they don't stick precisely to what they know.

Therefore, my conclusion from this is that we want to be very careful about prescribing what it is that social scientists ought to do more of or ought to do less of.   I think we also ought to remember that if you have too many surgeons it may be possible to know who shouldn't have become a surgeon.   If you don't have enough surgeons it is awfully hard to find the guy who didn't become a surgeon. You see, I copped out because I didn't go into philosophy, and I don't know why I should blame a philosopher for not doing what several people including me don't do, unless you simply mean he got so close to it that he should have done it.

And then the question arises from his point of view of whether he is doing something useful and, if he were to have to do your kind of philosophy, of whether he would have gone into philosophy in the first place. And the answer may well be no. Therefore, when you find people doing what you think is a waste of time in a social science, I think it does little good to propose that they do something different. They are doing their thing. They are doing it because that is their thing. If they had to adopt your method or your interest, they probably would find something to do other than the social sciences, including retiring early.

HACKER: May I ask you a question on this?

SCHELLING: Sure, go ahead.

HACKER: We at Cornell send a lot of our bright undergraduates to graduate school at Harvard. I see what happens to them in graduate study. My usual reaction is: "I knew him when he had an imagination and flair, and now he has become a discipline-based scholar." In other words, you are looking at a person at the age of twenty-six and saying, "Well, that's what he can do." I'm saying he could have done lots of other things until the guild got hold of him and changed his intellectual perspective.

SCHELLING: I don't mean that if you put in a different style in education it wouldn't be different, but simply that at my age, if I do things too mathematically or not mathematically enough, if I don't like to handle data or if data are what I find fun, it is awfully late to change me.

Let me wind up quickly about the union of social science and biology. It is worthwhile speculating as to what aspects, even of our political philosophy, depend on such facts as Mr. Bierstedt mentioned, such as that the fiction about all people being equal is tolerable. One reason it is tolerable is that the largest group of the acknowledged unequal—infants and small children—get to grow up and have their turn. If it turned out, as he suggested, that we went through stages like the gypsy moth that begins as a caterpillar—as speculated on in science fiction—we'd have a hard time deciding whether, so to speak, children were people and unequal, or not people and not to be counted in our political science.

We are discovering, particularly as we study environmental problems, many things that are common to the physical sciences and the social sciences. A big thing discovered with customs data was the "balance of payments." You could almost always identify every transaction as involving two parties and having double entries for each party, so you were engaged in quadruple-entry bookkeeping. Once you discover that, things you used to think were coincidence you now recognize to be determined; you find you have one degree less of freedom than you thought. You can sometimes even estimate a missing magnitude if you have a total for the rest of them.

In economics the big theoretical advances have often been the discoveries of what we call the "mere identities"—those equations that don't depend on how people behave but on the kind of behavior it is. The physical sciences are full of these. If you ask what happens if you put a room air conditioner on the floor, shut the doors and windows, and run it, there are principles of conservation that suggest it is about the same as if you ran a vacuum cleaner using the same amount of electricity.

Now we are discovering that in our economics, or in our enlarged social science, we've got to deal with a great many more "transaction budgets" and "balance sheets" than we used to. The earth's thermal budget—the heat exchange between the earth and the rest of the universe—is not altogether unlike a balance of payments. We are discovering a lot of "conservation principles" in the way the non-biodegradable things that we throw away or spread around travel though food chains or accumulate in particular organs, and we need a radioactive fallout budget, a DDT budget, and things of that sort, many of which are reminiscent of economic institutions and phenomena. This is not altogether different, say, from chain letters, corporate pyramids, credit expansion, the bond market, or the ship-construction cycle. You've got to trace the transactions through some system that shows closure; often you discover that, so to speak, what you used to think you could throw away is still there.

LINDBLOM: This theme has been sounded several times now—individual differences among scholars, the variety of circumstances that may lead to fruitful development, and the impossibility of being confident about what methods are best.   We all agree.

Granted that, we nevertheless want to look for patterns, regularities, dominances, modes.   Even if it is true that there are Marshalls with high temperature peaks in the morning and other generals with high temperature peaks in the afternoon, we might want to know whether most people have high temperature peaks in the morning or most people have them in the afternoon. Similarly, even if it is true that finally each of us has to go his way and do what he can best do, nevertheless we want to reflect now and then on what we have been doing and what we might have done if we'd had a different bias or training, and we want to know what to encourage our graduate students to do.

Your comment about the variety of styles that have to be indulged and protected is, therefore, only prefatory to the considerations that we want to move on to.   You may want to respond on that, but what I really wanted to get the floor for a minute ago was this.   I don't think we have responded to a specific request you made.   I understood you to say that you would like to have at least a few responses around the table on the question: Standing in one discipline and looking over the wall, what would we like to see neighboring disciplines do?

I would like to encourage some responses by making one myself.   Looking from economics over the wall, I want to take note of a healthy imperialistic expansion of economics over the wall into other disciplines.   It is the concept of the economic man, called to my mind because you made some earlier reference to it. Though the concept of economic man is, of course, always under attack as a now obsolete eighteenth- or nineteenth-century, intellectual creation, economists continue to get an enormous amount of mileage out of it.   Far from that concept's weakening in economics, it is making strides in the social sciences as a whole.   In *World Politics* (July, 1969) Harsanyi has described the extent to which the social sciences are making headway in analysis by postulating the highly rational individual and spelling out likely patterns of behavior on that supposition.   Down's work on the economic theory of democracy is a conspicuous example.   So also are such attempts to develop exchange theories of politics or of social behavior as Ilchman, Curry and Wade, Blau, and Homans. All are exploiting fundamentally the same concept as that of economic man and getting some very considerable insights into social behavior.

LAMBERT: Let's think for a minute about the difference in disciplines. Which of them have time series analysis of any sophistication at all, and which call attention to variables that might change and hopefully move between two static positions? Certainly in terms of the analysis of policy implications or even intellectually the question of the nature of changes over time in various disciplines is really very different indeed.

For instance, if you are discussing development side with the anthropologists, what you will get is a calling attention to the fact that people's cultures are complex and you have to watch out for them, both because they will block what you are trying to do and because the governments' plans frequently have troublesome cultural side effects. The sociologists, by and large, will say much the same thing as the anthropologist, only he tends to do it with the macro- versus the micro-level. Sociologists have a kind of demographic bookkeeping device which enables them to work in numbers; the anthropologists, by and large, do not.

You go on to the political scientists, dividing them between the tribes who argue intrastate determinants for foreign policy and these who emphasize external systemic determinants of foreign policy. However, in political science there are intradisciplinary imperatives which are very different from the anthropologist's and the sociologist's. On up you could go to the economists with their rather special kinds of measures of development, and so forth.

What I am trying to say is that I think a part of the agenda at some point is to take a look at the ways the disciplines don't intercommunicate because of these fundamental differences in viewpoints.

I was struck a couple of years ago—many years ago—by a very ingenious thing that Sol Tax did in one of his early volumes of *Current Anthropology*. He had an economist review the work of the anthropologists on village-level economic data and then sent this critique out to the anthropologists for a response to it.

It was one of the most delightful set of exchanges I think I've ever read.

What it did, I think, in a sometimes amusing, sometimes truculent, fashion was to dredge out a lot of really very different world views of the various disciplines.

CHARLESWORTH: Our discussion here has turned, appropriately enough, on what it is we want to discuss and why our particular topic was chosen for this conference. I have my arm resting an essay which I wrote on that subject that I did not circulate to this group because I did not wish to appear to foreclose a discussion—not only on the substance, but the procedure of our conference. I think it is all to the good that we should roam around saying, Now what is it that we are after? Is this the way to do it? Is it worthwhile even if we could do it?

The man for whom this hotel is named, in reconstituting the Junta, said it was for the purpose of the pursuit of useful knowledge. He emphasized the useful part which, of course, for sophisticated people like this group only begs the question on what is useful. If we go back to Cohen's celestial navigation, is that more useful than a good lifeboat? That doesn't dispose of the difference between useful knowledge and knowledge which is pursued just for the fun of the game. You ought to try to think that you are doing something useful. I say a pox on this guy who says, "I hope nobody can use this information."

I'm not going to read my essay, but I explored all of these alternatives, how you approach this integration business, and I also dwelt on the subject of whether integration is worth anything or not. If you will recall, one of the sentences in my letter of invitation said there might not be anything in this. If not, it is a good thing to find it out and let our colleagues over the country know it. So it doesn't worry me that we don't have an ordered, structured program here going methodically from point to point settling this and settling that. If, during our first session the general motif is flounder, well, flounder let it be. If a distinguished group like this, after trying hard and writing these papers and going to the trouble of coming to a distant city, can't do anything but flounder, then that's very useful information which we ought to put around.

LINDBLOM: The brightest possibility I see for integration that has been raised this morning is Schelling's when he begins to talk about the commonalities in various phenomena. You remember his somewhat figurative reference to budgets. He talked about the new budgets we need and the analogy between man and other physical systems. I would like to draw him out further by asking whether he thinks that there are, in whatever commonalities lead him to think of budgeting as applicable varied phenomena, possible, extraordinarily fruitful integrating generalizations to be developed. The reason I ask him in particular is that he seems most skeptical in his paper of any payoff in integration. I see him, therefore, on both sides of the argument.

SCHELLING: Is this a question you are asking me—which side of the fence I am on?

LINDBLOM: I don't want to pin you down particularly as to where you are. It isn't anxiety about your location that motivates my question. I just want to know why your own paper doesn't respond to your own suggestions that there are fundamental, integratable similarities, as illustrated by your references to varied applications of the idea of budgeting.

SCHELLING: I guess I want a weaker word than integration, and I don't want to integrate the *social* sciences.

LINDBLOM: We got that point. Very good. Are you not really suggesting, by the number of cases to which you have already applied the notion of budgeting, the possibility of a vast integration incorporating all the sciences, including the social sciences?

SCHELLING: There are many lines of theoretical thought that are useful to several social sciences but are not themselves social science. There are a couple on your list, for example, the theory of collective choice. This shows up in many places—in legal theory, economics, philosophy. But broad as it may be, it is an abstract, specialized, formal body of thought that doesn't particularly integrate with sociologists, economists, and anthropologists except once in a while to bring a few of them together if they are interested. Then there are some broader things like the "budget" concept where we do find something in common among the social sciences—or, I should say, among many sciences, including several of the social sciences.

If they are there to be found it is foolish not to look for them. If they are best found by putting people from two or more disciplines together, let us try it.   If they are best found by having people become voluntary exiles from their own disciplines to browse the literature of another one, let us try it.

When you find these unifying or common-use ideas, it is good. But if you do this with an ultimate purpose to integrate the social sciences—not to take advantage of things that may be common to them but to try deliberately to form a whole out of them, adopting a doctrine that it ought to be possible, and if it ought to be possible it is possible, and it would be good—you may miss a lot of opportunities and you misconstrue the goal.   The goal is to find a common concept, like "queuing," "information," "homeostasis," "growth," "balance sheet," or some other.   The goal is not to unify a particular handful of disciplines through the concept you find.

KARIEL: I am just as skeptical as you are about integration and about heroically enlarging disciplinary boundaries, but I would nonetheless be prepared to legislate and to move ahead if I had more evidence to go on.   The kind of evidence I would like is the kind that would enable me to tell whether those who work within particular disciplines find themselves needlessly confined and can tolerate some climbing over that fence, moving within enclaves other than the ones which presently exist.

What particularly strikes me is that doing disciplined work within narrow confines may actually contribute to the self-esteem of those who work within them insofar as they are professionals. Also, they are connoisseurs who know what is being done by professionals and how well they do it.   Those who work within a discipline can give one another recognition, even affection.   One ought to consider carefully before giving all this up.   How much to give up, I think, is a testable, practical question.   There is very little information on this.

I would be prepared to firm up the disciplines *and* facilitate movement between them; that is, not to freeze an individual to such an extent within particular professional postures that he finds it difficult to move from area to area.

SCHELLING: It seems to me what we agree on is the disintegration of the social sciences.   I am not in favor of maintaining the disciplines in the present boundaries, deliberately or otherwise. We don't even integrate my department.   People get so far off in one part of economics that they don't know what economists are doing in other parts. Once in a while they meet a lonely political scientist, team up, and find the fence separating a neighboring discipline no more impassable than fences inside their own discipline.

But we should distinguish between the idea that somehow, intellectually, we should integrate or disintegrate the social sciences, which is what Ed is talking about, and the more practical question of whether—dealing now with the social sciences as institutionalized occupations—we should integrate or distintegrate university departments or professional societies. It is one thing to go at curricula, organizations, occupations, and institutions and say that there we are either welding together, breaking apart, or building higher fences. It is quite another to talk about the relation among problems, issues, ideas, and methods independent of the floors of the building that people occupy.

LINDBLOM: I was talking about the way Schelling referred to the word "budget." I had in mind, you see, that he said explicitly that he thought of man as an input-output system. He thinks of the whole ecology as an input-output system just as economists think of economy as an input-output system. There are quite a number of political scientists who think of the political system as an input-output system.

So I am asking in effect: Schelling, do you think that there is, in your budget notion, some kind of potential integration? In his reply to me, Schelling doesn't quite answer that question. Instead he says that integration of that sort shouldn't be any particular scholar's purpose, or at least his main purpose. That still leaves my question unanswered: Would it be a good thing to have integration through such concepts as the budget, irrespective of whether it is any one scholar's purpose to achieve it?

That question, in turn, raises a larger question. Charlesworth, you were earlier denouncing the scholar who says that he hopes his material won't be of any use to anybody else. Might we not want, as a feature of social science or science generally, that it be integrative or not integrative, or that it be applied or not applied, or that it be useful or not useful, and yet treat as an entirely independent question what scholars' purposes ought to be since there is a great gap between results and purposes?

For example, even people who believe that all knowledge should be useful knowledge might still endorse some scholars working for fun on the grounds that scholars who work for fun produce useful knowledge. And it also might be that—though no one should pursue formally, explicitly, and deliberately any comprehensive integration as his purpose—it still might be that we ought to encourage scholars to pursue such purposes other than integration itself that would achieve some forms of integration.

I am making a methodological point that we ought not to lose sight of again—that we can distinguish between what kinds of results we want in social science or science generally, and what kinds of purposes we want to ask scholars to pursue deliberately.

GUETZKOW: In his opening remarks, Lindblom already indicated that results may differ from purposes when he endorsed my alternative formulation, that the pursuit of knowledge simultaneously by the social science super-elite and gifted policy analysts may inadvertently yield rich integrations of the social sciences. But he seems to grasp only part of the total picture, at times stereotyping my assertions about the qualitative as a desire "to move away from the verbal to the quantitative," and then continuing the century-old argument that a systems study of desalinization along the southern coasts of the Mediterranean is less basic than inquiries into the "fundamentals of social organization." My exposition is faulty if Lindblom was able to conceive that my comments on his essay argued an "automatic identification of the quantitative . . . with policy orientation." In proposing an alternative formulation for the conference's question in my remarks on "Integrating Social Science *With* Policy Analyses" I indicated,

Given knowledge formated as data and theory banks, with a capability of performing at various levels of aggregation and generality, one almost inadvertently moves toward integrations of social science within policy analysis simultaneously. As one works ahead, building theory banks and data banks, could it just be that the needs for knowledge of both the elitist social scientist and the professional policy analyst will be satisfied simultaneously? Each benefits from the other; each contributes to the other.

So then you will get integrations as such become useful, as we develop a technology of knowledge which enables us to generate other than eighteenth-century, verbal formulations of the single question variety.

LINDBLOM: Well, you may. I am quite open to the possibility that you may.

BIERSTEDT: Whatever the overt purpose—whether it is to solve a problem or to integrate the social sciences—psychologically, wouldn't you agree, Mr. Lindblom, that the pursuit of knowledge is to be explained by a need to satisfy curiosity, and that that may be enough? I know Mr. Guetzkow wouldn't agree with me.

LINDBLOM: Much of the pursuit of knowledge is financed in ways that call for another explanation. Obviously, the sources it finds are often looking for useful knowledge; they are not merely subsidizing intellectual curiosity.

HACKER: Empirically, that's not true. Recently there has been much more support for pure curiosity.

LINDBLOM: Where did the money come from?

HACKER: The federal government. It was given to the social sciences, and they didn't even ask us what we were doing with it.

LINDBLOM: But when we collected money through the March of Dimes, it was not to satisfy the intellectual curiosity of medical researchers. People were interested in preventing polio. If you want to explain the pursuit of knowledge, you've got to explain that too.

MACRAE: I'd like to come back to Lambert's question because I am afraid that it may be unanswerable. The question, as I understood it, was whether we couldn't move toward a particular integration of the social sciences by enumerating things that we found useful—an inductive method, so to speak.

But in distinction to that question, I would like to say that, like some others around the table, I fear we will never get anywhere that way. All of us would have rich experiences. We could list hundreds of examples which would accumulate on the ones that Lindblom and Lane and others have listed, but I don't think we would make much progress toward integration. However, if we ask the question, as some have, about how to facilitate integrations—in the plural—in the social sciences and other disciplines, we would move to the question of social structures that would encourage this sort of integration if we believed it to be desirable. We might consider making the boundaries or the walls between the disciplines more permeable, or requiring dissertation committees to include someone outside the discipline in question.

If we could cope with the questions that Kariel raised about the self-esteem and satisfaction that come from operating within a discipline, we could talk about how to facilitate these various integrations rather than the particular concepts that would furnish the one and only integration. Two means of facilitating various integrations might be the loosening of ties that bind graduate students to particular disciplines, and the establishment of various kinds of interdisciplinary structures within the universities, including generalized policy schools, such as are growing up around the country.

LANE: As I understand it, this is certainly very close to the illustration of policy analysis that I used—that is to say, it was a budget problem, an illustrative case of how to spend money for health research. So my guess is, if pushed a little bit, that budgeting is policy analysis in part. It is a conceptual apparatus for it—perhaps more than that. I take satisfaction in this and note it.

To return, though, to that integration which comes up most frequently, I noticed most often in the criticisms of my paper, but in other cases too, that we are concerned with this nondiscipline of evaluation and the empirical-causal modeling. This is where the policy analyst is criticized for three things. One is that the scope of his inquiries is too small. The second is that the agenda is too much set for him, and I don't agree to that. The third is that it is not properly systematized in terms of the implicit norms or purposes or values which are to be implemented.

One can state this, but the next step, I think, is how would one then elaborate this particular integration of normative thinking with cause-and-effect analysis or policy analytical cost benefit analysis or whatever, or effects of a given intervention on a system?

But is there something more to get said than that one should take account of it? I address this to Henry and Duncan and those who are saying it ought to be done.

MacRae: If you phrase the question again, I will try to feed back what I am getting from you in order to answer the right question. I think you are advocating evaluative discourse. You are asking: What more can you say than that you have to take systematic account of values?

LANE: Yes. We are talking about policy analysis. The first question may concern what policy should be pursued—and that is the evaluative one, perhaps—or ought we to advance, and then a series of other questions. But that one clearly is prior. And yet, having said that, is there more to be said?

MacRae: There are two kinds of additional things to be said. One is the intellectual content, and that runs the risk of boiling down to the personal assertion of how I would do it. The second is the social-structural. What kind of discourse do you want between people, in what roles, and with what sorts of reward and organization attached to it? I'd rather discuss the second, both in the area of evaluative discourse and in the area of the integration of the social sciences. I'd rather talk about getting people talking about these things than I would place myself in the position of a target by suggesting one controversial way of doing it.

So I think that merely getting welfare economists and democratic theorists, for example, talking to one another would move us toward coping with some of the half-articulate or semi-conscious assumptions that we make in talking about things like preferences. That's an example, but I wouldn't want to restrict the discourse to that.

LINDBLOM: One of your questions, Mr. Lane, was on how to relate evaluative components to empirical components of analysis. Two points on that. One is that it takes a great deal of energy and sophistication to drive them apart. They don't come apart easily. To bring them together we have merely to abandon certain efforts that we have invested in driving them apart. Secondly—I come back to my earlier point—they are automatically integrated because when we think we are talking evaluatively we are laying down empirical propositions. I grant that we have to be aware of differences between evaluative and empirical elements because there are ways in which unwitting mixtures cause trouble. Even so, the integration of the two is easy.

For example, suppose we raise the evaluative question: Should we try to control inflation? What can you or I say about it? We could say that inflation hurts people with fixed incomes. That is a sensible and relevant comment to make. It is also a factual comment. Or suppose we raise the evaluative question: Should democracy be more participatory? What can we say about that? We can say that participation makes some people feel better or that participation raises the level of responsibility that people exercise. Again, these are empirical propositions.

BIERSTEDT: I wonder what you would say about the encounter that Wesley C. Mitchell once had with Franklin D. Roosevelt, who asked for Mitchell's advice. He asked him at a particular stage in our economic development whether or not, given the situation he was facing, he should lower the gold content of the dollar.

Professor Mitchell said, "Mr. President, I'm very sorry, but I can't answer that question. I can tell you what will happen if you do lower the gold content of the dollar, and I can tell you what will happen if you don't, but whether or not you should, that's not an economist's question." Now doesn't that point out the distinction between a policy action and——

LINDBLOM: No. Professor Mitchell tells the president the economic consequences of alternative policies. He cannot evaluate—or so he says—those consequences for the president. How is the president to evaluate them? He will have to fill in—or turn to other advisors to fill in—further empirical propositions about the consequences of those consequences predicted by Professor Mitchell. His evaluation necessarily takes the form—largely, though not wholly—of empirical analysis of consequences, of consequences of consequences, and so on. The president finally comes, of course, to that end-of-the-line point where he has the consequences of the consequences and finally has to make up his mind. At that point there isn't much left to ethical discourse. Everyone has run out of things to say.

To be sure, at some point one has to take a position, and there are all kinds of methodological controversy in philosophical circles as to what to do at that point. My point is that discourse or analysis is pretty much finished.

Bierstedt: Taking that kind of position is indulging in a political or ethical, not empirical, kind of a thing.

Lindblom: At that point you have to act. However, my argument is that ethical discourse up to that point is almost entirely empirical—up to that end point—and ethical discourse is largely, therefore, in fact empirical discourse. When ethical discourse takes on a special non-empirical characteristic, it becomes methodological discourse on what to do when you can't talk anymore, when you can't analyze any further, when there are no other facts to be brought to bear, and where you have to fish or cut bait. That is the end of the discussion. The content of the discussion is the empirical proposition.

Bierstedt: But the end of the discussion is the beginning of the action.

Lindblom: Yes, that's right.

Kariel: I want to respond to Lane's question. He has asked really whether it is sufficient simply to take account of what is discovered in, or what conclusions are found within, normative discourse. My response is no. Partially we engage in normative discourse all of the time, but we disguise this and say that ours are methodological discussions or that they are narrowly policy oriented and value neutral, in which case the normative ingredients are merely repressed.

Now, I would argue against any segregated area in which we engage in normative discourse, the results of which might then be conveyed to, let's say, policy analysts who could learn what we have discovered. What one ought to do instead—and I am saying really what has been intimated previously—what we ought to do instead is to seek somehow to work toward ever greater explicitness, making the implications of whatever it is that we are doing increasingly more obvious, and providing larger contexts for whatever decisions or policy operations we engage in, so that we reach a great degree of lucidity as we act. Thereby we would be coping implicitly with value problems.

Charlesworth: Well, gentlemen, this has been a very stimulating discussion, but we are running out of time. I invite your attention to the room on the other side of that partition where we will have cocktails and luncheon. We will reassemble at this same place at the appointed time.

Integration of Political Science and the Other Social Sciences through Policy Analysis

By Robert E. Lane

POLICY analysis I take to mean the answers to the questions: What happens when we intervene in the social system this way rather than that way? The "we" is important because policy implies human decisions, not the unfolding of natural events—that is, it means this unless we have in mind God's or nature's policy. Normally the reference is to government intervention, but it might equally mean intervention by some other institution, such as a university, or perhaps private intervention where the pattern is repeatable and weighed against alternatives. In the definition, the term "this way rather than that way" excludes policy thinking that is not comparative. I believe the consideration of alternatives, including doing nothing, is an essential, hence definitional, part of policy analysis. By the reference to "social system" I exclude those technological choices of instruments or means that have few human consequences—though I suspect one of the virtues of policy analysis is that it reveals the latent human consequences of many seemingly innocent decisions, such as, say, the choice of copper versus aluminum, with its benefits for Chile versus Guiana.

Some Intellectual and Social Origins of the Policy Analysis Movement

To help place what might be called "the policy analysis movement" in current intellectual history and to indicate some reasons why it should not be regarded as a superficial trend toward applied social science, it may be well for me to mention briefly some of the intellectual and social background of the movement, as I see it. I do this hesitantly as an amateur in the field, but perhaps the commentators following will correct me where I am wrong. I will mention five contributing elements: (1) the development first of general systems analysis and then of applied systems analytical thinking; (2) the emphasis on governmental effectiveness, or outputs, as contrasted to line-item costs or inputs; (3) the concept of government policy as applied social science and of government programs as social experiments; (4) the "social indicators" or measurement movement; and (5) the concepts of cybernetics and the development of an information exchange capacity following an information explosion crisis.

From the main intellectual component of systems analysis and systems theory, policy analysis borrowed the idea that a change in one set of specified elements of a mutually influencing network of elements can be seen to change the other elements in a specifiable manner. (Policy analysis also has some roots in linear programming, but since my understanding of these matters is so shallow, I will not comment further on this.) If one looks at the governmental units as elements of social systems, and policies and programs as the element-changing forces, one is led to wonder what happens when the government spends so much money here rather than there, regulates this process, that price, and so forth. Segments of the government-society nexus come to be seen as systems.

The second theme, following from this, is the examination of outputs, effects, and impacts rather than inputs, such as personnel, supplies, travel costs, and construction costs of the line-item budgets. Here three terms for related elements of policy analysis are relevant, all of them sharing this output-oriented, system theoretical concern: program, planning, budgeting (PPB), cost/benefit or cost-effectiveness analysis, and program evaluation. Borrowing from work done at RAND and from RAND personnel, Robert McNamara employed program planning budgets in the Defense Department to give him new management tools designed to restore civilian control over the military as well as to improve performance. The devices or their spokesmen were so persuasive that President Johnson ordered them employed throughout the federal system.

The second related term is cost/benefit or cost-effectiveness analysis. The technique is best interpreted by an example, this one from the health field explained by Robert N. Grosse, then deputy assistant secretary for Program Systems, Department of Health, Education, and Welfare (HEW):

[In a] study in the health area . . . on disease control programs . . . we looked at cancer of the uterine cervix, breast, head and neck, and colon-rectum. We estimated cost per examination, the number of examinations that would be required before a case would probably be found. From this we derived the number of cases that would be found. An estimate was made of the number of deaths that could be averted by the treatment following detection of the cancers. Then we calculated the cost per death averted, which ranged from about $2,200 in the case of cervical to $46,000 for colon-rectum cancer. . . . We're about to begin answering questions such as—"If we have a budget to spend over this time which is $75 million, what do we do?" If we have only $75 million, we ought to put the money in cervical cancer; if we have, say, $115 million, we could pick up both cervical cancer and some work on breast cancer detection. Head and neck, and colon-rectum seem to be much too expensive. We recommended that these be restricted to research and development programs. . . . We see that cervical cancer is one of the higher payoff programs (in terms of cost of deaths averted) as are the largely educational programs in the use of restraining devices in motor vehicles.[1]

Additional studies took into account the ages of the persons whose deaths might be averted, giving information on life-years saved. The technique is applicable to cost effectiveness of most domestic government programs—vocational training, exits from poverty, family assistance, and so forth—even though the values to be maximized, or the evils minimized, may be subject to various interpretations. Being specific does not reduce the evaluative or interpretative component of policy-making; it merely makes it explicit and therefore subject to informed challenge by those who disagree.

Finally, the third related term is program evaluation. In the language of an important study, *Federal Evaluation Policy,* by the Urban Institute:

Evaluation (1) assesses the *effectiveness* of an *on-going* program in achieving its objectives, (2) relies on the principles of research design to distinguish a program's effects from those of other forces working

1. Robert L. Chartrand, Kenneth Janda, Michael Hugo, eds., *Information Support, Program Budgeting, and the Congress* (New York: Spartan, 1968), pp. 163–165.

in the situation, and (3) aims at program improvement through modification of current operations.[2]

In one sense this is that part of systems analysis and cybernetics that is called feedback. More practically, it provides the possibility of comparing the effectiveness of one type of program with another whose purposes are similar. Thus it provides cost-effectiveness data for the next budgetary round. The reference to "research design" in the Urban Institute's definition is important because it reveals the contribution of general social science method and theory to policy analysis. Without methods for eliminating the influence of "test variables" or third factors, policy evaluation would be impossible; without some theoretical ideas of what causes what, one would find it difficult to know what "other forces working in the situation" should be thus eliminated—given the frequent impossibility of randomizing experimental treatments.

A third intellectual element in this policy analysis movement is best summarized by reference to the recommendations of four books, including *Federal Evaluation Policy* mentioned before, and two conferences held in October, 1970. These recommendations have in common the premise stated in the definition of policy analysis—that public policy is an intervention in a social system. The authors of these books and conference recommendations believe that it follows from this premise that behavioral and social scientists with appropriate training should play a greater role in social and foreign policy-making. These books and conferences are: *The Behavioral Sciences and the Federal Government* (1968), commissioned and published by the National Academy of Sciences (BS & FG), *Knowledge Into Action: Improving the Nation's Use of the Social Sciences* (1969), commissioned by and published by the National Science Board (KIA), *The Behavioral and Social Sciences: Outlook and Needs* (1969), commissioned by the National Academy of Sciences and the Social Science Research Council and published by NAS (BASS), and a more technical book, *Federal Evaluation Policy: Analyzing the Effects of Public Programs* (1970), by Joseph Wholley and others of the Urban Institute (FEP). The conferences are the Brook-

2. John S. Wholley and others (Washington, D.C.: Urban Institute, 1970).

ings "Symposium on Applying Knowledge from the Behavioral
Sciences to Social Legislation Programs" (October, 1970, BS)
and the "Conference on Social Research and Foreign Affairs"
(also October, 1970, SR & FA) sponsored by the Department of
State, the American Foreign Service Association, and the International Studies Association.

I will summarize the recommendations, grouping together
those with comparable thrusts even though they may differ in
detail.

1. The federal departments and agencies should identify their
needs for personnel trained in the behavioral sciences, systematically recruit for the positions so identified, and train their own
personnel through in-house training and educational leaves of ab-
sence (BS & FG, KIA, FEP, BS, SR & FA).

2. The strategic science advisory agencies, that is, the President's Science Advisory Committee and the Office of Science and
Technology, should include more social scientists (BS & FG,
KIA, BS). The *Knowledge into Action* studies also recommended that the Council of Economic Advisory's staff should include more social and natural scientists.

3. The president and Congress should prepare annually a
statement of long-range research needs (BS), and the secretary
of state should establish a Secretary's Advisory Research Council
for this purpose and for implementing a more vigorous research
policy in the State Department (SR & FA).

4. The National Science Foundation should increase its support for basic and applied research (BASS) and training (KIA)
and the mission agencies should prepare long range plans for their
research needs as well as for their specific program needs, including program evaluations, and provide larger funds for grants and
contracts to carry out such research (BS & FG, BS, FEP, SR &
FA).

5. The government and the scientific communities should establish better liaison and information brokerage mechanisms for
informing social scientists of the government's needs on the one
hand, and for informing government in all its branches of the research capabilities available, on the other. Some of these suggestions include conferences, early notices of legislative and administrative hearings, publications, attendance of government officers

at the annual meetings of the social science associations, and so forth (BS & FG, FEP, SR & FA, BS). Specifically the Brookings Symposium recommended:

that appropriate professional associations and concerned universities increase their efforts to alert their interested members and constituents to researchable questions generated by public policy problems.

6. To improve the implementations of research findings, academic and other outside researchers should join with government researchers in common inquiries (KIA, SR & FA).

7. There should be established a Council of Social Advisers reporting to the president and Congress. This should either be privately financed (BASS) or established by the government (BS) in which case it might be joined with the Council of Economic Advisers into a Council of Social and Economic Advisers (BS).

8. The Library of Congress should establish a set of rotating professorships in the social and behavioral sciences to "advise members of Congress and the staffs of congressional committees" (BS).

9. There should be established and funded by government (1) a National Institute for Advanced Research in Public Policy (BS & FG) and/or (2) a set of Graduate Schools of Applied Behavioral Science on the university campuses (BASS) and/or (3) about 25 Social Problems Research Institutes throughout the country (KIA).

10. The final reports of all commissions, policy relevant research publications, and perhaps even papers like this one, should provide a section on the implementation of the recommendations. The report that made this recommendation failed to provide a section on implementation—and I will, too (BS).

11. "The social and behavioral science community [should] give consideration to the creation of a national social science organization, such as the National Academy of Sciences, which would be located in Washington" (BS).

There is another recommendation from this group of books and conferences which seems to me to represent a fourth intellectual source for the policy analysis movement. This recommendation itself has something of a history. Perhaps it may be linked to Harold Lasswell's concern for social observatories and developmental constructs. Curiously the National Aeronautics and Space Administration gave the movement impetus by funding a study of social indicators by Raymond Bauer and others [3]— but he and they were already concerned. Otis Dudley Duncan [4] and Bertram Gross [5] are fathers of important works in the area, and the social science data archives movement, sired in part by the Inter-university Consortium for Political Research, was important. But, most generally, the traditional interest of social scientists in such data as the census provides, the concern and practice of the economists with masses of self-generated data bases, including the early work of Wesley Mitchell in national income accounting, and the needs of the government for increasingly better data all played a part in what might be called the social indicators movement. As a consequence, one of the main themes of the books and conferences mentioned above is stated in the recommendation:

The government, with appropriate guidance from social scientists, should improve its data and information systems, records keeping and records sharing, and especially give more attention to developing social indicators as guides to national performance and public policy. (BS & FG, KIA, BASS, BS, SR & FA).

Finally, fifth, it seems to me, that the sophisticated concern for improved information exchange, born out of cybernetics and made possible by the computer, plays an important role in the thrust for policy analysis. We see this developed in the National Science Foundation's series on *Current Research and Development in Scientific Documentation,* which started publication in July, 1957, in the Committee on Scientific and Technical Information (COSATI) of the Federal Council for Science and Technology, established in 1959, in the Smithsonian's Science Infor-

3. Raymond A. Bauer, ed., *Social Indicators* (Cambridge, Massachusetts: M.I.T. Press, 1966).
4. Otis Dudley Duncan, *Toward Social Reporting: Next Steps*, Social Science Frontiers Series #2 (New York: Russell Sage Foundation, 1969).
5. Bertram M. Gross, "The State of the Nation: Social Systems Accounting" in Bauer, *Social Indicators*.

mation Exchange, which has traditionally received, organized, and exchanged information about research in progress, and in perhaps a dozen specialized government documentation and information exchange services. Of course, all of these are antedated by the Library of Congress, but the computerization of some Library of Congress services is of more recent vintage.

Today, Congress has begun to interest itself in its own information services—including a modest change in the title and role of the Legislative Reference Service—as is made clear in Robert L. Chartrand, Kenneth Janda, and Michael Hugo, *Information Support, Program Budgeting, and the Congress*. If anything were needed to reinforce the view that information exchange developments are part of the policy analysis movement, the discussion in this book will make it clear. Throughout these discussions, the term "knowledge is power" is employed to make this point, with the added edge that congressmen or their partisans believe that the loss of scientific information retrieval capacities inhibits policy analysis capabilities and hence is responsible for the loss of power by the legislative branch.

This brief review of some of the ingredients in the thrust towards more attention to policy and program analysis, while wholly inadequate as history, helps make several points: (1) policy analysis draws on some of the most important intellectual themes of recent times, themselves quite interdisciplinary, for example, systems analysis and cybernetics; (2) it is not, therefore, a superficial attention to social problems in a time of urgent concern, but rather an important convergence of ideas with important theoretical roots and consequences; (3) not only does the policy analysis arise from a group of interdisciplinary intellectual themes and movements, but it makes demands, as implied in the title of this paper, on the social sciences for collaborative and interdisciplinary thinking.

While the preceding discussion has touched on some intellectual origins of the policy analysis movement, there are some latent intellectual components of policy analysis that deserve some explication. I will argue that policy analysis is rooted in certain epistemological, psychological, and cognitive premises that inform it and make it possible. Since these have a bearing on the interdisciplinary nature of the work, let me briefly set them forth.

SOME INTELLECTUAL THEMES IN THE IDEA OF POLICY ANALYSIS

The Ends of Government

The emphasis upon governmental outputs in policy analysis involves statements of purpose, mission, and objectives. It thus leads to a sharpening of debate on the ends or purposes of government. Is it better to save lives through a disease control program, or to improve the functional literacy of the disadvantaged? How much defense risk should one take in order to improve the quality of life in a country? Since the heart of political philosophy is the discussion of the ends or purposes of government, policy analysis should sharpen and improve that discussion. Recall Grosse's question: "If we have a budget to spend over this time . . . what do we do?" By focusing discussion on this question and especially by providing the information on how much it costs to do the various things desired, policy analysis should lead rather soon into important philosophical, human, and of course, inter- and nondisciplinary questions of values.

The Ideas of Social Costs and Latent Effects

Ideology, as contrasted to philosophy, tends to argue for a limited set of values without adequate consideration of the value-cost, or opportunity cost, of the values chosen. To the egalitarians, Tocqueville's argument that social equality breeds anxiety is ignored or quickly dismissed. But if he is right, then one buys equality with anxiety, and the purchase price should be made clear. Similarly, to the libertarian, Fromm's argument that individual freedom, choice, and autonomy make people so insecure that they want to *Escape from Freedom* is heresy. The emphasis on the effects of social policies is very likely to bring these unfortunate costs to public attention, although within more reduced policy domains. Program evaluation, informed by these ideas in somewhat more technical terms, may feed back into political and social theory. Very likely, program evaluation studies will specify some conditions under which the alleged effects are brought about and others where they are not brought about.

The Emphasis on Alternative Means to a Given End

If program evaluation reveals the latent disutilities of a program, cost effectiveness reveals the alternative ways to a given end; it poses mixed questions of ends-means. There is a process of narrowing alternatives. Posit the promotion of the pursuit of happiness as the end of a group of federal programs: Shall this be through increasing enjoyment of the arts, better health, greater economic security? The question was always there, but cost effectiveness permits more exact questions. Posit one of these, say better health: Shall this be done by averting death for a specified period of time for a few or ameliorating suffering from nonlethal diseases, like arthritis, for the many? Posit one of these, say averting death for specified periods of time: Shall this be done by slightly reducing the risks for many or by greatly reducing the risks for a few? In some ways, these questions are nondisciplinary, yet very likely the experienced views of anthropologists and sociologists will be useful as they explore latent consequences of each of these policy choices.

Since government often proceeds by listening to advocates of one group or purpose at a time, the continued emphasis upon alternatives and competing benefits inherent in policy analysis is a useful corrective. For one thing, it may introduce into the discussion an argument for a poorly organized and poorly financed group whose members are unable to present their own case effectively.

Men Have Plural Values

It follows from the forced consideration of the competing values to be bought for a given expenditure that the plural values of mankind are brought more sharply into consideration at any given moment of decision. True, these are likely to be presented within narrow ranges by a single bureau or even department, but even this is a gain—especially when one considers the range of values embraced by a Department of Health, Education, and Welfare. In terms of interest groups again, this means that their single-valued arguments are somewhat weakened—men are not only motorists, sportsmen, patients, and so forth. In terms of disciplines, it means that disciplines with limited policy domains

—law and order, economics and wealth, education and learning—must consider matters outside their professional knowledge, a gain for humanizing the disciplines and, incidentally, for inter-disciplinary discussion.

The Nonrational Must Be Thought About

Lasswell once mentioned that politics is where the irrational basis of society comes to light, by which he meant not only that such emotions as aggression, ambition, and dependency have political manifestations, nor merely that such psychic processes as displacement of private emotions onto public objects have an important part to play in political choice, nor even just the importance of myths and symbols in political life. He also meant that ultimate values were at stake. These may be reasoned—though they may not—but they are hard to deduce from each other; they rarely have the structure of logic; they may not even be transitive.

Policy analysis, because it specifies purposes and ends and compares them, requires some consideration of these values. Because in its sophisticated form policy analysis is so new, I do not believe policy analytic thinking has greatly informed political thinking along these lines; but as the products of cost effective-ness and program evaluation studies come to light, they will compel consideration of the nonrational aspects of politics and they will do it in the light of much more specific data than have been available before. In some ways, this is the same point made about the purposes of government, but from a different stance. Here the point is not the improvement of political philosophy, but rather the de-mystification of government and politics.

Conventions Are Flexible

A standard finding of studies of the budgetary process is that once a program is funded, regardless of the changing nature of society or of the demand for the services provided, the budget for the program tends to grow at roughly the same pace as other programs. Cost effectiveness studies take the opposite premise: they start with a zero order presumption for each program and, unless it can prove its worth, out it goes. Of course, this procedure is not followed in the political world, but the very presumption is radical for it challenges conventions. The radicalizing effect of this kind of thinking is brought home in a set of studies reported in the medicine section of the *New York Times* (2/28/71). Here the presumption challenged—it seems to be Nixon's—is that the best way to improve the health of the nation is to increase medical services by increasing the number of doctors, helping people to pay for more medical care, and improving the distribution of medical services.

But, the *Times* reports:

Dr. Eli Ginsberg, Columbia University economist, points out that, "Despite the substantial increases in expenditure for medical care there has been no significant increase in male longevity during the past decade." Dr. Victor Fuchs, another economist, comments, "My reading of the health literature leaves me with the impression that the greatest potential for improving the health of the American people is not to be found in increasing the number of physicians, or forcing them into groups or even increasing hospital productivity, but it is to be found in what people do for themselves. . . ." Dr. Nathan Glazer, the sociologist, argues further in the current issue of *The Public Interest* that our personal, psychological and cultural milieu—i.e., the way we have learned to take care of ourselves—may be as important as better environmental conditions and certainly more important than doctors and doctoring.

This is partly because doctors are "helpless before the ailments that account for most of the sickness and death in America"—but see to the contrary Grosse's analysis of cancer above—partly because "at least four studies have indicated that annual physical check-ups do not decrease mortality or morbidity," and partly, it is alleged, because "in the modern world, housing, nutrition, accident prevention, sanitation—clean water, food, streets and homes—have produced more health than all the doctors and hospitals combined."

I would not argue that such an anlysis as this, or the careful studies on which it is based, goes very deep in changing conventions or mores, but these studies have a way of challenging fairly basic presumptions and conventions. Studies of the effect of a family assistance program that denied welfare payments to mother and children if there were an able-bodied man in the house found an important effect to be to keep the family separated and generated basic discussions on the ghetto family. Studies of the effect of guaranteed annual incomes found that the incentive to work increased with the provision of minimal security. Such findings are radical in forcing the examination and sometimes the rejection of some of our cherished assumptions. As policy analytical studies increase, we can expect more of these assumptions and conventions to be examined.

The Emphasis upon the Consumer of Programs

The academic social scientist asks: "How can I, we, or society understand social phenomena?" This might be caricatured as "autistic." With an emphasis on inputs, the bureaucratic social scientist asks, "What evidence can I find to support the program my agency handles?" and *he* is measured by program growth. This might be said to be "governmentalist." Policy analysis, with its emphasis upon end-effects and the requirement that the policy analysts be located at one remove from the operating agency, asks, "What does the consumer of the program get from this expenditure?" And this seems to be consumer oriented, analogous to the "consumerism" that has taken hold in many places recently. To the extent that social scientists write primarily for the members of their own discipline, consumerism changes the terms of reference, for a wider audience is likely to be listening.

The Emphasis upon Control over Men's Fates

Anthropologists have often found that Western man is distinguished from others by his sense of dominance over nature, although there has recently been much discussion of men's increasing sense of powerlessness. In any event, the thrust of policy analytical thinking is towards control, action, or, as we said earlier, "intervention in the social system." Lasswell once defined two modes of address towards social phenomena: manipulative and contemplative. Social scientists in academia may stress the importance of understanding and leave the matter there. This is, I think, the contemplative mode. Policy analysis rests on the assumption, if supported by evidence, that something can be done; it is manipulative.

Some Intellectual Consequences of Policy Analysis

Although it is not easily possible to distinguish origins from latent premises from, in turn, consequences, let us briefly look at some facets of the problem that seem to me to emerge under this head.   In the first place, I believe that *argument* for a policy is properly considered to be the very stuff of social theory, if the scope is sufficiently broad.   After all, Hobbes, Locke, and Marx were arguing the cases for certain kinds of social policies: monarchical and authoritarian political arrangements; contractual relationships and the defense of private property; communal divisions of goods and services, abolition of social hierarchies, and socialization of the means of production.   In much more muted terms the argument between a medical insurance plan that relies on employer payments and private companies versus one that relies on national public health insurance has some of the same properties.   The proponent of the latter plan, Senator Kennedy, now cites cost effectiveness studies to show that the Social Security Administration delivers health insurance with lower costs per unit of payment than either the private insurance companies or Blue Cross.   Since this bears on the general question of government versus private efficiency, it enters both into this specific narrow argument and into a larger social argument of which it is a part.

What policy analysis requires is good causal theory; it is not helped very much by taxonomic theory.   Thus, as I consider the plight of theory in sociology, anthropology, and political science, the requirements of policy analysis should prove helpful to the cause of better theory.

Policy evaluation studies have led to the belief that one gets better data from social experiments than from correlational studies.   Thus in HEW there is a strong effort being made to try out several different programs with similar purposes in different cities, controlling for as many exogenous factors as is possible. Up to this point it has been argued that one reason the natural sciences and psychology have made rapid strides is because they are experimental sciences while the social sciences are observational.   If, with the cooperation of the federal government, the social sciences now become experimental, social science generally should be improved—and this without regard to discipline.

Another consequence of the thrust for policy analysis will be the improvement of the data available for all social scientists, whether or not they are themselves engaged in this work. Thus academic social science will benefit directly. There will also be an indirect benefit, I believe, because new data often form the basis for new theory. Thus data on the costs of pollution have caused a revision of theories of national income, revisions of some figures on gross national product, and some new ideas on economic development. The study already cited on income maintenance provided new data to improve the theory of work incentives.

In policy analysis, it is important to reduce the domain labelled "all other things being equal" since they are not equal in real life and since real life consequences follow from the results of policy analytical studies. This has a direct bearing on interdisciplinary research, since the "all other things" are often in another discipline's province.

Finally, policy analysis is a stimulus to social invention because it focuses on how to bring about social change. Thus, Charles Schultze—as reported in a talk by Henry Riecken to the American Academy of Arts and Sciences—lists a few:

> The concept of effluent charges in pollution control, incentive contracts and subsidies in manpower training programs, efficiency-oriented reimbursement schemes in medical insurance programs; experimental voucher systems, individual student and performance-oriented pay scales for teachers as a means of introducing incentives into stuffy and rigid educational bureaucracies, mandatory flood insurance with premiums adjusted to flood risk as a method of inducing rational flood plan development, charging the military budget for the current cost of atomic weapons and the present values of currently accruing veterans' benefits as a means of inducing more rational resource allocation, providing military decision makers with incentives to avoid the gold-plating of weapons; designing grant-in-aid programs with more flexibility and with incentives for mayors and governors to bargain with the federal government about an optimum mix of local grants, designing a system of congestion charges for airports to spread traffic, reduce delays and provide investment signals.[6]

6. *Bulletin of the American Academy of Arts and Sciences,* vol. 24, no. 6 (March, 1971), pp. 7–8.

I cannot imagine the development of these incentives and costing schemes without considerable further interdisciplinary work, work that would both benefit from the several knowledge domains and contribute to them, jointly and severally.

SOME FORMS OF INTERDISCIPLINARY INTEGRATION

Interdisciplinary integration, like other meta-scientific goals, is important or valuable only as it helps us to understand something better or more efficiently or do something better or do it more efficiently.   The assumption of its advocates, no doubt, is that such integration will do the following:

1. By mutual comprehension and borrowing, the practitioners of each integrating discipline will discover intellectual tools and findings useful in explaining matters they have traditionally explained less well.   By borrowing concepts of collective choice from economists and group dynamics from sociologists, political scientists can explain legislative behavior better.

2. By synoptic and integrative efforts, the practitioners of each discipline will be able to state old problems in a broader way, employing more powerful theories, and will discover latent patterns invisible when approached on a single discipline basis.   Thus political scientists who have familiarized themselves with work in social anthropology have developed a sub-field of political culture, restating and broadening their concepts of public opinion and political attitudes.

3. By familiarizing themselves with the language and concepts of other disciplines, the integrating disciplinarians may both reduce the redundancy of multiple special languages and, more importantly, discover the connotative values of the "foreign" language that had been omitted in their own terminology.   Further, by comparing the references of the same terms employed in different disciplines, they enrich their understanding of their own body of phenomena through comparison and contrast.   The term "value," as employed in the anthropologists' value orientation, Lasswell's base and scope values, and economic value, is used to refer to partially different and partially similar matters; the comparisons are illuminating.

4. The range of explanatory independent variables in the several disciplines reflects their knowledge domains, but often the

dependent variables are common: social change, institutional instability, alienation. Thus explanatory models are improved by the wider search that interdisciplinary integration provides.

5. Most disciplines have distinctive methods and research traditions, but some they share in common. A political scientist may discover that he can "get at" his material better through borrowing the psychoanalysts' depth interviewing, the sociologists' survey, or the anthropologists' participant observation. But he can do this better if he has familiarized himself with how the original masters go about their business. The same is true, of course, of particular statistical and mathematical tools.

Finally, integration happens in many ways; the grand synthesizing theory is only one, but an important one as the work of Talcott Parsons reveals. There are emergent patterns of integration as well as revealed ones, as is true, for example, in the intersection of sociology and political science in political sociology. The importance of this perspective is revealed by two questions. If one asks who the great social scientists are today, to compare with Max Weber, one is led to think of the decline of social science. But if one asks, do we today understand the problems of legitimacy, leadership, occupational choice and structure, and the sociology of religion better than Weber did, one is led to believe, I think, that the theories and findings of the past half century have been enormously fruitful. Policy analysis, with its narrower view of social scientific explanation than is encompassed in the great works, is, in my opinion, likely to contribute substantially to interdisciplinary explanations and accountability and to the development of a more mature social science. Anyway, by requiring social scientists to work together, policy analysis presents this opportunity.

Commentary on Lane's Paper

By David Easton

OUR problem is to inquire into the utility of policy analysis as a means of integrating the social sciences. The statement of the task already presupposes that there is some probable value in achieving such integration. I assume that among the numerous possible benefits, improvement of our capacity to apply the knowledge of the social sciences looms largest for this conference. I shall not at the outset question this assumption, but I shall conclude first that policy analysis is no more likely to provide for the organic integration of the social sciences than a long line of illustrious predecessors, and second that this type of integration, although helpful, is not really necessary if we wish to apply our knowledge effectively.

The social sciences are analytic. Social problems are totalistic, to borrow a term from Sartre. This contrast reveals the critical difficulties contemporary social science has in putting its knowledge to work effectively in the service of society. The social sciences have learned how to analyze social behavior with a view to generalized understanding. They have yet to discover adequate methods for reintegrating their knowledge. Nor are there any really hopeful prospects on the horizon for effectively reassembling the social sciences for these applied purposes.

The policy analysis movement described in Lane's paper is the most recent effort in this direction. The literature in this area shows a strong preference for dwelling on immediately identifiable but theoretically only secondary issues, such as output effectiveness, benefits as against costs, the identification of problem areas in space and time (social indicators), and structural arrangements for facilitating collaboration among social scientists—institutes for the application of knowledge. However, as Lane's paper indirectly confirms, the literature fails to address itself to one fundamental question: Can we ever hope to reintegrate the social sciences organically? Are there any theoretical barriers—meth-

odological, cognitive, or epistemological—to the integration of
analytically derived social knowledge?

Analysis is a central characteristic of the social sciences. Each
social science seeks to analyze a more or less specialized aspect
of social reality. In itself, human behavior is an undifferentiated mass of activities. The moment we seek to bring some
order into these activities for purposes of scientific understanding,
we are compelled to select or abstract out those aspects that are
of particular interest to us. As social scientists intent on understanding the generalized relationship between phenomena, our
criteria have tended increasingly to become theoretical or selectively problematic within broad theoretical limits. That is to
say, the generalizing social scientist will select out of the apper-
ceptive mass of social reality those aspects that relate to some
concept or hypothesis. And where he has more practical considerations in mind, the specific problem, within the framework
of the theoretical criteria of his discipline, will dictate the type of
variables and data to be isolated from the total situation. In
either instance the scientist deals only with a limited aspect of
the concrete social reality as it is filtered through and interpreted
by his own discipline's intellectual structure.

It is of the very nature of the tools of the social scientist that
he decomposes a total life situation into those elements with
which he can deal, given the concepts at his disposal. Even where
social scientists have sought to differentiate between the analytic
as against the concrete system, seldom have they argued on behalf
of an approach that would allot to any single discipline the task of
understanding an event or institution in all its aspects. Rather
it is assumed that any concrete group or, more appropriately, any
entity unit—as contrasted to an abstracted but empirical property
common to many units—needs to be investigated with the specialized tools of each discipline if generalized understanding is to
be achieved. Each discipline orders the same experiential world
according to its own theoretical criteria.

Urbanism, for example, is a major focal point of dissatisfaction
in contemporary mass society. Political science can shed some
light on the way in which authoritative decisions are made and
implemented in the city; economics, on certain consequences of

the use of resources within the city; sociology, on the urban social structure, its integration and cleavages; and so on for the remaining social sciences. But no one discipline, and not even all of them in combination, is able to look at the city as a total phenomenon, identify its central problems, prescribe for them, and take into account all the ramifying effects of any policy. Indeed, for the social sciences there is no single object out there called the city. Each discipline sees a somewhat different set of variables as the city. Hence the dependent variables at the core of each discipline constitute an analytic system, not an entity or total system made up of biological persons and all of their interactions.[1]

To achieve generalizable understanding of the phenomenal world, social science has fractured reality into seemingly useful pieces. This fragmentation of knowledge, inescapable for purposes of scientific understanding, has left us with major cognitive difficulties when we come to apply our knowledge for the resolution of practical social problems. This is a central theoretical issue made salient by the pressures today for the application of our knowledge. Of course other difficulties also stand in our way as we seek to put our understanding to use: the paucity of generalizations in most disciplines, the dubious validity of those we have, their apparent lack of relevance to urgent concerns, and even the very shortage of adequate data. Yet even if these impediments miraculously disappeared tomorrow, my point is that the central cognitive problem of applying our knowledge, which is dispersed among the analytic disciplines, would remain a major hurdle.

This deficiency of social knowledge, associated as it is with the very nature of scientific understanding, has provided an important base for the major assault being launched against the behavioral sciences today. The critics argue that the utility of social knowledge has been undermined because, through analysis, social sci-

1. Misleadingly these entity or totalistic systems are sometimes called "concrete" units. But an analytic system is just a set of empirical (concrete) behaviors abstracted out of the intuitively known total (concrete) reality. Hence the analytic system is no less "concrete," that is, no less knowable to the senses, than the undifferentiated, intuited reality called the whole entity. See my *A Framework for Political Analysis* (Englewood Cliffs, N.J.: Prentice-Hall, 1965), chapter 3.

ence has destroyed the intuitive unity of the acting, feeling human being and his society. The whole intuitively perceived reality, like the whole person, has been lost from sight. The actor, in a role defined by its theoretical relevance, replaces the whole human being as a repository of the stream of experience. Everything the social scientist touches crumbles into analytic pieces which he is unable to put together again for practical purposes. To gain increased knowledge, the social scientist has pushed Humpty Dumpty off the wall. His pieces are carefully and quantitatively scrutinized. But when it comes to putting him back together again for purposes of action, social scientists, even collectively, are virtually helpless.

The scientific condition of man, it is argued in this vein, creates the very consequences that Lindblom identified. The myopia that comes from concentrating on bits and pieces of the total realm of experience is apt to reconcile the social scientist with the status quo, or at least incapacitates him for launching broader attacks. Each discipline has assigned itself the responsibility for generating indicators reflecting what is happening to its own variables. No one has responsibility for the whole. Even where policy advice is sought, the social scientist offers it in terms of the values associated with his own discipline. He is thereby encouraged to convert policy questions into technical problems of means, rather than to sort out the value implications in the questions themselves. Since no social scientist is called upon to consider the whole, no social scientist feels impelled to challenge the broader social context within which his advice is being asked.

To the major critics of the social sciences today these deficiencies are not just accidents of inattention or of the immaturity of the disciplines as we social scientists might be inclined to argue. The incapacity to deal with the whole reality is presumed to be inherent in the very assumptions of the analytic model of science as applied to man in society. To cope with this inherent flaw in science, alternative cognitive procedures are suggested designed particularly to come to grips with the total experience of the real world. These resemble, in many respects, the *verstehen* sociology of Weber; or they take the form of phenomenological Gestalt perceptions. Both are proposals that cannot help but appear to anyone trained in empirical science as a return to intuition.[2]

The critics are correct in their description of the problems that the urgent crises of society have revealed in the body of knowledge produced by contemporary social science, unconvincing as their remedies may be. The policy analysis movement represents the beginning of our latest response. This movement is well enough along now so that we may begin to question its plausibility as a means for reintegrating the social sciences.

At one time, as early as a few decades ago, demands for the application of knowledge available to the social sciences were considered premature. We had insufficient confidence in the reliability of our generalizations to risk inflicting them on the public. The rapid growth of scientific research about society in recent years has increased our confidence somewhat. And even if diffidence is still the rule in most social sciences, the current social crises have forced the pace of our efforts to justify our increasing claim on social resources.

What are the probabilities that the new policy analysis movement will be able to overcome the inherently analytic divisions among the social sciences? Can the social sciences be reassembled in an organic, meaningful whole that does not decimate the reality in an effort to understand it? We may get some help in answering these questions if we glance briefly at the experience of some past and continuing efforts toward integration.

Concern for integration of the social sciences, for purposes of understanding as well as of application, is at least half a century old.[3] But time has not left the problem any less recalcitrant to solution. Most of the major alternatives have been found wanting although they persistently reappear in the literature dealing with policy analysis today.

1. Theoretical integration. For purposes of ultimate application, it has been argued, integration can be achieved through the

2. See the following articles and the bibliography therein: P. F. Kress, "Self, System, and Significance: Reflections on Easton's Political Science," *Ethics,* vol. 77 (1966), pp. 1–13; and J. G. Gunnell, "Social Science and Political Reality: The Problem of Explanation," *Social Research,* vol. 36 (1968), pp. 159–201.

3. See L. Wirth, *Eleven Twenty-Six* (Chicago: University of Chicago Press, 1940).

construction of some overarching social theory. Such a theory would provide a base of common concepts and acceptable generalizations upon which each of the social sciences could build its specialized enterprise. Action theory, general systems theory, and perhaps rational choice—social decision—modelling are the best known efforts in this direction.

No one of these modes of analysis shows much promise of providing an interesting reassembly of the social sciences even as the first step on the road to coping with practical problems of society. Of all efforts to formulate overarching social theory, general systems theory has perhaps one advantage. Its point of departure is sympathetic to the criticisms of analytic social science. General systems theory assumes that it is appropriate to deal with whole entities, that these constitute the units of systems. These entity elements will differ only in scope, moving from the cellular to the global society level.

At best this theory holds out a promise for the distant future. The level of abstraction is today so general, the orientation of general systems theory for the social sciences as a whole is so limited, that there is insufficient evidence to pass judgment upon the ultimate relevance of this approach as an integrative device to facilitate the application of knowledge.

2. Multidisciplinary education. A second alternative has been to recognize the inaccessibility of general social theory at the present stage of development in the social sciences and to opt for selective interdisciplinary integration. This has taken a number of forms but it appears most frequently as a curriculum that encourages the training of students in two or more disciplines.

Experience indicates that scholars seldom achieve sufficient expertise in more than one discipline, if even there. They often acquire sufficient familiarity with other disciplines to be able to work on the boundaries, but this seldom contributes to the theoretical intermeshing of the disciplines. At best it is likely to provide for a more coherent attack on certain boundary problems, and these interstitial experiences may feed back important new concepts and methods to the parent disciplines. This, at least, has been the experience in political science with the new political economy, political sociology, political psychology, and political anthropology, pedestrian names for innovative and exciting marginal fields.

3. Problem orientation. The argument has been made that social scientists will best be able to handle practical social issues if they begin with such issues at the center of their research. Two proposals have appeared. One suggests that students be instructed in courses devoted not to abstract theoretical issues but to concrete social discontents such as poverty, pollution, liberty, war and peace, and ethnic tensions; another that the conceptualization within a single discipline, such as sociology or political science, should be elaborated around the understanding of social problems directly.

As an instructional device, a problem orientation has much to commend it. Indeed, it may be inescapable. In curricula developed along these lines, students have been presumed not to know of the existence of specialized disciplines. Thereby they might be sensitized to the fundamental unity of all knowledge. They would be innoculated against the disease of analytic decomposition. Their motivation for the study of social science would be heightened, and the social sciences themselves would be under constant pressure to organize their knowledge so that it might have more immediate practical uses.

Nonetheless the problem-oriented curriculum has offered no real solution. Student disappointment soon sets in. Knowledge about social causation is not so well advanced that its practical utility is overwhelmingly persuasive. Much scepticism is generated about the value of social science as a whole. The inherent limitations of each social science for understanding the total human experience even in a selected area cannot be concealed. The problem-focused curriculum is apt to leave the student more acutely aware than ever, first, of the relative isolation of each discipline, one from the other and each from the total phenomenal reality; and second, of the ad hoc character of efforts to build a composite curriculum around social problems. Problem-oriented courses composed of mixtures of knowledge from various social sciences tend to lose even minimal intellectual elegance and coherence both for faculty and students. Nevertheless, even in the face of these insufficiencies, this kind of curriculum is valuable for maintaining the pressure toward a more useful integration of knowledge.

As a means for advancing generalized and integrated understanding of social phenomena and for bringing the social sciences closer to the real world, the selection of practical social issues as focal points for research within a discipline, rather than just for instruction, appears even less promising. We all know that on occasion basic theoretical considerations may dictate the utility of examining transparently practical issues. More frequently, social needs may compel inquiry, under government or other auspices, into various pressing areas regardless of theoretical requirements, although theoretical benefits may be incidentally derived or salvaged. But the normal tendencies and needs of basic science have been toward the identification of theoretical problems that appear to be increasingly remote from the world of immediate intuitive experience.[4] The logic of rigor in research moves irresistibly in this direction. But here again, despite the needs of basic research, periodic reference back to real social problems is undoubtedly necessary if only to test the ultimate practical utility of the knowledge being sought.

4. Team cooperation. All else failing, the hope has been held out that under the constraints of the hard task of applying knowledge in specific situations, the social sciences would somehow be brought together again in a coherent way by social scientists acting in concert through appropriate combinations of teams. The benefits of this procedure are self-evident, but its shortcomings are equally apparent for those who have participated in such team efforts. For example, each discipline tends to define its problems differently so that members of the team may be working at cross-purposes. Scholars have difficulty in understanding each other's concepts. Criteria of adequacy and validity vary enormously among the disciplines. Differences in the methods of analysis yield apparently incompatible conclusions, as Coleman's paper clearly indicates. Little wonder that prescriptions for action also remain in dispute. The probability of achieving useful degrees of integration of the social sciences

4. T. S. Kuhn, *The Structure of Scientific Revolutions* (Chicago: University of Chicago Press, 1962).

through team work in the resolution of practical social difficulties is not very high, if past experience remains as a guide.

It is clear that as much progress as we have made, the challenge to apply our knowledge has not yet shown us the way to reassemble the analytic social sciences. We are still struggling painfully and awkwardly to find a useful prescription to overcome the nature of the divisions that scientific rigor and effectiveness have imposed on us. The policy analytic movement is but the latest surfacing of a deep vein of discontent that has run throughout the history of the social sciences in this country.

Does the new interest in policy analysis hold out a realistic hope that the problems will be overcome and that through it some useful form of integration for applied purposes will be achieved? By implication I have been suggesting that to the degree that policy analysis directs its attention to such mechanical operations as multidisciplinary training, disciplinary problem-oriented curricula, cross-disciplinary team coordinated efforts at application, and the infinite combinations of these academic gadgetries the main issue will be avoided. No inventory of the state of the nation through the massive accumulation of accurate social indicators, no efforts at costing the benefits of proposed programs, and no institutional reorganization under imposing titles asserting that knowledge has been organized for action or for social engineering will magically overcome the abyss that separates the analytic systems of science from the totalistic or entity systems of social reality.

All this can suggest one of two things. First, we can interpret this failure positively, as it were. We could argue that it is not likely that the cognitive issues will, in fact, be fully appreciated except through the laborious failures at trying to apply what knowledge we have. We might conclude that it is one thing to adopt these mechanical devices as makeshift inventions under the pressures of the moment in the search for useful answers to urgent social problems. It is quite another to expect these measures to overcome the barriers to organic integration posed by the analytic character of social science. Only when we acknowledge that policy analysis and similar movements in the past do not go to the heart of the matter, will we have taken a vital step toward identifying the real issues at stake. Only then will integration of the social sciences be seen to involve a challenge to the basic analytic assumptions upon which the search for reliable knowledge has been based in modern times.

The historical experiences with efforts at integration suggest a second and alternative conclusion however. Perhaps integration, in the sense of creating an organic unity out of the social sciences, will be attainable at some point in the distant future. But it may be that this kind of intellectual coherence, however helpful, is not really necessary for applying our knowledge sensibly in the here and now.

To be sure, organic or theoretical integration would give us a more powerful tool for understanding various aspects of social behavior. It would enable us to trace out more easily some types of causal interrelationships now concealed or complicated by the division of labor in the social sciences. Yet even though such an integral body of knowledge would require some general laws underlying all human behavior, these would only provide a base on which specialized areas of study would still need to be elaborated. These specialties might continue to focus on subject matters identical with those of the current social sciences, or they might require a general reorganization of content. Regardless of the specific structuring of the disciplines, however, the very nature of rigorous research would still call for a high degree of specialization of labor and, therefore, of analytic decomposition of reality. If this is so, an organic integration of the social sciences through a generalized theory of human behavior would not really resolve the problem of application. The same kind of problems that we have today in overcoming the division of labor among the social sciences would remain. Probably we are pursuing a will-o'-the-wisp in our search for an integration dubiously related to application.

It would appear then that the problem for the present conference might well be of questionable validity. I assumed at the outset, you will recall, that we were to be interested in the contribution of policy analysis to integration because in one way or another one might share the prevailing conviction that such integration would resolve many of the major, recognized hurdles in the way of application. If integration is not a probable panacea, whether or not policy analysis leads in that direction is less interesting than the question as to whether it makes some other, more direct contribution toward overcoming difficulties in applying our social science knowledge.   Rather than worry about the relationship of policy analysis to organic integration, we would probably be much better advised to adopt a more pragmatic, less architectonic view of integration.

To this point I have interpreted integration of the social sciences in its fundamentalist sense, that is, as the organic reformulation of our knowledge into an overarching general theory of human behavior.   But it is possible to consider integration at less ambitious levels of architectural unity if we are prepared to accept the demonstrable utility of selective interlocking of the social sciences for applied purposes.   At the present stage of development, this would seem to be a more feasible and modest objective.   Essentially this is what the policy analysis movement implies from the point of view of the relationship among the social sciences.   It calls for an effort to draw together relevant skills and knowledge from the various social sciences for coherent application, on a pragmatic basis, to specific totalistic problems.

The papers have brought out various types of difficulties and shortcomings encountered as social sciences are applied to specific situations.   Recognition of their existence is, of course, the first step.   Aside from those proposals offered in the various papers to compensate for or overcome these weaknesses, several additional strategies might be followed.

At the more general level, there is an urgent need for the practising social scientist to familiarize himself with the most profound criticisms about the validity or adequacy of the cognitive assumptions about contemporary social science.   Both we and our students need to understand better the philosophy of science in terms of which we seek to validate the whole social scientific enterprise.   At the very least this will prevent a smug acceptance of analytic science as the only conceivable path to reliable understanding.   At best it might ultimately help to produce a reinterpretation of social science that will permit us to transform our generalized knowledge more easily into an applied form.

Simultaneously we are now in a better position to appreciate the full implications of the incidental but continuous efforts we find over the years devoted to the search for general social science theories. No one can dispute their very limited success if we look for universal concepts and valid generalizations. But we can now see more clearly and convincingly that, strange as it may seem, such abstract and apparently remote theorizing is, in effect, one kind of response to the pressure for demonstrating the utility of social knowledge. If we did have a body of common concepts and some universally accepted generalizations about human behavior and if each of the social sciences used these as a base for its own more specialized explorations, the difficulties of conversion from generalized to applied knowledge would be reduced, even if the reduction were considerably less than the optimists would have us believe.

However, even if general social theory were the panacea it is not, to await its development today is clearly a counsel of perfection. We need instead the specification of additional particular reforms that will help us move toward efforts at partial reassembly or selective interlocking of the disciplines. Several measures would seem to be appropriate, if extremely modest.

First, interdisciplinary training and team work by varied social scientists needs to be continued. We now find them in many different settings, such as in the new schools of administration and management, in institutes of public affairs and policy analysis, and in centers of urban and regional planning. They all seek to assemble the relevant social sciences either mechanically, through juxtaposition of the disciplines, or organically, by efforts at piecemeal theoretical integration.

However, a set of procedures needs to be invented through which the applied scientist can contemplate the total consequences for society of any proposed set of policies. The training of social scientists needs to cultivate a capacity to look beyond parochial outcomes as identified by a discipline or two so that the applied scientist will feel the need to trace out a long, involved, and proliferating chain of causation as it relates to variations in policy. In place of disciplinary pride and commitment with its attendant, limited vision, the applied scientist needs to develop an emotional investment in amelioration of the experienced social problems regardless of disciplinary conceits. In the socialization of social scientists in their profession, the status and esteem of the applied social scientist needs to be sharply improved so as to draw and hold a high level of talent.

Second, the applied scientist needs to be trained to consider himself as an expert in social experimentation. Policy recommendations are, in effect, proposals to achieve specifiable outcomes through determinate manipulations of the social environment. Policy interventions constitute experimentation in the classic sense.[5] But because of the scope and consequences of policy intervention in social processes, the experimentation tends to be on the grand scale. Once we recognize the experimental character of policy implementation, small-scale innovations, under more easily controlled conditions comparable to pilot studies, might become a practical skill in which the policy scientist needs special training. The policy analyst might profitably see himself as the architect of small, innovative social experiments to pretest the validity of his proposals and their total consequences for the values he expects them to achieve.

Third, a policy environment needs to be created that would encourage the applied scientist to compare the ramifying consequences of policy intervention with specific preferred states—as recommended by MacRae—as well as with overall normative images of society. Only in that way will there occur a continuous link between policy formation and normative assessment. The social scientist would bring his knowledge and expertise to bear not only by providing technical assistance for goals established by others, but by independently considering the consequences of his own proposals for alternative images of what a whole society could do and be.

Finally, social scientists require far more experience with the consequences of actual intervention in social processes—the essence of policy planning as Lane appropriately remarks—under actual field conditions during the period of his training. We educate students in one or more disciplines. We teach them how to reassemble small areas of knowledge from various social sciences in order to cope with specific social problems. What they still lack is field experience in actually applying solutions to living

5. From a communication presented by H. Riecken at the Stated Meeting in January of the American Academy of Arts and Sciences, Brookline Station, Boston, Massachusetts.

situations which can be fed back immediately into their learning situation. We have little by way of political "clinics" to parallel the clinical experience of the physician, a central ingredient of his training.

For this purpose I have proposed modifying the structure of the universities to incorporate what might be called Academies for Action. These would permit both students and faculty, as part of their normal training, to experiment with the actual implementation of alternative solutions to major social ills. It would permit the university in one of its aspects to become an active agent in fostering social change, that is, to provide social clinics as part of its educational services. To some extent this is already under way. Universities have established urban development centers, open medical clinics in poverty areas, experimental school systems among disadvantaged groups, and the like. I am proposing more formal adoption of these service structures. Not only would they meet actual needs in the community, but they would also help to elevate the status of applied research and to feed training in application back into the disciplines.

The Academies could take many forms—an Academy for Urban Action, an Academy for Ethnic and Racial Action, an Academy for Action on Ecological Pollution, an Academy on the Peaceful Uses of Military Forces, an Academy for the Delivery of Community Medical Services, one for legal services, and the like.

These Academies for Action would be open to all students and staff. The members would be full time or they would share their time in the traditional ways with other departments and schools within the university. The walls between the Academies and the other usual parts of the university would be permeable. Both staff and students would shift between Academies and other divisions of the university as their interests, skills, and programs dictated.

Clearly there are many difficulties in the way of operating such Academies. Not the least of these would be the tendency to politicize the university.[6] However, in the process of attempt-

6. There are structural devices available to minimize these risks. For example, each Academy would be part of the university but it would need to be viewed as dispensable. Each Academy could act not in the name of the university but in its own name. If it got into troubled political waters,

ing to apply knowledge in true "clinical" settings, both faculty and students would gain essential knowledge about society. Social scientists primarily interested in basic research would have something to learn from such applied efforts. Those concerned with the application of knowledge would add to their understanding of the difficulties in the way.

In conclusion, application may contribute to integration, even if it has as yet failed to do so. Application may, in turn, be helped by integration of the disciplines, even if as yet there is little evidence to document this. But integration will still leave analytically divided disciplines. This is of the nature of science as we still understand it. Integration is therefore no panacea. Both institutional and intellectual devices need to continue to command our attention to bring about some selective interlocking of disciplines for specific applications.

---

it would be expected to extricate itself through its own efforts. If it failed to do so, the university would set it free to sink in its own muddied waters. In short, part of the task of each Academy would be to learn how to survive as an engaged and committed part of an academic institution. If any Academy could not do so it would suffer the fate of all failures—retrenchment, until it learned better, or extinction. And simultaneously, of course, the public, including government and politicians, would need to be educated about the nature and purposes of the Academies as new elements of a university. This proposal for the continuing structural adaptation of the university to the needs of the late twentieth century for the application of knowledge is made in full recognition of the political risks it entails. On the other hand, the dangers that confront the world are considerably greater and the need for whatever expertise the universities can bring to bear on these problems is urgent. See D. Easton, "The Political Obligations of the University," *AGB Reports,* Association of Governing Boards of Universities and Colleges, vol. 14 (1972), pp. 4–9.

Commentary on Lane's Paper

By Henry S. Kariel

I F ALL goes well—the assurances are those of the United States President in 1971—America will "come out of this searing experience with a measure of pride in our nation, confidence in our character, and hope for the future of the spirit of America." The national consensus may have been shaken for a moment—invisible victims actually became visible in political arenas—but we may yet pull ourselves together again, realize we are one nation dedicated (the words are still stunning) "to form a more perfect Union, establish Justice, insure domestic Tranquility, provide for the common Defense, promote the general Welfare, and secure the Blessings of Liberty. . . ." Assured by proclamations about the massive, pervasive agreement on ends—each end properly capitalized—we can concentrate on means. Nor is there reason for the social sciences to abstain. Duly integrated, they can profitably focus on policy analysis.* More precisely, they can converge and engage in concerted efforts to specify the unambiguous pleasures and pains of alternative means for achieving authoritatively given ends. In public life as well as social science, the means-ends schema is alive and well.

Robert Lane serves to make it attractive. He shows it to be endowed with a respectable intellectual tradition; for some time now, various theoretical movements have made unwitting contributions to it. Its main benefit, it would seem, is that it will allow us to do more efficiently and economically what, on reflection, we—all of us, really—want to do. It will enable us to identify common objectives, clarify concealed costs ("latent dis-

* This seems to mean all sorts of things, including description of governmental programs in such fields as agriculture, evaluation of the rationales for alternative policy recommendations, specification of costs and benefits of alternative policies, speculation about the consequences of governmental decisions, predictions of the impact of prototypical intervention in society, explication of policy norms, or, more fashionably, casual mixtures of these.

103

utilities"), and perceive alternatives. It would be odd, therefore, if policy analysis should fail to make us more ingenious and effective in our commitment, as Lane explicitly reminds us, to the pursuit of happiness.

Lane's paper serves, too, to do justice to some of the manifest utilities of integration and synthesis in the social sciences. Interdisciplinary work, his paper permits us to realize, will surely conserve energy. If research exhausts the industrious practitioner, this will, in any case, not be because he will be constrained to agonize about the ends of policies. He will be free to use his intellectual resources so as to widen the range of options for those with power to decide. Since the decision-makers may be assumed to exercise power legitimately, since, in the final accounting, they are Americans whose hearts and minds have been won long ago, one may faithfully serve them. Bringing irrational aspects of life into the open, putting the stress on policy alternatives, calling attention to previously unperceived benefits and beneficiaries of programs, one can count on the emergence of just public policy. One can safely underwrite governmental intervention, supporting what Lane calls the manipulative mode.

This faith, some may feel, should not be without useful results for social scientists: the replacement of mere correlation by experimentation and of contemplation by action, the promise of agreement on uniform measures of utility, the accumulation of data useful as social indicators, and the growth at last of a body of systematically interrelated propositions. On another level, the benefits to the social sciences may be even more dramatic. Insofar as it comes to constitute the coherent basis for diverse operations, a common frame of reference has the virtue of rationalizing the social science labor market and facilitating the classification and placement of specialized talent. Certified "useful" by governmental agencies, policy analysis should open up new sources of revenue. Furthermore, initial agreement on the ends of analysis should make scientific work attractive to individuals who are disconcerted by the ambiguities of speech and the frustrations of politics, by intellectual procedures which annoyingly impel the continuous identification and weighing of one's interests. There will be rewards for technicians who line up to solve problems posed by others.

Such professionalism does not mean that policy analysts must ignore their own values or betray their moral sensibilities, for they can simply keep their work divorced from their values and their politics. On the one hand they can appreciate the objective reality of science and on the other the subjective one of politics. For them, scientist and citizen, fact and norm, theory and practice can be conveniently segregated.

Not surprisingly, the less dramatic and more ambiguous results of entertaining the means-ends schema are harder to appreciate. As those engaged in policy analysis distinguish between an impersonal world of facts and a personal one of values, and as they scrupulously treat the former world as open and the latter as closed, they keep part of themselves out of their work. Doing policy analysis, they repress their political capacities and absorb the logic and purposes of the dominant elements of the system. They sway with the prevailing winds of doctrine, the mood of the time, or more precisely with those who set the mood, those who have been free to formulate goals and define problems in relation to them.

To be involved, for example, in peace research—one might readily substitute research in health, education, or welfare—is to understand peace as what is authoritatively regarded as such, that is, as a condition which in practice is acceptable to those who have the power to shape opinion, to define words. It does not matter whether analysis demonstrates that some specific policy would entail nurturing or repressing disruptive elements as long as the end—the achievement of an equilibrium defined as peace—is external to analysis. Nor does it matter whether it is a vicarious or actual experiment, comparative study, or systems analysis. The end is unavoidably extrinsic—as it must be to any operation predesigned to come to an end. We move, are expected to move, in the prepolitical world where, if our minds are in good repair, all is technique.

Protected against having to give life to his theory, undistracted by the impulse to play the role of citizen when doing his research, the practitioner of policy analysis helpfully reinforces the objectives favored by those currently in power or previously built into established institutions. There is no reason, of course, why he might not find this a congenial task; he may well share the prevailing definition of public ends. Not suffering from role strain, he can then unreservedly proceed to inquire how we can "make democracy work" or "bring peace to nations" or "reduce violence in inner-city ghettos." Agreeing on the meaning of key terms— not only *democracy* or *violence* but also *decision, event, fact, system,* and *reality*—he can seek to find economical solutions to what are called problems, welcoming whatever public or private agencies promise to implement the results of his work. Thus he is apt to find the distinctions between citizen and scientist or between political ideals and political reality as pleasing to live with as they are easy to proclaim. Alienated from politics during his most productive hours, he may be spared the knowledge that the consecration of reality could hardly cost less, that his service is cheap.

Attuned to a settled, predefined political reality, trusting it, policy science remains effortlessly on the side of accredited interests. Its practitioners, themselves not disposed to interfere with established definitions of reality, perceiving such transactions to be unscientific, readily make the prevailing problems of society those of their science. It becomes their proper task to search for the type of knowledge which can be used to govern effectively within existing political frameworks, to integrate men in established systems while instructing them which of their experiences they are to accept as part of political reality and which they are to dismiss as unrealistic, as excessively costly, dysfunctional, and hence disreputable.

Of course, policy analysis in practice need not be anywhere near as tidy. It may well be premised, as Lane allows, on the belief that it will lead to sharper debate on governmental objectives and not merely to the consideration of courses of action which are technically feasible or minimally wasteful of available resources. It may presume to become politically creative and postulate objectives not previously envisaged and conceptualized. It may also come up with new reasons for striking out in new ways. But this is merely to concede that it may lose its integrity, subverting its epistemological foundation.

Not socialized to doing applied research, not fully loyal to the means-ends dichotomy, policy analysts may admittedly engage in contradictory operations. Their sense of injustice alerted, they may even find themselves arrogantly redefining given problems.

Or mere boredom combined with adequate salaries may induce them to become politicalized, to wonder after hours, perhaps playfully, about sharing in the pleasures of policy-making. They may then resolve, like Dostoevsky's underground man, to fuse means and ends, becoming truly pragmatic and experimental. They may, in fact, go further and acknowledge the pre-eminent imperative of a pragmatic orientation—treat research like every human venture, as performance, as demonstration. They may then be led to conclude that research consists of language acts which test and disrupt given states.

It may yet become possible to see what is entailed by defining research as a form of action—the *full* presence of the researcher in his field of concern. Present in a field that includes his multiple unrealized parts, ideally his entire self, he is impelled to realize, moreover, that he simply cannot know what is least costly to actual and potential human possibilities without involving whoever is affected by policy, himself included, in the designing of their society. He would agree with Amitai Etzioni: "Ultimately, there is no way for a societal structure to discover the members' needs and adapt to them without the participation of the members in shaping and reshaping the structure." Participation, in other words, becomes an epistemological imperative; action and knowledge are inextricably one. To be in action is to learn of one's capacities and thereby to realize precisely what one can successfully manage; what new reality can, in fact, be made true; and what boundaries, laws, and promises can be broken without unbearable losses. It is to do violence to all prefigured ends to action, scorning every authority stationed somewhere outside or above the field of operations.

Such a transactional paradigm—which, as Paul Kress has recently shown, owes more to Bentley and Dewey than to Marx—makes a shambles of the entire means-ends schema. After all, a coherent transactionalism demands a discipline—including a disciplined respect for the uses of linguistic ambiguity—against which cost-benefit accounts and systems analysis as conventionally conceived must discriminate. It insists on the continuous injection of one's own diverse values into the research process—a process which, like politics, has no predefined end whatever. It directs the actor—man, as both political animal and political scientist, to remain involved not in knowledge-accumulating projects alleged to be beneficial someday but in an inherently rewarding, reality-constructing activity.

Cost-benefit analysts may yet tell us precisely how costly a consistently sustained transactional persuasion would be for entrenched interests in American society. We might learn from their accounting what we already know—that privileged orders display little affection for the means-ends distinction in their own lives, that they enjoy being fully in politics, and gladly pay for instant gratification. In fact, they find their political action to be so pleasurable that they keep the gates closed and the price of admission high while assigning nonpolitical roles to outsiders. Few of them are likely to mind if the others outside decide to serve them by learning how to integrate and engage in policy analysis.

Commentary on Lane's Paper

By Sol Tax

T HE latest paper to interrupt my thoughts in finishing my comments on the paper by Robert Lane is that by David Easton, which causes me to start all over in somewhat too personal fashion since I realize for how long and how much I have been spinning wheels on the questions before us. This autumn it will be 24 years since David Easton came to the University of Chicago to join a small faculty group developing a course in The Scope, Methods and Interrelations of the Social Sciences. For some years Social Sciences 200 was required of all students in what was then a three-year M.A. program for the large influx of excellent students in the post-war generation. Our small, interdisciplinary, younger group called upon our best senior faculty to ask and answer questions about the ways the social sciences together relate to society. Most of us had already served some apprenticeship in integrating social science knowledge for undergraduates in the Hutchins College, but now we became self-conscious as practitioners of the disciplines.

My personal history in these enterprises goes back even farther. When I came to Chicago as a graduate student in 1931, it was into a newly organized Division of the Social Sciences designed to break down barriers between departments. In 1932 the first dean, Beardsley Ruml, invited distinguished faculty and a few graduate students into a fully interdisciplinary Dean's Seminar; there must have been thirty of us together for two years. But in that period there were also problem-centered seminars. I best remember the one that later came to be called the Race Relations Seminar in which Ph.D. candidates in economics, sociology, anthropology, psychology, education—these are the ones I remember—described their researches to one another and to an equally mixed faculty. For twenty years, including my years of intermittent field work in Guatemala and Mexico, this ongoing seminar was for me almost as much home base as my Department of Anthropology.

109

I also recall the postwar Social Science Research Council's effort to deal with values, by asking five universities to conduct interdisciplinary seminars on how the social sciences should deal with them, and at Chicago we met over dinner for regular bi-weekly sessions. We took in stride the problem of how to study values empirically and devoted most of our attention to relating non–value-free social science to society. Finally, I recall a very busy year chairing our Ford Foundation-sponsored, interdisciplinary "self-study of the behavioral sciences" at the University of Chicago.

Through all this institutional history dealing with problems of the social sciences both as intrarelated and as impinging on society—which I don't doubt was in some degree matched by happenings in other universities—of course I had a personal history. As an undergraduate at Wisconsin in the late '20s I switched from political science and economics to sociology and anthropology and was also firmly entrenched as a leader of the campus noncommunist radicals. Social action was pushed aside during the thirties while I learned anthropology at Chicago and in the field. In 1942–43 I taught in Mexico, where new colleagues, action programs, and radical students forced me to face questions of science and society. In 1948, back at the University of Chicago, I permitted a group of students to plunge with me into a major experiment of social interference in an American Indian community—or did the students drag me into it? As far as I know none of us have been sorry for the experience and the development of what came to be called "action anthropology," which faces the problem of science and values explicitly and deliberately mixes them. The problems of American Indians were quickly reinterpreted as a problem of the larger society in which they find themselves powerless, and attention quickly turned to that larger society.

At this time, also in the early '50s, professional duties in the American Anthropological Association suggested that we, as a whole, must respond more to human needs, and I became aware of the structural difficulties which kept the professionals from doing so. As president of the association, a critical meeting with highly placed and sympathetic officials of the Association for International Development gave me the beginning of a hypothesis on which I have been since acting—that anthropologists require their own definition of research problems and are too small and powerless to influence those who make budgets and policy. Later I served on the U.S. National Commission for United Nations Educational, Scientific, and Cultural Organization, and its inter-disciplinary Committee on Social Sciences. The Natural Sciences Committee was chaired by Roger Revelle, who understood the need for a strong human sciences component in action programs. We therefore agreed that the two committees should meet together and encourage UNESCO policy-makers to take a similar view. We hoped that the development programs might begin with people. The result was rather—if this was our influence—to weaken the social science component in UNESCO, which combined it with humanities, while not changing development formulae at all.

The point is that technology, including engineering, economic planning, and even mass education, necessarily requires so much operating budget and personnel that with the best will in the world anthropologists could not be noticed. Anthropology starts with problems as defined by the grass-roots people we live with. "Government anthropology," as it was practiced in the colonial era, had put off most of us. The postcolonial programs, whether managed binationally, by international organizations, or by local elites alone, were put by us in the same class. We thought they couldn't be effective, and we lacked the power to change anything. We ended up essentially as Monday morning quarterbacks and otherwise retreated to pure science. Here we could control our destinies; and if we did our friends little good, at least we felt we were not contributing to their genocide. This position was not comfortable for the many anthropologists in the world who believed that we had an essential ingredient to offer to the positive solution of world problems.

In 1958 I was given the opportunity to meet with colleagues all over the world. The result was development of a community of scholars—which has since grown greatly in strength—who seemed to want everywhere not only to develop our science but also to be more effective in the troubled world. It also became evident, long before Camelot and Thailand, that anthropology couldn't continue to develop unless it operated cross-nationally and reciprocally, and that a major need was to develop professional resources as quickly as possible in all countries. Since 1958, at least, my personal stance has been non-national; therefore, I cannot be an "American." The most satisfying result of this is to see that my fellows in the United States, by almost any definition home to nearly half of the world's anthropologists, by and large wish to take this same stance. The way things are in the world, only such a stance permits us to work, even at home, on social problems; indeed, most of us argue that we are unable to do "pure anthropology" in our own country or cities without separating ourselves from all of the controlling establishments. The easiest way to do this is to take a "mankind" point of view, which is anyway comfortable to a discipline which purports to study the entire career of the genus *Homo*.

The world community operating through *Current Anthropology* consists of individual scholars whose efforts can be coordinated by somebody who "reads" their wishes and needs and in whom they have confidence; and until we succeed together in our effort to depersonalize and routinize the process, I personally am "it," with a choice: either to help something to happen, or not. As if to make the choice in the positive direction easier, my colleagues, in September of 1968, gave me the presidency of our International Union for a five-year term. At a recent meeting of the Permanent Council of the Union, it became evident that they would prefer action. Meanwhile, in May of 1970, a way through the wilderness opened up. Under sponsorship of the Smithsonian Institution's Center for the Study of Man, an international group of colleagues, organized a year earlier, saw how to coordinate research on social problems facing the species, beginning with the problem of population. As I write this, that research is well under way. A similar effort concerning the environment has begun, and exploration has been started on the worldwide problem of education. I find myself in the keystone position, and clearly the luxury of free choice no longer exists for me.

Having been for a dozen years so largely immersed in the problems of my own discipline and means of making it effective in policy, nothing could have been more welcome than this opportunity to come out of the water to see how my never forgotten cousin-colleagues were faring with the same problems. Indeed,

I feel a little like Rip van Winkle returning to his old town. On the road I met, first, Charles Lindblom, whose book *The Intelligence of Democracy* I had happened to read and use in another context. I had to restrain myself from writing at once an enthusiastic comment without awaiting the paper from which I had agreed to take off. Next I met my former colleague, James Coleman, whose famous report had also interrupted my slumber. And then came Robert Lane, who was quite new, and with whom I could legitimately converse.

Lane first described the policy analysis movement in which, if he is indeed an amateur, I am a duffer. I had, of course, heard of the elements described, and had given some angry thought to so-called cost-benefit analysis. But I came to this integrated movement quite from the outside, and it seemed to me too extraordinarily valuable, powerful, and dangerous a part of modern technology to be left in the hands of the technologists. The second part of Lane's paper was somewhat reassuring, for, while it does not view these technologists with alarm—his purpose in presenting a sketch of policy analysis is to show that policy problems have already stimulated and drawn on interdisciplinary work—the major part of the paper raises questions and provides a larger context for that technology.

Needless to say, Lane's context was still, for me, surprisingly narrow, beginning with "the ends of government" rather than with the needs of mankind or even of the part of mankind living in the United States. I hasten to say that I appreciated greatly, nevertheless, each of the seven points of the discussion which followed. I found agreeable the pluralistic and relativist positions which he takes and which I hoped would be philosophical bases of this entire discussion. I was equally appreciative of the major point that attention to measurement of costs forces us to think through the alternatives; of course, we must all accept a rational technology, and no matter how fearful we are, reject that of the ostrich. Finally, I found profitable the general discussion of the relation of theory to policy, the way the disciplines are likely to support one another, and the place of policy analysis in their mutual development. I wondered a little here at our general assumption that our disciplines are to be considered coordinate; perhaps economics and sociology, for example, are like horses expected to pull the wagon in tandem. But why in tandem? Maybe one is horse and another is harness, and in that figure one has to ask about who or what is in the driver's seat. It seemed to me that a useful outcome of our discussion could be a more subtle and realistic picture of the structural interrelations of the disciplines. But my main concern as I read Lane's paper was to see if we could not approach our question in terms of a different conception of policy.

Then along came the other commentaries, and finally David Easton's, to make me realize that thought along these general lines had not stopped while I slept and that along this axis I could only contribute these few views from anthropology. The two terms of reference—*interdisciplinary* and *policy*—have been treated differently in anthropology. We live on the first. Anthropology is a point of view with some unique data which at every boundary lives off the product of one or another discipline. The boundaries look to all of the other sciences—physical and biological as well as the humanities. On the social science edge we nurture psychological anthropology, political anthropology, economic anthropology—some turn the phrases about—and, of course, we are at least as much a historical as a generalizing study. Our relations with sociology are confused; we seem to have the same subject matter but different prejudices. We are sometimes too competitive or hostile to profit, each from the other. They say we study simpler societies, and we say we study all societies; indeed, our fastest growing field is "Urban Anthropology." We say they are immersed ethnocentrically in the one case of our Western society, but they have moved as fast into the other two-thirds of the world as we have into our own society. And anyway, what of Japanese, Indian, Latin American or African sociologists?

The head of the Institute of Ethnography of the U.S.S.R.'s Academy of Sciences tells me that Soviet scientists have solved the identity problem by accepting ethnography as the discoverer of the ethnic in any society. In a society that is a pure strain, so to speak, this is easy; but in any part of a society where many ethnic strands have become intertwined in a single society with a single economy and polity, the field anthropologist first has to do the work of the sociologist, unless this has already been done. This division of labor has become possible only within the past five or ten years, since earlier ethnography but not sociology existed in the Soviet Union. In the United States we are less disciplined and want to work in domains of other social sciences because we think we do the work differently. Nor do we struggle with the problem which the Institute of Ethnography has solved, partly because in our pluralistic value system our tolerance for ambiguity is great, and perhaps because there are enough of us to provide the illusion that we must be right.

On the policy side, I have already indicated that applied anthropology has neither achieved status nor been successful. Anthropologists have made their contribution indirectly through general education in the cross-cultural, relativist perspective. Perhaps that will always be our largest contribution. Perhaps, also, anthropology never has been, or should be, coordinate as a social science with the others represented here.

I concluded as I finished reading the comments that we are a group precisely qualified to work out the interrelations of our disciplinary contributions and their bearing on policy. Our disciplines, considered strictly as social segmentary institutions, clearly have important uses in socializing apprentices; in providing a common language for close intracommunication, and a set of values for common identification and action; and in providing a platform of received knowledge—both substantive and methodological—to which creative additions can be made. They are also conservative with their inherited paradigms which outlive their uses. An opposite model of complete individualization of scientists and scholars is unlikely to be achieved in any case, but its disadvantages would be great. At least the entrance to a large system would seem to require a small-group structure. The compromise to which we appear all to have been committed is maintenance of changing disciplines with as much movement as possible between them of individuals and of information. For all our commitment to that effort, we are evidently still dissatisfied with the amount of interchange that occurs today. We shall probably agree at this conference that given the disciplines as at least a secure entrance point for the uninitiated, then the greater the communication among them, the better, and we probably shall continue to say, as forty years ago, that any devices that assure greater interchange among practitioners of disciplines are good.

Working together on public policy is clearly one such device, with the added advantage of a dual function. (I have learned the need for the social sciences to consider increasing knowledge and improvement of society as coordinate goals.)

What I am proposing is that we are opportunely situated to discuss, analyze, and understand the entire social process. Since in the past years we have, as Lane emphasizes, developed new tools in the social sciences which are useful for policy analysis and which I know little about, I am curious to know why we cannot use them fully on ourselves in relation to the largest whole in which we operate. What better opportunity to study the question asked than this conference which is at once interdisciplinary and a consideration of policy?

If we are to do so, I presume that in the '70s we must take the world as a system of which governments, mobs, and scientists are all parts to be described in the flow chart, and accept our disciplines being treated partly as social segmentary interest groups with some power in some places, partly as systems of ideas. But we would also see that the collective influence of each discipline might hide more important inputs from individuals—for current examples, take Kissinger, Mead, and Nader—and from ideas, the history of which would be complex. With respect to the formal social sciences, meanwhile, if we begin with individual activities and ideas, we will eventually come to groupings that will remind us of some of the subdisciplines with which we are familiar, and these may even loom important. It is unlikely that, except as structures in the establishment, our disciplines themselves will seem as essential to the whole as we like to think, but the knowledge of the part that we do play would hopefully suggest how we might become more effective.

I have deliberately burdened this comment with several pages of autobiography, not only because reminiscence is pleasurable, but to show that there is, indeed, a history to discussion of the problems posed for this conference. Easton's practical suggestions would carry us some steps beyond where we are, but they are still within the paradigm of the discussions of the long past. Perhaps I am the only one who has slept through the gestation period of a new and promising paradigm, but I want to make evident that one who has been in a vortex of these problems has

indeed not noticed it until now. Doubtless on that account I
think more of the novelty than it deserves, but there can be little
harm in bringing to the table even a foolish hunch.

Whether or not our conference turns in these few days to the
task I suggest, I hope that we shall discuss whether this is a step
that can and should be taken, whether such concepts as "social
science" or "the social sciences" or such juxtapositions as "science and society" hide more than they expose, and whether—as
Easton, Lane, and others teach me—we have sufficient theory and
method with respect to policy analysis as applied to government
decision-making to enable us to apply it to ourselves.

Commentary on Lane's Paper

By William M. McCord

ROBERT E. Lane's paper makes a distinct contribution to our knowledge of the intellectual origins of policy analysis, the current themes which pervade it, and the unexpected intellectual benefits which it confers upon particular disciplines. I fully share his enthusiasm for an interdisciplinary approach, and clearly, in my own work—ranging from studies in criminology, to issues concerning developing nations, through analyses of ethnic conflict— I am also committed to the basic concerns of policy analysis.

I wish to make this essential agreement clear at the beginning, for I would like to proceed to raise certain cautions, some red flags, concerning the utility of applying social science to political or societal problems. Dr. Lane has already made clear in his paper that those of us engaged in policy analysis must necessarily consider such issues as the end of government, the latent effects of our efforts, and the irrationality of man and society.

From my own experience, I would like to emphasize some of the underlying themes which Professor Lane has considered. Specifically, I wish to examine briefly five philosophical and empirical themes which Professor Lane's paper either explicitly or implicitly has brought to our attention:

1. Should social scientists intervene in public policy?
2. If so, what goals or ethical principles should guide our behavior?
3. Do we have sufficient knowledge of the latent effects of our actions to intervene in a fashion which would serve the public interest?
4. What impact have social scientists actually exerted on policy?
5. Assuming the value of policy analysis, how can social science best integrate it into the body politic and into its own educational and research programs?

These topics are obviously interrelated and interdependent. I have separated them only because my own experience indicates that in real life they arise independently of each other. Let me begin with the most fundamental issue: Should we attempt consciously to change society at all?

SHOULD SOCIAL SCIENTISTS INTERVENE IN PUBLIC POLICY?

Many writers on both the political right and left have vehemently argued against any intrusion of "the academy" into policy. George Orwell in *1984*, Aldous Huxley in *Brave New World*, anarchists from Emma Goldman to Sir Herbert Read, and conservatives as diverse as Joseph Wood Krutch and William Buckley have all conjured up the spectre of omnipotent social scientists manipulating people for their own ends. A few developments— the use of subliminal advertising, Project Camelot, and ill-fated Head Start programs—lend support to those who question whether social science might be used as an instrument of human repression as well as human liberation.

Let me cite a few examples. During the Second World War, Arnold Rose and others demonstrated that American infantrymen fired their rifles only 25 percent of the time in combat situations —even though the soldiers found themselves in secure positions. Various investigations suggested that the troops refused to fire because of a conflict between military ethics—whose supreme command is, of course, to kill—and their earlier socialization which had taught them that killing was the ultimate crime. Subsequently, the army high command called in social scientists to advise the Chaplains' Corps on effective means to convince soldiers that killing was moral. The advice worked. After a series of pep talks from the chaplains, the rate of fire of American troops in Korea and in Vietnam increased dramatically. Today, infantrymen fire their weapons approximately 75 percent of the time when given a safe opportunity to kill the enemy. The question which I would like to raise is whether the proper use of social science is to implement a policy whose sole goal is to exterminate human beings.

Guilt over the misuse of social science is not, of course, confined to our side of the Iron Curtain. If press reports and the petitions of Russian scientists can be trusted, psychology and psychiatry in the U.S.S.R. have been perverted into an instrument of political repression. Apparently, dissenters to the current regime—including distinguished generals, physicists, and novelists—have been subjected to psychological examinations which invariably lead to the conclusion that these political outcasts are crazy. They have, so the reports go, then been subjected to imprisonment in mental hospitals and subsequent psychological conditioning. Here, it seems to me, is an ultimate instance of the subversion of social science to political goals which are directed towards suppression rather than liberation.

Even if we review less blatant examples of the misuse of social science for specific policies, the American experience raises a degree of hesitation. Most social scientists, for example, applauded the use of their data as pertinent evidence leading partially to the 1954 Supreme Court desegregation decision. The testimony of Kenneth Clark and others concerning the deleterious effects of school segregation marked one of the most significant and properly lauded interventions of social science in the policy-making process. Leaders of the White Citizens Councils, of course, decried the invasion of sociology and psychology into an essentially constitutional decision. Yet they, and at times we, forget that social science can often be used for ethically questionable purposes. Conveniently, the Southern opponents of the Court failed to remember that William Graham Sumner's views vitally influenced the *Plessy vs. Ferguson* decision of 1894 which first enforced the separate but equal doctrine. More contemporaneously, we ignore, to our peril, the possible influence of a McGurk or a Jenson in providing an intellectual base for accepting a belief in innate differences between blacks and whites—and of the policy consequences which flow from such views.

These examples should caution us concerning the goals which policy analysis serves—at times social science has acted as the handmaiden of policies aimed at the suppression of revolution, the degradation of an ethnic group, or the conversion of ethically torn men into killers. I suggest that the basic goal of policy analysis must always be kept in mind—to extend freedom, not to suppress or deceive human beings. Accepting that position, I would answer, "Yes, we do have a right to intervene." But the issue still remains: What specific principles should guide our behavior?

What Principles Should Guide Our Behavior?

As Professor Lane states in his paper, "Policy analysis involves statements of purpose, mission, and objectives. It thus leads to a sharpening of debate on the ends or purposes of government."

This point was brought home most forcefully to me in Egypt during the years 1964 and 1965. An anthropologist, an economist, and I had been hired to advise on the future of the Aswan Province. The development of the High Dam precipitated a number of policy questions: What should be done with 80,000 Nubian peasants who would be displaced by the new Lake Nasser? How should the 35,000 workers on the dam be relocated after they had fulfilled their primary mission? Should fourteen new industries, tapping the minerals of the area, be established? In rebuilding the city of Aswan, what would be the role of the present population of 135,000?

We approached the task with high expectations and a genuine hope that social science could contribute at the beginning rather than at the end of a massive experiment. We were often disillusioned. It became immediately clear that the government of Egypt had not decided on its own priorities. Should, for example, the water held back by the High Dam be released for purposes of irrigation in August or for purposes of generating electricity in the winter? The Russians had almost completed the dam, but no one in the highly competitive, jealous Egyptian hierarchy had made the basic decision concerning the use of water.

Other problems soon arose, directly connected to the goals of the entire project. The Nubians, traditionally a people who send their men off to cities as servants, refused to be relegated to a status of peasant. Consequently, they refused to move to new land which had been promised to them as fertile relocation areas. After much cajoling, and naturally, direct bribery, the 80,000 moved. All of the policy analysis available was brought to bear in convincing them that the migration was desirable. What happened? The Nubians arrived on their new lands which were indeed equipped with relatively decent housing, schools, even clinics.

But somebody—a bureaucrat in Cairo, no doubt—had neglected to order certain crucial items. For example, the new settlements lacked irrigation pumps. Thus, it became impossible to bring water up from the Nile to irrigate the potentially fertile lands above it. At this point, the Nubians generated a potential revolt. They were angry, stalled in the midst of a wilderness which might have become a garden of Eden. What could the so-called policy analysts do? There were only two choices: (1) support the government, explain the lack of irrigation facilities and try to "quiet the natives," or (2) openly oppose the government and side with the Nubians, either in their protest or in their nearly impossible wish to return to the lovely villages which they had deserted.

What would you do in this specific case involving thousands of people? It was impossible for the policy analyst to maintain some kind of pure, value-free position. A decision had to be made. Clearly, on the one hand, the government had some degree of rationality on its side for no high official could have really prevented the mistakes of his subordinates in not ordering the required pumps. Yet, on the other side, if one truly obeyed the democratic wishes of the majority of Nubians, it would have required sending them back to certain death as the waves of the new lake rolled over their old villages. It is in this type of case where policy analysts must take their stand: Are they in favor of rational decisions, no matter how irrational their basis may be, or do they favor democracy, no matter how disastrous the consequences are?

One more example from the Aswan province of Egypt. The government assigned our same group to survey the existing city of Aswan in order to determine the actual occupations existing in the town. The goal was utterly acceptable. If, for example, the population turned out to be primarily fishermen on the Nile, then obviously our plan was to furnish them with a relocation along the river which would allow the continuance of their present occupation. Alas! This did not prove to be the case. It required only one day to establish that most of the working population subsisted on smuggling goods from the Sudan. Carefully organized caravans brought cigarettes, liquor, transistor radios, and all other sorts of merchandise via camels from the Sudanese border. To relocate these merchants meant the destruction of their occupation.

Again we, or rather I, faced a decision concerning our goals. Everyone, including the director of our research institute and the governing officials, knew exactly what was happening. As policy analysts we had been sent on a fool's mission—to determine the occupational distribution of a district which was well known to anyone acquainted with the Middle East. What should we have done? Report in a properly somber fashion that the city of Aswan was made up of smugglers? Or, conversely, make up a report which would protect our informants but mislead unknowing but well-meaning officials in Cairo. Here the choice lay between explicit truth, our highest canon, and lying. Whatever the decision, the people of Aswan would be hurt. We had placed ourselves in the middle of the dilemma by accepting the assignment in the first place. Yet the choice was made out of ignorance, a sheer lack of knowledge concerning the Arabic culture, the nature of bureaucracy, and the economic situation.

Without confessing to our solution of either the Nubian problem or the issue of smuggling in Aswan—both decisions, of course, had to be made despite the bunglings of our superiors in policy-making—and without acting as stool-pigeons on our sponsors, I wish to point out that both decisions involved a serious consideration of the goals for which we intervened: rationality or democracy? the immediate happiness of a people or their long-range welfare? truth or lies? These incidents in Egypt also raise the third question of which I have been aware since I first paroled a murderer in 1950 from San Quentin, only to see him commit more homicide: Do we have enough knowledge in policy analysis to intervene successfully?

THE LATENT EFFECTS OF POLICY ANALYSIS

The failure of the war on poverty, the dismal results of many programs in urban renewal, and the total lack of success of various presidential commissions on crime—all informed, if not well-informed by policy analysis—suggests that we should be quite humble in making claims that the application of social science will necessarily serve the public interest.

Indeed, under some conditions, policy analysis will have latent unanticipated results which actually worsen the problem. I have long been associated with the Cambridge-Somerville program, just one example of a project which had ill effects. In 1935, a physician and social worker, Richard Clarke Cabot, founded a program aimed at preventing delinquency. He selected 1000 young boys from Cambridge and Somerville, Massachusetts. Teachers and others had predicted that 500 of the boys would become delinquent and that 500 would not. Utilizing the very best medical, psychiatric, and social scientific advice then available, Cabot then split each group down the middle and placed 500 boys in a treatment group. These boys received counselling for an average of five years, medical and psychiatric care, membership in various camps and clubs, special vocational training, and educational tutoring. The other 500 were placed in a control group which received no special attention. Cabot assumed that early intervention in the lives of young children would prevent criminality.

Various follow-up studies some twenty to twenty-five years later indicated the converse. By any measure—self-admitted crimes, arrests, court appearances, incarceration in reform school or prison—the boys who had received treatment committed *more* crimes than the control group. The difference was not statistically significant, but nonetheless, the treated children committed more crimes and more serious crimes in absolute number than the children who were left alone.

Why should this be so? Perhaps the boys in the treatment group were involuntarily labelled as future criminals. Perhaps the actual counselling process harmed them. We do not know, but one point is clear: despite the best in scientific advice, Dr. Cabot's program did not achieve its aim and may actually have contributed to a higher crime rate. We could argue that better, more sophisticated policy analysis would have prevented this result. However, we do not possess much empirical evidence to support this belief. I am not saying that we should eschew the task of intervening in serious social problems, but simply that we must do so in full recognition that even the best intentioned, best-advised programs may backfire in ways which we cannot yet anticipate.

UNDER WHAT CONDITIONS WILL POLICY ANALYSIS HAVE AN IMPACT?

As Professor Lane has indicated, policy analysis is also inhibited by the irrational behavior of individual men and societies. We cannot and should not control the actions of others, particularly of elected political leaders. And we cannot predict when a rational policy analysis will later be used for irrational, even violent, ends. Let me give two illustrations.

In 1961, when I first went to Nigeria, a Royal Commission carried out a thorough review of the future educational needs of that nation. They recommended the establishment of several new universities scattered throughout the country. They did not suggest the building of a new university in the Eastern Province because of the immense expense involved. Peopled by brilliant, energetic Ibos, the East protested vigorously and finally, through political pressure, sucked the revenue from the federal government to create from nothing a new university at Nsukka. The rest of Nigeria, particularly the Northerners, did not forget. One of the first actions of the civil war in 1968 was for Northern troops to burn down the new university, a symbol to them of "Ibo arrogance."

My point is simply this: the prior political conditions were so inflammable that a rational policy decision made by the Royal Commission could not possibly be implemented. If, somehow, the commission had prevailed, the Easterners would have been alienated and the Northerners mollified. The train of events going as it did, the Easterners temporarily got their way but only at the eventual cost of Northern wrath and a total loss of investment. There are times when the choice is only between the devil and the deep blue sea. It is under these conditions that policy analysis must be suspended.

Under even worse political conditions, policy analysis may be downright harmful. In 1967, as one example, I was in Houston, Texas, during a racially tense period. The mayor asked two psychologists and me to serve as assistants in charge of riot prevention. Some may argue that this was just another Project Camelot, but knowing the atmosphere of the city and the temper of the police, we believed that any outbreak of violence in the ghetto would lead to a bloodbath. Consequently, we served as a buffer between the black ghettos and, particularly, the chief of police who more than once urged the mayor to move in with force.

We fought for moderation and, fortunately, won in at least ten incidents. In the so-called Lucky Hill case, for example, a white policeman shot an alleged black robber with no provocation. After a large crowd had gathered, the police officer refused the aid of a black nurse and arrogantly dropped a lighted cigarette in the man's face. Except for counsels of moderation and the influence of several black ministers, the incident could easily have exploded into a violent confrontation.

One night in 1968, students at the predominately black university gathered for a rally. Police roughly arrested one of the speakers. The rally took a dangerous turn towards a riot situation and the chief of police surrounded the area with upwards of 500 policemen totally untrained in riot control. Militant students barricaded themselves in a dormitory. Various black leaders were negotiating with them while, at the same time, we advised the mayor to hold back his troops. Unfortunately, the mayor took the advice of his chief of police and the officers moved in to restore order. What was, in essence, a street festival became a battlefield. Among those killed was a policeman, shot from the ricocheted bullet of a police rookie, and various students. One of the black leaders whom we had asked to serve as a negotiator was wounded, and various student leaders received stiff jail penalties —including a thirty-year term on marijuana charges for a student who had actually been with me during the battle.

Here my functioning as a policy analyst not only failed to prevent the riot but directly harmed a number of individuals. One can, of course, argue that if our advice had been heeded the incident could have been avoided. That, in my opinion, is true; nonetheless, in such a politically volatile atmosphere, we should have realized that asking black leaders for their help was virtually sending them to jail or to their death.

How Can We Implement Policy Analysis?

Keeping in mind all of the inhibitions which I have mentioned —the misuse of policy analysis for repression, the sparsity of social science knowledge, our inability to gauge latent effects of our action, and the possibility that the political climate can turn policy analysis into a neuter or even harmful exercise—I still agree with Professor Lane's endorsement of the general approach. Unlike Professor Lane, however, I fail to see the utility of any specific measures designed to implement the introduction of policy analysis as an integral part of our government or of our profession. Professor Lane cites eleven recommendations concerning the future of policy analysis. Frankly, I have yet to see convincing evidence that the establishment of new commissions, institutes, or advisory agencies will have a demonstrably beneficial effect upon policy.

On a very modest level, I would prefer that we start at the other end, the education of social scientists who can conceptualize any policy problem in a broad, interdisciplinary fashion and thus be equipped to face a multitude of issues. Such individuals will, of necessity, have to possess a passing knowledge of psychology, sociology, political science, and economics regardless of the particular discipline in which they concentrate. I realize that such people will be regarded as dilettantes by their stricter colleagues, yet if we do not produce such "Renaissance men," all of the commissions and conferences in the world will—as they usually do—prove to be fruitless.

Conference Discussion II

CHARLESWORTH: We're all here, thank goodness. Nobody's gone over the hill.

Brother Lane, shall we hear from you?

HACKER: May I ask you, is Coleman going to be here to-morrow?

CHARLESWORTH: No sir. He is in Europe. I heard from him just a few weeks before this meeting. He had tried to make arrangements, but couldn't.

LANE: I don't know whether Lindblom's law applies to the afternoon. There is a special soporific quality about afternoons. (Laughter) It isn't a throat-clearing operation, but something else. Not a mind-blowing one, I'm sure, but in any event I am willing to provide background music for you for a little while until we all come together again.

I really said in my paper pretty much what I have to say—in fact, a little more than what I have to say. This is not a special field of mine. Perhaps a few preliminary comments. On the question of integration, it does seem to me that the discussion this morning was more clarifying in the sense that we are not saying that policy analysis is the only way. It is one of many ways. It isn't really spelled out in what way it points to the integration of the social sciences. In fact, I think probably the variety of words used—clustering, bilateral treaties, unification, cultural borrowing—these all suggest ways in which integration takes place, and my guess is that each of them is probably suggestive of a different method but that we really haven't thought about what it is that makes one idea next to another idea catch fire, or a set of concepts find a means of leverage against some experience. I think that that really deserves more analysis, and it probably deserves more than we can give it right now. What I really mean to say is that we haven't developed that very much.

For the policy analysis part of this discussion, it might be useful to think of this as four different stages. The first is: What should we do? This is really, in some ways, an evaluative-normative question. But I would argue that this is best discussed, partly as Ed was saying, in terms of empirical information and that inevitably the question is: At what cost do we want to buy what values? What values do we give up for some other set of values? This may be exchange theory. But whatever it is, nothing is free, even if we are talking about time, effort, energy, and so forth.

Given that, it doesn't do any harm to attach weights to these. In fact, it eliminates the discussion to attach some weights: How much happiness, as I said in my paper, or how much cultural achievement, or vice versa? Without the weights you really are unable, I think, to give a fair exchange rate or really come to a reasonable decision, in that measurement is new. It is just that it is either latent or it is manifest, and better it be manifest. To improve that first question in policy analysis—What should we do?—is really an integral part of this policy analytical framework.

The second question after that is: What are we trying to do? This is the statement of admission of an agency or a bill. And the requirement that it state its purpose is the institutionalization of an enormously fruitful first step—that is, to specify what the objectives of that program or policy are and what it is going to give you. At least without it, you can never say whether it is a success or a failure. You could say, I suppose, whether it does what you want it to or not, but you can't say whether, within its own terms, it is a success or a failure. Therefore, the exact specification of a mission—What are we trying to do?—is one of the features of a policy analytical mode of thought, which is, I think, so late that it is surprising it has not been required earlier.

Then, are we doing it? This is program evaluation. If you know in advance that that question is going to be asked, you will have set up those measures in advance which indicate whether or not you are achieving. Without that, you don't have a base-line. It is certainly a better way to proceed than to talk about numbers of people, and numbers of typewriters, or numbers of trucks, or whatever it is that used to go into a budget; therefore, these two things—"What are we trying to do?" and "Are we doing it?"—are improvements in our social thought as well as in our public policy.

Now then, the fourth question is: Are we doing it better this way than another way? This requires that you consider alternatives. It is an experimental approach, and it means that the single program evaluation is inadequate because it can't answer that question.

Well, those are very simple points. They merely spell out in the most general terms what it is that we are talking about. Now let me turn briefly to some of the comments made on my paper.

Dave Easton, who isn't here, talked about the inherent impossibility of universal integration, and of course he is right. All theory is analytical, that is, it abstracts from experience. But then it doesn't really tell us the answer to the first question, namely, what criteria do we establish for interrelationships of ideas and data, cross-disciplinary if you like, for answering questions that you want to have answered?

I found McCord's comments enormously helpful in the sense that they revealed the complexities, the real paradoxes, of entering into this, plus some cautions to people who start situations so out of their control as the Aswan Dam. My guess is that here the next step is to develop some classes of things which should be used as cautions. The systematization of thinking about entry into reservations, about taking on this role, might be a useful step. This has to do with acting out policy analysis and not so much with the integration of the social sciences.

I sought to draw out Henry, and to some extent Duncan, on the question of what Henry puts as the sort of citizen role which goes side by side with the professional analyst role. You are a person with your values at the same time. Let us recognize this.

As I listened to the answers to the questions this morning I found several things stated. One is that evaluative analysis is dialogue. This is the same answer, in effect, which a philosopher gave me when I said, "Now what good is political philosophy?" and he said, "Well, it is a discussion." He is a natural law political philosopher, and he said, "It is the process itself." It is the process plus the clarification.

So Duncan was saying that the welfare economists and the democratic theorists should have a dialogue. My guess is that it really needs more than that. That is to say, it needs to have specified segments of a dialogue so that one can recognize when one is going down one track as compared to some other track, and so that one realizes each of them is likely to have its consequences.

The British Analytical School is really throwing imagined examples up against an idea to test its margins. What they don't realize is that this is inductive in the sense that the imagined examples really are building up a case law and that it would be more helpful if they were to take the findings of empirical research and use those rather than their own bizarre examples, such as supposing Napoleon buried a bomb which one hundred years later explodes and kills somebody: Is he morally responsible? I think, perhaps, it would be just as well if they had spent that time talking about the research which might be available—I don't know that it is—on responsibility and real cases of responsibility. I think, in other words, that their selection of cases by this bizarre method really biases the findings that they come to.

HACKER: When you say research, do you mean research on moral responsibility?

LANE: Yes. For example, cases of research on dilemmas of a high school superintendent. What is it to be morally responsible within the findings of role conflict?

HACKER: I just remembered a question that was once put to me, and I forget what the answer was. Is there such a thing as moral research? Can we do research on morals?

LANE: Well, I mean research which reveals the dilemmas which real people have, role dilemmas if you like, responsibilities to this group and that group and the means which are employed or the criteria used for selecting one against another.

HACKER: Well, that is empirical.

LANE: Yes. This can clarify it better I think than the bizarre cases that I saw employed. You find out something about moral responsibility by talking about moral responsibility—by talking about a man who has been entrusted with a farthing by a friend and is held up. Is he morally responsible for not giving it to the man who threatens him? Suppose somebody pushes his elbow so he holds out the farthing. Is he then morally responsible? All these are clarifying, but I thought that they really were off on the wrong foot.

LINDBLOM: If I may just interject a point. Those examples which you call bizarre are excellently suited to permit philosophers to discuss how to discuss moral questions, while the kind of things you talked about would plunge them into moral questions which they do not want to get into. They want to discuss the method.

LANE: Well, what they wanted to do at that point was to clarify through this illustrative method what we mean when we talk about moral responsibility—the concept, not how we should go about clarifying it.

LINDBLOM: I think you'd say methodological inquiry.

LANE: It is definitionally something like that.

LINDBLOM: Yes. So you are asking them to change the whole character of philosophy by choosing different examples. You are not just asking for slightly different examples. As I said this morning, I think they are not really very competent to do that; they don't have the empirical competence. I think we can do it better.

LANE: Could be.

LINDBLOM: The method is all right, but somebody's got to practice it.

LANE: I agree. It is particularly suitable to legal problems, I think.

HACKER: Some colleagues of mine, who are more or less disciples of Leo Strauss, are dedicated to adumbrating moral principles. They deduced from Plato and Aristotle, for example, statements about the evils of pornography. I don't know whether you call what they do research or not. What is more important, however, is that everything they say is unverifiable in that you either agree or disagree with their conception about the good life. There is no empirical input with which one can argue about their conception of the good life. Now, is this what you are suggesting?

LANE: The point I took off from was, I believe, several of the criticisms of my paper including, I think, yours, which had to do with its failure to be explicit on the normative-evaluative components of policy analysis, which I take seriously.

Asking the question "How do you do that?" I got several answers. One was dialogue. I'm saying here that so far this is a blunt term; that is to say, I am willing to believe that dialogue is illuminating, but I would like to see some explication of manners, style, consequence, and categories—the usual thing that we do when we explicate a concept of that kind. I also got a second answer, which holds it isn't a question of how are they integrated but how they can be separated. This is really, in some ways, the same question asked in a different way because what I am asking is how are they related, not are they separate or integrated.

I think I would also like to take some exception to what Ed was saying, that nine-tenths of evaluative discourse is empirical statement. I think a larger fraction is definitional; that is to say, it is statements of meaning. They are intimately interlocked because meanings have references; however, they are not really what is common usage, but rather what is plausible to our kinds of meanings. In any event, I am addressing myself to this set of criticisms which were properly addressed to my paper about these relationships of evaluative to policy analytical ways of thinking. It may be this is not the first time this problem has come to a sort of sudden halt, but I am not quite satisfied that we have explored it as fully as we might.

I would like to raise the point again, as Sol Tax did in his comments on my paper and his question this morning, of whether this policy analytical frame is not suited to self-analysis—that is to say, self-disciplinary analysis. I think it is, and it might start from the comment "What is our mission?—the beginning of program evaluation." Then the answers come—to satisfy curiosity, to develop knowledge, to be useful. These are knowledge-referential or social-referential products. Perhaps the answers can be classified that way. My guess is that here, as in all sorts of statements of purpose, the proper way to think about it is not only what the values are, because anybody can posit an ultimate value, but rather how we talk about any value in terms of other values.

I think to say we satisfy our curiosity is too self-indulgent. It has about the same moral worth as for the head of a transportation organization to say, "Well, my mission is to transport people." Or perhaps he might say, "My mission is to do my job." But transport people for what? I don't think it is fully sufficient for the individual who is talking about his own curiosity to say this is a statement of purpose, because it is consumatory for him only. It must have value, I think, in some other terms. If it is consumatory for others, this has a different moral purpose. But I think also there is almost always latent in somebody's mind the sense that it is socially useful and has some set of values, such as that people live better, or are happier, or are less sick. There is always present, I think, something to fall back on. If that is so, then I think that it should be explicated, that satisfying curiosity is not enough, and that knowledge for its own sake is only a stand-in for more fundamental argument.

Therefore, I would say to Sol Tax that the policy analytical program evaluation of our discipline and those questions that come of that frame of thought are really terribly useful to force us back into some kind of thinking about what ways and how to justify it. I am not satisfied with the common answers on this.

Some other sets of problems have come up in relation to theory, policy, and data. My guess is that where policy analysis is concerned, there are many hypotheses for most interesting, large questions—for example, the question to which the Coleman study was directed—and that what policy analytical questions do is to give weight to some of the many propositions and devalue others. In other words, it is accounting for variance, in a sense. This is likely, then, to restructure theoretical statements, and it should.

Further, I think, as I mentioned in my paper, that asking practical questions, such as what happens when people have minimal security as in the negative income tax, is very likely to produce a major theoretical finding, for example, about the work incentive curve.

Also, I think that the data generated in these ways are very likely to, by serendipity if you like, generate theoretical propositions, in just the way that Schelling was saying that early data about trade generated a theory of international trade. It doesn't go the other way all the time. So there is an interaction there.

These comments are partly specific to queries, partly restating what I said before, and partly answering or questioning some of the discussion this morning. Now we will see if anyone is awake. (Laughter)

KARIEL: After listening to you, Bob, I think I would still like to have you try to tell us how one must define policy analysis, whether it is integrative or not, so that it is not likely to enforce the prevailing way in which we define a political situation and so that it is not merely left up to a popular consensus or to whomever has the influence to define the popular consensus for us.

Also, I would like to have you tell us what is really meant by such pleasing abstractions as happiness—your happiness possibly being my misery. I still cannot get from you a definition of policy analysis that would keep those with power from filling in these amorphous terms.

To dramatize this opposition of mine, I would think it might be useful to reflect on alternatives and argue that we ought to surrender some conventional distinctions within the social sciences, the kind of distinctions which I think sustain the remarks that you have been making. These are very familiar ones: The distinction between policy analyst and citizen, the distinction between useful knowledge and theoretical knowledge, between fact and norm, between practice and theory, and an overriding one, the distinction that you insist on between means and ends—the belief that analysis must come to an end.

The notion that analysis could be interminable is, as I see it, an elite-sustaining one insofar as an elite can afford interminable analysis while the lower orders of society cannot. Further, as I understand your definition of policy analysis, for those who engage in policy analysis it does come to some sort of an end. For that reason, as I see it at least (and this reinforces points that have been made here by others) it is just not scientific. Or if you like a softer term, it is not scholarly.

CHARLESWORTH: Would you like to respond?

LANE: Yes. On the first point, is it necessary that those who serve the government as policy analysts become the servants of the rulers of society?

Let me say two things about this. I suppose you can define the rulers of society in several ways. If you describe them as upper-class Republicans, when the Democrats are in you don't. I would say there is a difference between stating problems and asking questions. It is possible that the problem is stated by a department of research, or some undersecretary, or perhaps someone higher than that. In the Department of Health, Education, and Welfare, the question is stated as "Our problem is that there is a high drop-out rate in the ghettos," and they think it is a question of the integration of the schools, or the bussing pattern, or something like that. You might rephrase this. You might say, "No, this is a question of the self-esteem of adolescents."

So you have changed the question where they have defined the problem.

Now, I would say this is not infrequent, and that this is a crucial role of a policy analytical assistant. Is he then the servant of the government? Well, he is working within a framework.

KARIEL: Let me pursue this because I think that the problem lies deeper than that, and that it is in the acceptance of terms such as "drop-out" and "ghetto." We agree on them, and this agreement is not put into jeopardy. All the other things that you refer to become then subject to analysis and re-analysis, and we can then, as social scientists, redefine them.

If we accept "drop out" as a term—not a bad one—there is no reason that we cannot assume, at least I see no reason why we cannot assume, that all those who are diligently enlisted within the—let's call it vaguely for a moment the American system—are not really drop-outs from the ideal republic.

LANE: Granted. Fine.

TAX: One calls the other drop-out, and the other replies that he is a cop-out. (Laughter) This is the basic problem, and this is why I think that we need to consider the social sciences in the whole system of the universe, so to speak—where we are in relation to the power structure as well as to the biologist, to the real world, and to our made-up world, and so on—to see if we cannot map our place in the whole. Since there are new systems analysis methods for doing this, let us think of ourselves as part of the system. Doing so would knock out immediately the notion of disciplines as entities. In fact, we are individuals who combine in different ways for different purposes, but it is characteristic of the universe that different people will classify us in different ways.

Sociology and economics are unreal in the same way that Nordic and Alpine races are nonexistent ideal types. The individuals within our disciplines accept the cubbyholes in which they are placed by the establishment which rewards them, for the disciplines are characteristic socio-cultural systems like others in the larger whole. Indeed the whole range of things that we talk about in the social sciences all applies to us but, characteristically again, we do not easily see them as applied to us. We can't study ourselves.

My comment asks what Kariel is asking—that we not stand like a group of gods above the universe that we are studying. By pretending not to be part of it, we are being a particular kind of part, in this case supporting some status quo, which raises a moral problem for us. The paradox of our position is that we don't apply our empirical knowledge to ourselves enabling us to see ourselves as we might be seen by other groups in society. If we don't see ourselves that way, if we don't understand our own role, and if yet we are the people who are supposed to understand the nature of the social world, we are obviously in an extraordinarily weak position with respect even to protecting ourselves as social scientists, much less doing any positive work.

HACKER: I know a very bright girl at Cornell who is going to drop out after finishing her sophomore year. I sat down and tried to talk her out of dropping out. She looked me square in the eye and said, "You stayed in, and look what it did to you." (Laughter) Now, I don't know how to handle that.

BIERSTEDT: Well, there is one way to handle it. Our mutual friend Herbert Deane was asked by one of his students in the History of Political Theory why he had to sit in class and learn this stuff, and Herbert replied to him, "You really don't have to, but if you are asking me why I am doing it, it's because it is my thing, and you're certainly going to let me do my thing." Now why shouldn't this girl let you do your thing?

HACKER: She'll let me do my thing, but her response would also be to say that we accept the roles of the system at an early age and decide to play by the rules of the game, thus becoming certain sorts of people. So here we are, playing tiddlywinks and calling it a scholarly career. That's what she would reply.

BIERSTEDT: That's pretty relevant to what Mr. Lane was talking about. Something worries me about this whole position here. It seems to me that Mr. Lane has conferred a moral quality upon knowledge itself, and I am not quite sure about the logical processes in terms of which he has done this. He is not satisfied with the acquisition of knowledge as a process in terms of which the individual satisfies his curiosity. He seems to imply that there is a certain immorality about this, that this is an entertainment, that this is fun. I suppose he would have to say the same thing about tiddlywinks and chess and various other kinds of things.

I am wondering if it isn't really the itch of curiosity that has gotten this intellectual tradition started in the first place. I can't imagine Socrates making such a nuisance of himself wandering around the streets of Athens asking "What is justice?" and so on, for any other reason except that he wanted to know. Of course, when he acquired the knowledge it had deleterious consequences for himself.

I'm not sure about the relationship between knowledge and morality. I had always assumed, or I had always tended to assume, that knowledge is itself morally neutral and that it can be used for good purposes and bad purposes and so on. But that is a debatable question, I suppose, and, as Hobbes said, to every argument one equally good can be opposed. I think we might debate this.

But let me turn the situation around a little bit. We have been worried about at what stage in our discourse or in our research or in our policy analysis, empirical judgments or empirical propositions turn into statements of value. Let's turn this one around and ask if there are not certain situations, very important situations, in which a priori moral preferences have something to do with the kind of knowledge we pursue.

Let me give you two illustrations of that. I am almost certain that everyone in this room would be appalled by a discovery that there are, in fact, genetic differences in intelligence between races. We are all liberals, so to speak—I'm sure of that, although I am meeting some of you for the first time—political liberals. We would not enjoy this conclusion, even if it should happen to be true. Consequently we would all be in a situation where we would not engage in that kind of research simply because we do not like the moral consequences of a scientific conclusion. There are other differences between races, after all, and there might be this difference.

Suppose we discover that there are differences in intelligence between the sexes—that although there is great overlap at the top end of the intelligence curve there are ten times as many men as women, as, incidentally, seems to be true also at the other end of the curve, so that there are perhaps ten times as many morons or idiots among males as among females.   Now, I think that we would not be happy to accept conclusions of that kind, even though perhaps we could find evidence to support them.

The question I want to pose, therefore, is: Aren't there certain moral preferences that serve to inhibit the acquisition of knowledge?   This is a reverse kind of relationship between morality and empirical propositions as compared to the one that we were talking about this morning.

TAX: I don't think, in fact, that any of us, no matter how liberal or anything else, would object to learning the facts of the matter.   The chief problem is that the people who are looking for the facts have a different kind of moral purpose in looking for them, and they don't really get the facts.

If it were true that either in the case of race or sex there is some clustering of differences in different parts of the population and we acted on the basis of these facts, it wouldn't hurt anybody's morals at all because we would then not be discriminating against people by race or sex, but by intelligence, which is what we all pretend that we are doing all the time.   But the people who want to make those studies do so to find data to justify discrimination on the basis of race or on the basis of sex rather than on this basis of intelligence.   So I don't think that we are being inhibited by these moral things at all.

BIERSTEDT: I think we are being inhibited by the very people who are anxious to find that kind of a conclusion when, on the contrary, we would not like to have that kind of conclusion.

TAX: Well I would like to have the whole spectrum of the differences in populations exposed to the public eye, provided the knowledge is not misinterpreted by those who want it exposed to the public eye for a reason different from mine.

I don't think the objection to which you refer is to making some studies, but rather to the people who want to make the studies and the uses to which they intend to put them; theirs is not an intellectual problem at all, but a political problem from start to finish.

LINDBLOM: You, Bob Lane, are saying that policy analysis is a useful way of integrating social sciences.

LANE: It provides a way for it.

LINDBLOM: Yes. Now what I want to know is how far you are pushing the claim that it is worth any special attention or special emphasis as a method of integration. Are you saying, since you have been asked in this conference whether policy analysis is a useful way of integrating, that you have to say in all honesty that it is, or do you single it out in your mind as an especially promising method?

LANE: I think it is the other way. The variables go in the other direction. I don't really care whether the social sciences are integrated or not. I do care about the capacity to identify, dissect, and analyze social problems or causes of grievances. I think that on many such occasions it is necessary for the social sciences to borrow from one another because the nature of the problem requires multivoiced analysis.

LINDBLOM: So you are saying that to get some good policy analysis we need some integration.

Again, then, I ask a question. Do you think the need for policy analysis is an especially high-priority need to which social science should be responding as against other things it might be doing? Are you really saying that we ought to make the social sciences deal largely with policy, or more than at present, or about the same as at present, or less than now?

LANE: Well, I guess what I am saying is that the intellectual development of the university out of the Middle Ages has given a mode of address to problems—a rationale, which has chiefly to do with individual scholars and the development of knowledge for what is called its own sake. So what I was saying is that this is a camouflage for something else.

It was true all along—but it is now more patently true, or we recognize it as true now in a way which we didn't before—that there is something else which this body of talent and these skills can do, and that is to help guide society through difficult passages. Because of the history of the university, this has been under-valued, and we now think it should be valued more. I would say that the criteria for its limitation is at that point when it begins to entrench upon research and thinking whose applied quality is unknown. I would use that as a definition of pure science. It's not that it isn't useful but that we don't know what uses it will have. So as soon as policy begins to entrench upon that, then I would say that is the stopping point.

LINDBLOM: May I just pursue this line a little further? Consider work like your own on political and economic equality. Might it help us through some kind of impasse?

LANE: I think so.

LINDBLOM: Well, it is quite different from the kind of work you are endorsing in your paper.

LANE: Extremely different.

LINDBLOM: What is there is your paper that defends the kind of work that you endorse in your paper as superior to your own kind of work for the very purpose you mention, helping society through some of these emergencies, crises, and impasses? Or what is there about that kind of work that you are endorsing that is better than a great deal of work that is not at all of the style you endorse—for example, the kind of work that Durkheim did on suicide?

LANE: These can all be argued to be works of potential value in helping society get through one of its problems.

Guetzkow spoke of valuing the term elite. Let me go him one better. A fair assessment of the members of my profession, I'm sure it is different in all others, is that there are some statements which may occur to an individual, and he may do nothing further along those lines; and there are some statements which have the characteristic of illuminating a whole series of problems to which they are not addressed. But this is not characteristic of most of the work done in the discipline. That is to say, there is a lot of work which really doesn't do this—just narrative accounts of something very small without any cumulative payoff. The great risk in this policy analytical thing that I am talking about is that you divert the seminal mind. You divert the person who is going to make that statement from saying it, and that is a great shame.

An example would be the person who is doing his dissertation. He doesn't have a problem, but he has a topic, and he is cranking out a piece of research which really doesn't mop up very much just because he is paid to do it or he gets a promotion out of it. What I am saying is that directed research to social problems, and probably the director himself, ought to be better quality, but that directed research should be set by an agenda which is not the individual's own. Often people are not the best judge of what they ought to be doing next.

LINDBLOM: Bob Lane—I must exaggerate a bit to make clear my point—you are saying you are sure there is a much better kind of social science research that an elite can do since most social scientists are cranking out something close to garbage or journalism. (Laughter) If that is your position, say yes to that. (Laughter)

LANE: Well, I said that knowing that that would be. . . . Let me put it this way. (Laughter) You know what we do. We discriminate and set up sets and subsets and so forth. It is a modified yes. Supposing one thinks in terms of manpower utilization, and that then one thinks in terms of payoff of several different kinds. One is seminal ideas. One is a sort of ordinary science, but important. And the third is something that doesn't even qualify for that.

And then there is another set of things which have to do really with eliminating given tasks of program evaluation and analysis of, not the statement of the research design because this is often a major intellectual task, but the work of given research tasks. If you think in manpower terms of maximum social utility, my guess is that we can employ a larger number in the applied field. This is only part of it. I also think reframing public policy questions is as interesting an intellectual task and requires as much ability as many of the theoretical problems. So I am hedging because I think that some of the talents should go into that.

McCORD: I agree with what Bob says. I think I would even go somewhat further. Let me give my answers to what I think are the two sides of the question.

First of all, I think the integration of the social sciences is absolutely necessary and extremely useful. Secondly, by attention to policy, used in the broadest sense, I don't mean just evaluating whether an anti-poverty program worked on——

GUETZKOW: In other words, Bob is endorsing a narrower sense.

McCORD: Yes, I think so, but I wouldn't even draw a distinction between seminal minds versus the masses because it seems to me if we think of policy in a broad sense, we would consider the seminal minds of the nineteenth and twentieth centuries in the social sciences to include Freud, Durkheim, Weber, and Marx. All of them were directly concerned with trying to solve some type of practical social problem. From their work there was, of course, a spin-out into theory. I think if we actually went over the great men, the seminal minds, we would find that they were concerned, not with developing theories or with pure sciences, but rather with solving practical problems.

KARIEL: Let me respond to that directly. I don't think that they were concerned with solving so-called social problems. They were concerned with solving their own problems. We have Weber's testimony on that. He tried to find out what he could bear, having been sensitized by his environment and having felt uncomfortable in it. He tried to recapture his balance, and he did it in part by writing. This can be equally well demonstrated with regard to Freud, Marx, and Durkheim.

McCORD: Well, yes. One can investigate their personal motivations. But Durkheim's goal, it seems to me, was to try to reintegrate a society that he saw as collapsing. Freud's goal was to try to find a solution to neuroses.

KARIEL: I think he tried to find his own bearings, balance, and equilibrium.

McCORD: Oh yes, but that could be said of any human being.

KARIEL: Then I think it is all right to go ahead and say it of anybody and tell graduate students and others that they ought to solve their own problems, not those problems that are predefined by those who tell us what happiness consists of.

McCORD: I see your point about serving the status quo. Nonetheless, it seems to me that a truly seminal mind, such as Marx's, was devoted to solving problems of poverty and industrialization—perhaps, too, his own personal problems. Yet, he was obviously outside the status quo. He was not a policy analyst in the usual sense of the word.

KARIEL: But we are all proud to be outside of the status quo. And I would resist the definition of these characters you have identified here as somehow distinctively seminal, unlike the rest. All minds are seminal. Some are more seminal than others.

McCORD: No, I consider myself very much a part of things.

LINDBLOM: The distinction isn't so much between people who have an interest in policy and those who don't. It is the immediacy of the policy concern and how relaxed, fundamental, and desperately ambitious they dare to be in thinking about social problems. A Marx does not believe that he must solve this problem tomorrow. He can take his whole life if he needs to, to work out fundamental relationships. Freud must have had something of the same sense. Scholars of that kind back off a great deal, as I say, from the immediate responsibility to give advice on policy. They take their time and they go for great goals. Their style is what Mr. Lane seems to oppose.

As I understand him, Mr. Lane is recommending a more pedestrian, non-elitist attack on problems, which he thinks is the level at which most of our social scientists can best function. You gave a qualified yes to my question, Mr. Lane, about whether we'd better do policy analysis because otherwise we will waste our time. You would like to see more social scientists doing your kind of policy analysis. I guess I would too, if I could also see more social scientists doing more of many other kinds of analysis —but not, however, if I had to transfer social scientists out of other kinds of work into your kind of policy analysis. I doubt that you have made a convincing case, or even cast your problem in those comparative terms so that we can see what your argument is.

As I look at economics, it seems to me that the intellectual tradition of economics puts most economists to work not, to be sure, on the grand issues that Marx or Adam Smith grappled with, but on unravelling complexities of monetary mechanisms and that sort of thing. What economists typically do is more useful to society than if economists were transferred to cost-benefit or systems analysis, as you seem to propose.

Perhaps we really ought to rely largely, for your kind of policy work, on nonsocial scientists—that is, on political commentators, journalists, staff assistants, practical decision-makers, and so forth. I am raising the question of whether your kind of analysis, Mr. Lane, is worth the time of social scientists in view of the payoff that social scientists can get by backing off further from policy and working on the kinds of things, for example, illustrated by your own work on equality.

Is it true, as you seemed to have suggested, that if they don't do your proposed kind of policy work, most social scientists would do worse work and therefore they should do your kind? Social scientists could do, I think, more ambitious work than they do do, and I am reasonably well convinced that somehow we take the ambition out of many budding social scientists in graduate school. I don't know quite how we do it, but I am deeply impressed at how much is lost in intellectual zest, creativity, and drive in graduate school. When I look at some of the characteristics of graduate education, the extent and kind of bureaucratization and standardization of it, I get some clues as to what is happening. It is true, for example, that in the Yale Economics Department a young man would have to be tough and confident to dare to pose what you would call a highly seminal question for his dissertation. He might be considered to be audacious to the point of irresponsibility. The fact is that such a person would be audacious, would probably be biting off more than he could chew, and would eventually fail in his project. To permit him his ambitions, we would have to be willing to put up with ten, or even ninety-nine, losers for every winner. Apparently we are not prepared to do that in graduate education.

MacRae: I can't tell whether it is Lindblom's or Lane's characterization of the problem, but I felt a moment ago that you, Ed, had trapped Bob into a position that he really didn't want to take, so let me defend his position a little bit.

It seems to me that by citing examples, particularly such distinguished pure scientists, we are restricting ourselves to the present system of evaluation and stratification within social sciences. If we publicly define policy analysis as superficial, trivial, and lacking in insight with respect to the fundamental alternatives available, then, of course, it is not worth doing. Second-rate people will do it, and we may have to have that coordinated hierarchical system that Bob seemed to be agreeing to.

But I don't agree to it. I think that if policy analysis is done at an abstract level rather than being limited to a particular skill to deal with a particular given problem, then top-notch people *will* go into it. Perhaps, too, they will eventually be recognized as top-notch and seminal even though they are not recognized as such in our present stratification system.

LINDBLOM: Would you say that the picture you had of policy analysis is strikingly different from the one laid down in Bob's paper?

MacRAE: Well, he said a lot of things. Maybe I am engaging in selectivity, but I think he was on both sides. I'll let him answer that. I thought there was a certain amount of what I am looking for in his paper.

LANE: I think there was intended to be.

MacRAE: So just to round out this argument, I would say that if we don't think of policy schools in terms of social welfare, business administration, industrial relations, international relations, and journalism—or even medicine, agriculture, engineering, or environmental studies—but think of them as general policy schools, we may find they will provide the environment within which seminal minds can deal with these problems and be recognized as outstanding.

GUETZKOW: Thank you, Duncan. Let me now return to Henry's ideas as a second base for the comment I would like to make. You may not want to join me, Dunc, but I certainly endorse what you have been saying.

If one describes values as static and without alternatives, as Henry implies, one is cornered. If one characterizes values as enduring, identifying with the status quo, as Andy seems to do, once again one has a stereotyped way of looking at policy analysis. But scholars may look at value problems per se when engaging in policy analysis. Remember there is the Institute for Policy Analysis in Washington, D. C., as well as the Stanford Research Institute in California. We now need institutes which refuse to allow their work to be cornered unwittingly by unanalyzed positions. Using Tom Schelling's style, we need to seek out excuses in the value problems encountered by policy analysts and disciplinarians. We also need to develop specialists who know something of both value philosophies and the social sciences so that we may develop a conjunction between the two approaches as values are implicated in integrations.

One needs bridge-crossers at the theoretical and empirical level too. In parallel to those concerned with values in social science and policy, the facilitation of the work of elitists and professionals in generating integrated knowledge is a concern of the organization of our academic and policy establishments. The day of the Renaissance man is long past because of the explosions in information and methodological technologies. Now it seems necessary to develop bridge-crossers between areas of academic and policy concern, just as we are beginning to create opportunities for the venturesome to float among the social sciences. If we are to reap benefits, these intellectuals will need to give five to ten years of their lives in such border enterprises so as to exploit the seminal developments they encounter.

LANE: It seems to me that it is possible to agree that the clarification of values, the analysis of the system within which they are to be maximized, and the causes and effects in a discriminating way are all things we normally do or should do. Now that to me is no less of an intellectual challenge. It is something we don't normally say. It doesn't require a lower order of intellect, and yet I would like to see it turned more to that kind of task.

SCHELLING: I just want to make a small remark, and that is that I think our thoughts about this subject contain very interesting metaphors—fences and bridges and that sort of thing—as though we are dealing with a plane surface that is exhaustively divided into compartments known as disciplines with the notion that you can only get from one to the other through a structure like a bridge.

It may be that there is a lot of no-man's-land and that some of the best of what looks like integrating the social sciences is getting outside them altogether. Or it may be that there is a lot of common ground surrounded by the disciplines and that what looks like multidisciplinary research is people going out on the commons to graze rather than digging in their own backyard. Or it may be that the structure is a line rather than plane, and each discipline has close neighbors and more distant neighbors; yet we are acting as though we were all equally distant from each other in a non-spatial way.

If we use other metaphors, such as all being on the same telephone system rather than being divided by fences on a plane surface, we might have very different notions about what constitutes integration. Metaphors such as physically moving over by way of a bridge would give way to such things as leaving the switch on after five o'clock at night and hearing what they are talking about next door.

I mention this because I am still very much confused about whether anybody here means by integration what I am now intimidated to believe is my original notion of what the word meant. I just wonder two things: first, whether our thoughts about it are very much constrained by our very traditional vocabulary, and second, whether we aren't engaging in a strange sort of evaluative policy analysis that I feel we got, or at least I got, seduced into without being told what my role is. I have the impression I am now trying to discover what the elite should be doing, what those who can't quite make the elite should be doing, who should be hiring out to the government, and who should be setting up Stanford research institutes in different places.

I guess what we are doing is a means-end analysis, allocating social science resources. Some of us are thinking that government is worrying about problems and where to go to get help and what is the most cost-effective way. Others of us may be secretly indulging in our own notions about what the true worth of knowledge is and trying to express it in terms that sound honorable and moral, as if, even though we are in it for fun, we must justify it, in addition to its being fun, as also being socially useful.

I'm not sure what most of us have in mind as the character of the resource. I am inclined to feel, getting back to Harold's notion of fun, that I put in about a forty-eight hour work week doing plain hard work, and if there is any time left over I engage in what I call my own social science research. I am inclined to think I do it on my own time or on my family's time, not at public expense; and if it's no fun, I won't do it. It's Sunday morning, and I work six days a week on stuff that isn't fun. On the other hand I can imagine being at a different institution or on a different kind of contract or under different circumstances where my attitude toward what I should do as a social scientist would be quite different because I might have some obligations.

Now I have a secret hunch that Socrates was just a show-off and a compulsive problem-solver like the rest of us. He was doing his thing, but this puzzles me because I am inclined to think that it doesn't matter what motivated Socrates. I don't care what his values were. What matters is that when I read his

stuff something comes through that is independent of whether he
had a compulsive desire to die young as a martyr, or whether
he was really hoping to get some of those boys after hours by
finding an excuse to get close to them.   I am inclined, then, to
think that there may still be for some of us something about
knowledge that is independent of the values which lie behind it.
It is unlikely to contaminate things that it comes in contact with.
It is clean, pure, and useful.   It's not dirtied, and it doesn't have
fingerprints on it.   And it may be that washed, sterile knowledge
is better than the kind that—I don't know; it depends on the
metaphor.

We've had a dispute in my department.   A small minority
insists that since all appointments are political we should make
them explicitly political rather than pretend that they are non-
political.   Now it is an interesting question whether——

TAX: All which appointments?

SCHELLING: All faculty appointments in the department.

At what degree of failure do you decide that it does more harm
to try than not because of self-deception?   Is it the case that if
you try to have non-political faculty members, if you try to have,
let's call it, if not value-free research, at least opinion-free, preju-
dice-free, or nondeceptive research, how unsuccessful do you have
to be before you decide that it does more harm than good to try?
I think part of the problem here is that it is like becoming secretary of the Treasury or a congressman.   We demand full dis-
closure.   We want to know what a man's interest is.   We want
to know what his stakes are.   If he advises us on what to do
about schoolteachers' salaries, we want to know how much stock
he owns in companies that make money.   We want to know
whether he has kids in the school.   We want to know whether he
is worried about a rise in the property tax.   We want to know
his prejudices and which side he is on—I guess, because not knowing quite how to use what he tells us, we are going to fall back
on his authority.

It is a little like the Wesley Mitchell thing.   Wesley Mitchell
could have said, "You wouldn't trust me if I told you because my
values are not your values."

Roosevelt might have answered, "I can teach you my values
more quickly than you can teach me your economics.   Therefore,

I will tell you my values, and then I will trust you to use my values and answer the question. It is faster that way." But if it turned out that Wesley Mitchell held a lot of gold bonds and was terribly interested in seeing the price level fall forever and ever, I think Roosevelt would have wanted to know that and might not have even trusted the man to give him the advice on the trade-off between employment and inflation.

So I guess what I am getting to as we talk about what the social sciences should do is the question: Whom are we representing? Are we representing the government's thinking about going through Bob Lane's difficult passages and wanting to know how to get help from the social sciences (supposing that there is actually help there to get), or do we think of ourselves as custodians of the great national resource known as the professions of the social sciences, or are we in it for ourselves the way most conventions meeting in this hotel are probably in it for themselves, whether they sell insurance or fur or are collecting money for firemen's benefits? Whom do we represent, and how do we take care of our own values in this business? Is it primarily that we must make full confession so that I know how to interpret what Bob is recommending because he has a book that will come out and it will be embarrassing if we conclude the opposite of what is in the book, or that I suddenly realize that I am going to lose a good office at Harvard because when we consolidate with the other social sciences we are going to equalize office space as well as income?

LANE: I am going to answer that. I posit three values for the enterprise we are in: the enjoyment of doing it, the pleasure other people have in listening to and reading it, and the degree to which it helps people attain self-actualization, growth, and the realization of their capacity. I attach ten percent importance to self-enjoyment of what one does, fifteen percent to reading and listening, and seventy-five percent to self-actualization. Of that seventy-five percent, some is for current generations and some is for future generations. When I say pure research, I mean seminal for long-term self-actualization and probably future generations. When I say applied, I am talking about more immediate self-actualization for more immediate generations.

I will take the ten percent and the fifteen percent as given, and I won't touch them, but I want to consider changing the mix of the seventy-five percent. I would like to see it go from, say, twenty-five percent trying to do the seminal, longer term kind of thing, but only five percent doing it well, to fifteen percent doing it. I would then like to add the least good of the longer term kind of thing to the shorter term kind of thing. I would then have the best fifteen percent doing seminal work, and the remaining eighty-five percent, short-term, applied work. All right? (Laughter)

LINDBLOM: We still don't know what your reasons are. You haven't given us a positive reason for using social scientists for the ten percent increment. Why not practical decision-makers and their staffs instead? Some of them are excellent at it. Nor have you really met the question of the danger of conservatism and superficiality, which is a point I also made in my paper, if social scientists do that kind of social science.

LANE: As you know, study findings show that for the most part the best guide line is that everything increases by some general increment at about the same rate. This is more true of municipal than national budgets. Now this means that some new infusion of an idea or critical analysis has to come which takes the purpose of an organization or restates the purposes and discovers whether it is being done. It is a radical notion that a bureau be abolished if it is not serving the purpose it is set up for. In this sense I think you are wrong about its being conservative.

So I think the only people who can really do that are people who are equipped to establish observable criteria, measure their achievement, and then appraise whether it meets its purpose and whether it does it more expensively or less expensively. I think only social scientists can do that. It's a relatively small operation, but I think there ought to be more people doing it.

LINDBLOM: Really now, Bob, is there any evidence that social scientists have done this any better than so-called practical people? For example, take the record of cost-benefit studies and systems analysis for PPBS. It's not an unquestionable success.

LANE: True, but its predecessors weren't either. I think if I knew more about this I would either be less positive, wouldn't have said this, or could answer your question. In fact, however, I don't know that much.

HACKER: Did PPBS come out of social science? Just because it came out of a building in Santa Monica doesn't mean it is social science.

LINDBLOM: It came out of programmed budgeting, which came from a practical background.

HACKER: That wasn't my question though. Did something come out of social *science*? Getting a man on the moon did not come out of physical science. It was an engineering feat.

I have the feeling that I, among all the people here, am least impressed with the accomplishments of social science over the last thirty years. I am more and more impressed, as I said in my paper, with our incapacity to understand. This is not because we lack technique, but because we are born with small minds compared with that which has to be understood. Therefore I disagree with a number of people about integrating the social sciences, the disciplines. I don't think we are up to it. Maybe another race on another planet would be but we aren't. We're not bright enough.

TAX: So do you think we should be smart enough to go out and find those other planets where there are people who are smart enough to do this?

HACKER: Do what you can do, and don't pretend that you can do more than you can do.

TAX: If we are smart enough to see that we are not smart enough to do it—understanding our capacities and our limitations —that's the smartest thing we could be. I don't think we are putting that smartness to work now. Somebody some day will point out that we have been monkeys playing a game. You asked if we were successful in any of these things. When the world finally blows up, on what scale could one measure whether Santa Monica was a success? We haven't even begun to ask that because we've been caught in the means-ends trap, a very parochial scale. When you ask what an institution is for, try asking instead, when a child is born, what his end is and whether one can talk meaningfully at all about means and ends in human life.

Suppose we made it one of the rules of the game here that we couldn't think of a means-end continuum at all. There are people, existentialists to the core, who don't think linearly. Would we be able to get a new paradigm for ourselves by which we might more successfully encompass the problems of humanity, and so on? You don't think so.

HACKER: No, I don't. We've got some suggestions here about how we could do this and do that. I wouldn't for a minute say to any government bureau, "I have knowledge which can help you with your policies." I would be lying through my teeth.

TAX: Talk to a Navaho Indian for awhile instead of to a government and think of what you would say.

You know, I'm trying for a different paradigm here by which we wouldn't be thinking in the system in which we have been thinking, but rather would get outside ourselves so that we could see ourselves.

HACKER: I'll tell you, I've been trying that with some students of mine, and it has been an absolute failure. They have determined that I have nothing to offer them.

Now I would only indicate here that I don't know whether we are going to correct certain unbalances that we have, but at this point I would be more pleased to leave the decisions to any random Black Panther or Hard Hat than I would to anyone at this table.

LANE: I would like to answer the second part of Ed's question having to do with effectiveness. In the bluntest terms, people with the values from the academe are more likely, on any set of measures I've seen, to have humane values which I share than are people in the bureaucracy or on legislative staffs. Journalists may be a little different. So that my guess is, just in those blunt terms, the infusion of people into the bureaucratic cohort has a humanizing effect. Furthermore, they are less bound by the question than the bureaucrats, so in that sense they are more liberal.

Moreover, I would say that the transfer of that ten percent which I wanted to make into applied policy analytical types is not a conservatizing influence. The only way you could make it conservatizing would be by not taking into account who is doing it.

LINDBLOM: No, you misunderstand me. It is the conservative effect on disciplines, the professions, not on the government.

LANE: Right.   Then let me take the other side.

HACKER: Did you see that book which came out recently on prisons, asylums, and orphanages in the Jacksonian period?   This was, in effect, their equivalent of social science.   Men of humane knowledge decided that the country needed asylums, orphanages, and prisons.   We have also helped create the Vietnam War.   Our track record is no better than anyone else's.

LANE: I think the comparison should be between, say, wardens and penologists or criminologists or sociologists.   There the reverse would be the case.

Let me return to Ed's question.   I have taken ten percent of the people from the value which comes from the use of knowledge for social purpose, which I have defined as self-actualization. Twenty-five percent of those I said were working on enduring, long-term, and therefore seminal or pure research projects.

I've taken ten percent of those and put them to work on applied problems in order to decrease the number of people who are working on more radical concepts.   The equation then is: To what extent for society, both public policy and the disciplines, do you increase the liberalization of society through applied social science on the public policy side by somewhat decreasing the capacity of reflective, long-term research on the social investigative side?   I guess our difference occurs in our relative evaluation of these two types.

MACRAE: I would like to draw together in a small way something that Andy Hacker said with something that Sol Tax said. Suppose we think of our bad track record.   Suppose we also adopt a certain amount of humility, such as McCord's case studies would lead us to have.   I think this would lead us to integrate academic with non-academic knowledge, another dimension of integration.   This leads us, then, to a slightly broader perspective on the relation between political sciences and the outside.

Now one of my colleagues, who is a political philosopher, made what I think you might consider a wise suggestion.   If we set up policy schools, we ought not to give the academics an unfair advantage over the students.   We ought not to bring in the civil servants and have them sitting in the classroom while the professor is standing up and lecturing; rather we ought to bring in the practitioner and the academic on an equal basis and let them integrate equally.

HACKER: Non-academic knowledge is considered non-knowledge. We are the custodians of knowledge. A discipline decides which facts, gathered and analyzed in a certain way, can be knowledge. There are perceptive people outside the academic disciplines—journalists, poets, the Beatles—but I don't think we can synthesize with them. One reason you set up a discipline is that it is internally consistent with rules established for handling information.

Many of the great minds we have been hearing about, like Freud and Marx, didn't belong to disciplines. Some of the earlier ones, like Adam Smith and Hegel, belonged to university faculties, but those were before the days of disciplines. I just wonder whether we are really good for anything other than fooling around inside our discipline. All the seminal work that Bob talks about is seminal only in a disciplinary sense. We have been seminating and reseminating inside a discipline.

KARIEL: But we do provide others with opportunities to rebel against the discipline, which is true of the so-called seminal mind.

HACKER: We have to make our own decisions here. Personally, I'm quite happy to move into the realm of non-knowledge.

McCORD: I agree with you entirely; we should be humble. Obviously we don't have much knowledge, but don't you think that we might have *negative* knowledge to contribute? For example, the Supreme Court recently reinstated capital punishment. At least we can say that this won't affect the homicide rate at all, and if that goal was in the court's mind, it was wrong.

KARIEL: I very much like your concept of negative knowledge. In fact we need merely to encourage ourselves to be more descriptive, to be more precise, in characterizing whatever it is that ails us or the institutions that surround us because ultimately, if we push this to its logical conclusion, we provide ourselves with some version of dialectical alternatives. It becomes then a mirror image of what is an intolerable situation.

CHARLESWORTH: It may be we got the wrong kind of people for this conference. (Laughter) I mean, it doesn't happen very often that a profession will reform itself. It may be that we should have gotten some high-level journalists and some enlightened executives of foundations.

SCHELLING: Only by luck did we choose two or three economists, none of whom has spent half his life working for the government.

UNIDENTIFIED VOICE: I've spent seven years in the government. I don't know how much time Ed has spent. Between the two of us I think we are unusual in being very academic, as academic economists go, and I think it is even remarkable in the economics profession that the better ones often go into the government for one or two or five or ten or fifteen years. This means that rather than talk about whether the good ones should go into the government or the good ones should stay behind, I think very often the answer, for a lot of economists, is that you do both. Life is long enough. If you want to communicate, you communicate with somebody with whom you went to school and with whom you have been in touch all along. A lot of the profound, non–policy-oriented work is done by people who spent five years in government, got a whole new conception of what interested them, and spent the next five or ten years doing non-policy work stimulated by——

CHARLESWORTH: I couldn't agree with you more. At luncheon I wasn't at your table. I was telling a story about some old ladies during World War II. They were psychometrists and were constructing tests for artillery officers. When I asked them what they knew about artillery, they said I was impertinent, claiming you didn't have to know anything substantive about a given thing to construct a valid test for it. Now, as you can see by looking around this board, this group was selected with great care because they do know what they are talking about and they do have perspective.

At a previous conference some years ago, one of the members actually said that a political scientist didn't have to know anything about government. So I said, "Well, would you hire a football coach who had never played football?"

"Sure," he said. "You don't have to play football in order to be a football coach."

Now, I feel very strongly about this. Nobody should be an economist if he hasn't been in the government or some related public activity, and nobody should be a political scientist unless he has been out in the field. They should boot him out every five years and tell him to root, hog, or die, and come back and know better what he is talking about, or at least become less top lofty in his statements. I couldn't agree with you more that social scientists should be practitioners.

HACKER: We got Adam Smith's *The Wealth of Nations* without his being a practitioner, and I'm sure that we wouldn't have gotten it had he worked in accounting.

SCHELLING: As you said earlier, it works for some and not for others.

HACKER: I'm just questioning whether that has much to do with it.

CHARLESWORTH: Well, let me take Hamilton and Madison before Madison became president. Whom do you think—I'm not quizzing you, I don't take that position—whom do you think really was a greater man and knew more about government, regardless of whether you agreed with him or not?

VOICES: Hamilton.

CHARLESWORTH: That's what I think. You see, he didn't steer by the stars; he steered by the headlands. That's the kind of person I think we need.

HACKER: Well, for example, Jean Jacques Rousseau was not a practitioner——

CHARLESWORTH: You can find examples for anything.

KARIEL: This gives me the opportunity to make my point again. Here we are accepting the distinction between theory and practice, as if Adam Smith were not engaged in some practical activity, as if the writing of his book had not been a form of action.

CHARLESWORTH: Now, Henry, if it isn't good practice, is it good theory?

SCHELLING: I would like to go on with the economists in government. What Hacker suggested was that you could not only allocate people between activities, but also allocate years of people's lives between activities. Most economists who deal with policy questions do it that way; that is, it is intra-career allocation rather than allocation of the top ten percent to this kind of activity and the next twenty-five percent to that. I think this

means that people inside and out are often congenial. Therefore, it may imply that on the question concerning whether we
would have gotten *The Wealth of Nations* if Smith had worked
in an accounting house, the answer might well be, if he worked
for only five years, yes. If he spent his life there, no.

But I think it may well be that economists are different from
other social scientists in that economists very often, when they
have an influence on policy, have it by hiring out. They go to
work in the Treasury, the Council of Economic Advisors, the
Federal Reserve Board, the International Monetary Fund, the
Department of Commerce—there are places loaded with them.
Most of them are pretty good economists, and as I said, most of
them go back into academic life.

This suggests that there is not a strong incompatibility, so
that when you talk about whom you leave it up to, you find that
if you leave it up to the bureaucrat, he is probably a bureaucrat
who went to graduate school with me, taught for nine years at
Stanford, and expects to teach again. Therefore, we are not
talking about whether you will loose the Rousseaus by this. We
are talking about whether the guy in government is the antithesis
of a Rousseau or whether he went to graduate school with him.
I think the answer is that they very often are somewhat congenial.

LINDBLOM: I sense a certain loss of momentum in the discussion. In the last fifteen minutes we seem to have not been moving very fast, which, at this time in the afternoon, is not surprising. It tempts me to raise again the question that I raised this
morning about what it is we want to know.

I still carry in my mind from graduate school days a vivid
recollection of Arthur Compton's telling a group of students what
physicists at that date—1938, I think—wanted to know, what
they needed to know. He was able to say, not speaking idio-
syncratically for himself but for the profession, what physicists
at that date had succeeded in doing, what they were doing reasonably well, what they had yet to tidy up, and what they still
needed to know. I have never heard a social scientist talk that
way. I want to invite somebody to——

CHARLESWORTH: Do you want a reply to that?

LINDBLOM: Yes, though I'm going to suggest that there is
good reason for our inability to do what Compton did.

Would anyone like to try his hand at indicating what we know? It would give us a good sense of concreteness. We have been working all day with what is, in some respects, a tired view of social science, as though social science has exasperated us or eluded us for most of our lives. No one here has spoken with a great sense of mission for the social sciences. If anybody has any concrete vision about what it is that social scientists need to know, he can help us develop a sense of what kinds of analysis—policy oriented or not—we need.

KARIEL: Well, it seems to me that, to a large extent, we need knowledge of the variety of processes by which we can keep moving, by which we can propel ourselves through whatever is the span of our lives. Substitute methodologies if you like for processes—or paradigms, to take an even larger word. Our preoccupation is not really with conclusions or findings or knowledge that can ultimately be put to some sort of use depending on who has the power or the opportunity to use it. Instead, it is simply with an ongoing activity. And it is this which to a large extent motivates us, whether we confess it to ourselves or not.

LINDBLOM: Let's suppose we grant your explanation. I'm sure that I, in fact, agree with it. But just for the sake of the argument, let's grant that it explains what we do. However, whatever your explanation of why we are what we are, we nevertheless feel the need to justify the jobs we have, the money spent on us, and the attention given to us. We then must look for a different level of explanation than yours. It is that other level of explanation which I want.

KARIEL: On this other level I do think we would like to know what it is—empirically, institutionally, and concretely—that makes this truth-seeking process likely. What facilitates it, and what alternative conditions are likely to promote activity of a scholarly sort, of a scientific sort, of a humanistic sort? Under what alternative kinds of conditions are individuals likely to actualize themselves, to gain in self-esteem? What are the social settings within which individuals thrive?

LINDBLOM: Now, push yourself further if you will. If you define social science problems at that level of generality, it appears that we want to know everything you can say. Can you be more specific? Much of what you say we want to know, we know from the most casual kind of empiricism. We don't want to treat all topics as major social science projects. Could you be a little more selective and pick out of your big basket the specific pieces of knowledge that more precisely represent social science aspirations?

KARIEL: Well, you could reduce this kind of problem to the levels of the existing school or prison—any enclosure. Under what conditions are you more likely to get individuals discharged from schools, hospitals, prisons—whatever the asylum might be?

BIERSTEDT: I don't think it is possible to answer your question, Lindblom, in substance. Everyone has different interests, and there are many, many different sectors in social sciences. One possible answer is that we need a lot of descriptive knowledge about the things that happen which interest us or which might have something to do with policy.

On a theoretical level it seems to me quite obvious—and it is mentioned in somebody's paper, not mine—that what we need in the social sciences, and especially in sociology, are more causal propositions. We have a great many taxonomies, but we have a dearth of causal propositions. This is the most embarrassing thing we confront. One of the things we ask ourselves once and awhile is: Do you have any laws, any principles, any universal propositions in sociology? The answer is that we do not.

LINDBLOM: Some cause-and-effect relationships describe core social science phenomena; others are personal and unimportant. Moreover, there are some causal propositions that are really terribly important for us to get; others we need not bother with. In other words, to say we need cause-and-effect propositions is not enough.

BIERSTEDT: I can only answer that in an abstruse manner by saying we need causal propositions about social change, but that is not a very satisfactory answer.

LINDBLOM: No.

TAX: I have a feeling that at the time I knew what we were up to in the social sciences as well as Compton knew what we were up to in physics. I was trying to understand what men were like in the same sense that he was trying to understand what the forces of nature were like. Was Compton more specific than that?

LINDBLOM: Oh yes.

TAX: What did he say?   Tell us what he said, and we will try to get an analogy.

LINDBLOM: That was a long time ago.

TAX: Well, it doesn't matter.   Did he say we were going to have fusion and fission?

LINDBLOM: He talked about very specific findings—names and dates.   As for the then future of physics, he discussed, for example, the uncertainty principle—what was known, what was puzzling, and what new questions it had opened up.

CHARLESWORTH: The tape is finished, and it is time to adjourn until tomorrow morning.

Integration of Sociology and the Other Social Sciences through Policy Analysis

By James S. Coleman

IN THE past several years, I have observed an extended confrontation between several social sciences in a single area of policy. This case has sufficiently shaped my views about the relations between the social sciences in matters of policy that I will confine my discussion to this case and the suggestions it holds for integration or alienation of the social sciences through their work on policy problems. The case is a survey that was carried out in the U.S. Office of Education in 1965 and 1966 to examine equality of educational opportunity by race. The disciplines involved are sociology, economics, statistics, and educational psychology.

In July, 1966, a report to Congress and the president on the survey, *Equality of Educational Opportunity,* was published. The survey was designed and carried out principally by sociologists and statisticians. The two sociologists most involved were Ernest Campbell and I. The statisticians most involved were Alexander Mood, who, as assistant commissioner of education, played a principal part in the overall statistical design; John Tukey, who, acting as a consultant to the survey, helped shape the design of the regression analysis which constituted the major analytical tool of the survey; and Albert Beaton, who did most of the computer work which implemented the regression analyses and worked with me in carrying out specific analyses.

Major controversies developed after publication of the report surrounding the results of the analysis and the methods used to achieve these results. The principal protagonists in the controversies were, on one side, the authors of the report and, by implication, those who took part in the design of the analysis. On the other side they were the three pairs of economists who wrote critiques of the survey and carried out some independent analyses of the survey.

The first of these critiques was by Samuel Bowles at Harvard and Henry Levin, then at the Brookings Institute, who wrote a paper titled "The Determinants of Scholastic Achievement—An Appraisal of Some Recent Evidence," which was widely circulated in Washington in draft form and then published in the *Journal of Human Resources*. The second was by John Kain and Eric Hanushek, who carried out at Harvard an independent analysis of the survey data and wrote a paper titled "On the Value of *Equality of Educational Opportunity* as a Guide to Public Policy," published in a volume edited by Moynihan and Mosteller titled *On Equality of Educational Opportunity*. In addition, Hanushek's Ph.D. thesis involved further analysis of these data. The third pair was Glen G. Cain and Harold Watts, both at the University of Wisconsin, who published a paper titled "Problems in Making Policy Inferences from the Coleman Report" in the *American Sociological Review*.

A third force was a group of analysts within the Office of Education headed by George Mayeske. Their fields are statistics and educational psychology. This group carried out extensive further analysis of the survey data and has written two volumes based on the analysis: *Our Nation's Schools* and *A Study of the Achievement of Our Nation's Schools.**

What makes the controversy of great interest to the present discussion is the fact that the issues which emerged were issues on which not merely the persons involved differ, but on which

* References for the above-named works are: Samuel Bowles and Henry M. Levin, "The Determinants of Scholastic Achievement—An Appraisal of Some Recent Evidence," *Journal of Human Resources,* vol. 3 (Winter, 1968), pp. 3–24; John F. Kain and Eric A. Hanushek, "On the Value of *Equality of Educational Opportunity* as a Guide to Public Policy," in Frederick Mosteller and Daniel P. Moynihan, eds., *On Equality of Educational Opportunity* (New York: Random, 1972); Eric A. Hanushek, "The Education of Negroes and Whites," (Ph.D. diss., Massachusetts Institute of Technology, 1968); Glen G. Cain and Harold W. Watts, "Problems in Making Policy Inferences from the Coleman Report," *American Sociological Review,* vol. 35, no. 2 (April, 1970), pp. 228–242; George W. Mayeske et al., *A Study of Our Nation's Schools* (Washington, D.C.: U.S. Government Printing Office, 1969); George W. Mayeske et al., *A Study of the Achievement of Our Nation's Students* (Washington, D.C.: U.S. Government Printing Office, 1971).

there appear to be differences among the general approaches of the disciplines involved. There is no way of firmly establishing that this is so, but the consistency within disciplines and the divergence between persons of different disciplines strongly suggests this premise.

The major descriptive question of the survey was the question of just how much, and in what ways, children of racial minorities in the United States experienced lesser educational opportunity than did children of the dominant Caucasian race. In order to answer this question, particularly the "in what ways" portion, it was necessary to examine a more analytical question: What factors in schools as they are currently organized in the United States contribute most to a child's educational experience? It was the answer to this analytical question also which could provide the most extensive avenues for policy, for this would indicate what kinds of policy changes in schools might be most effective in increasing educational opportunity. And as subsequent events have shown, the period following the report's publication has been one of much policy discussion and many policy changes in education in the United States. Consequently, the emergence of a potentially policy-relevant report at this time meant that the report and the discussion surrounding it played a greater role in social policy than is ordinarily the case for social research.

A major result of the survey, which was, perhaps, the source of the disquiet that provoked the controversy, was the finding that most of the traditional indicators of "quality" that school administrators have used to describe school quality were nearly unrelated to achievement of students in these schools if the family background of these students was controlled. Some characteristics of teachers were found to show some relation to their students' performance, but these characteristics were not related to teacher's salaries—one of the most frequently used common sense measures of school quality. Other standard measures of school quality, such as per pupil expenditure, textbook age, size and quality of the school plant, laboratory facilities, and most striking, classroom size, were among those characteristics shown not to be related to student performance when their backgrounds were controlled.

Multiple regression analysis was used to show these effects—or, as it turned out, lack of effects—and the way it was used constitutes the first dimension of disagreement among members of different disciplines. This first disagreement turned on the particular measure of effect used in the survey. Regression analysis provides as its basic measure of effect the raw regression coefficient, which has a dimension, units of change in dependent variable per unit change in independent variable. These regression coefficients are not directly comparable for different independent variables because their size is a function of the units of the independent variables.

A second measure, however, corrects this fault—at the expense of introducing certain other difficulties, which Cain and Watts' paper points out—by standardizing the regression coefficients so that they have a maximum of 1.0 and a minimum of —1.0. This provides a measure which does allow comparison of the relations of the different independent variables to the dependent one.

A third measure differs in concept from both of these. Called the "unique variance explained," it measures the additional variance in the dependent variable which is accounted for by adding a particular independent variable to the set of explanatory or independent variables. As a measure of the effect of an independent variable upon the dependent one, it has the same property of comparability among independent variables that the standardized regression coefficient has. It differs from that coefficient, however, in that it is more conservative; it is unaffected by any variance in the dependent variable that could be explained either by it or by another independent variable in the explanatory set. The unique variance explained by variable x_1 measures just that variance which can be explained only by variable x_1; any variance which could be accounted for by another independent variable is not included in the measure. The standardized regression coefficient, on the other hand, is decreased by the existence of such shared explained variance.

There is an extension of the unique variance explained measure, which is the variance uniquely explainable by a particular pair of independent variables, a particular triplet, and so on. The measure for variables x_1 and x_2, for example, shows the amount of variance in the dependent variable that can be accounted for by x_1 and x_2 together, beyond that uniquely explainable by x_1 or x_2.

The properties of the three measures are related to the general style of use of regression analysis, in a particular way. There appear to be three general styles or strategies in the use of this statistical technique, and they can be described as follows:

1. The use of regression analysis as a technique for estimating parameters in a model. Ordinarily this model has a linear structure, but there are other models, such as a multiplicative model, whose parameters might also be estimated with regression methods by use of appropriate transformations. This approach implies the existence of a well-specified model, with a structure that is known, but with unknown values of parameters. It assumes also that the errors of measurement and collinearity among independent variables are small enough so that their effects on regression coefficients are not great. Raw regression coefficients are the proper measures to use in this approach, for they are the required estimates of the parameters.

2. The use of regression analysis as a technique for uncovering the causal structure in a set of variables when something is known about, or some prior assumption can be made about, the causal priority in a system of variables, and when the coefficients in the causal structure can be put in triangular form in a matrix. That is, we suppose it is known or assumed on substantive grounds that although x_1 *may* effect x_2, and x_1 and x_2 *may* affect x_3, x_3 *does not* affect x_1 and x_2, and x_2 *does not* affect x_1. When such partial knowledge about the structure of relations exists, then a method has been developed by a population geneticist, Sewell Wright, for measuring the relative effects of different variables in the structure and eliminating those paths which do not show any effect. The method, called path analysis, uses standardized regression coefficients as path coefficients to measure the relative strength of different causal paths.[1] Thus, with this strategy, the appropriate measure is the standardized regression coefficient.

3. The use of regression analysis as a method for obtaining as much information as possible about the structure of relations

1. See Hubert M. Blalock, *Causal Inferences in Nonexperimental Research* (Chapel Hill, N.C.: University of North Carolina Press, 1964).

among variables when nothing is known or assumed about the independent variables other than that any relation between them and the dependent variable is not produced by an effect from the dependent variable to the independent variables. It is assumed, in accord with the two preceding strategies, that the structure of effects is expressed by a linear model, but there is no assumption that the structure of relationships is known. In this strategy, there is much more concern about the effect of errors of measurement on estimates and about the joint consequences of collinearity among the independent variables and varying amounts of measurement error for different ones of these variables. For this strategy, the appropriate measure is the set of unique-variance-explained measures. These measures allow one to partition the variance in the dependent variable between that uniquely explainable by $x_1, x_2, x_3, \ldots, x_n$, that uniquely explainable by x_1 *or* x_2, x_1 *or* x_3, $\ldots, x_{n-1}$ *or* x_n, that uniquely explainable by x_1 *or* x_2 *or* x_3, $\ldots, x_{n-2}$ *or* x_{n-1} *or* x_n, and so on. A first approximation to this approach is to obtain merely the measures of the variance in the dependent variable uniquely explained by each independent variable alone, $x_1, x_2, \ldots, x_n$.

In the controversy, the line-up concerning measures to be used was this way:

a. Raw regression coefficients
   Supported by Cain and Watts, economists
b. Standardized regression coefficients
   Supported by Bowles and Levin, economists
   Supported and used by Kain and Hanushek, economists
c. Partitioning of explained variance into components explained by combinations of variables
   (1) Unique variance for single variables
       Supported by statisticians involved with the project, and used by sociologists and statisticians in the report
   (2) Unique variance for single variables and combinations
       Used by educational psychologists and statisticians in U.S. Office of Education's further analysis of data

In the arguments for particular measures by the various protagonists, it is clear that belief in the use of one or another measure has been dictated by the general strategy in use of regression analysis in the different disciplines.

In economics, there is frequently an assumption that the form or structure of the causal system is well known and that the empirical question at hand is to estimate values of coefficients for that structure.   The strong argument of Cain and Watts for the use of raw regression coefficients is consistent with that general approach.   The argument by Bowles and Levin, and by Kain and Hanushek for standardized regression coefficients appears to reflect this approach less strongly, but as explained in the next paragraph, standardized coefficients for their assumed models perform the same function as raw coefficients do for Cain and Watts with their assumed models.

This use of strategy by the economists is shown by related evidence as well.   In both the Bowles and Levin paper, and the Kain and Hanushek paper, there was a proposal that a particular other model be used, one in which the value of the dependent variable depended upon the product of the independent variables, each variable raised to a power given by some coefficient.   The coefficients to be estimated in the regression analysis were these powers.   Why is such a model proposed?   It is clearly because this is the most frequent form of the production function in economic theory.   The Cobb-Douglas production function consists of the product of capital and labor factor inputs, each raised to a power which represents its marginal productivity.   These coefficients, interestingly, are regression coefficients without dimensions and are thus comparable, in contrast to the raw regression coefficients obtained in a linear model which have dimensions and thus are not directly comparable.   In proposing this model—which is transformed to linear regression by taking logarithms—the two pairs of economists are clearly proposing the use of regression analysis to estimate parameters in a previously well-specified model.

There is still other evidence of this use of the first strategy by economists.   Both Bowles and Levin, and Kain and Hanushek, especially the latter pair, argue strongly that one important defect of the report was the lack of an explicit model showing the assumed causal structure—again, implicitly arguing that the major empirical result to be sought was the estimation of parameters in a given causal structure.

In sociology, the strategy in use of regression analysis that is most prominent is the second one. Sociology contains less theoretical basis for deriving specification of models, but nevertheless there is often willingness to specify such a model to the extent required for path analysis. Given this general approach, one might have expected to find use of standardized regression coefficients in the report since sociologists had a large hand in preparing it. However, it appears that the statisticians, who are less model-oriented and better described by the third strategy than by the first or second, shaped the report's policy in this respect. The general orientation to use of regression analysis among statisticians—though it is less safe to generalize here than in economics —is less causally oriented, less tied to specific prior assumptions about a causal model, but more sensitive to errors of measurement and multicollinearity. All these orientations point to the statisticians' use of the third strategy with regression analysis.

The statistically oriented educational psychologists also differ sharply from the economists, just as the statisticians do, in their lower likelihood of assuming a well-specified structural model. Their general strategy in use of regression analysis appears to be very close to that described for the statisticians. This leads to use of the variance-explained measures, which partition the variance, showing how much can definitely be attributed to each variable alone and how much must be left undecided between particular pairs, triplets, and so forth of variables. Their general use of regression analysis appears to be as an aid in the specification of a casual model when little is known beforehand about this model. Consistent with this assessment, two of the three places using the method of partitioning explained variance among variables, pairs, and so forth have been in literature frequently cited by psychologists.[2] The third is in the first Mayeske volume, in

2. See R. G. Newton and D. J. Spurrell, "A Development of Multiple Regression for the Analysis of Routine Data," *Applied Statistics,* vol. 16 (1967), pp. 51–64; and Richard B. Darlington, "Multiple Regression in Psychological Research and Practice," *Psychology Bulletin,* vol. 69, no. 3 (1968), pp. 161–182.

which the method is attributed to Alexander Mood. (It appears that use of the method was independently proposed about the same time in the late 1960s in these sources.)

Another event in the history of this survey shows well the difference in strategies by economists and educational psychologists with whom the statisticians will be grouped in subsequent discussion because of similarity of approach. The event was a conference held at the U.S. Office of Education, chaired by Alexander Mood, on the topic, "Do Teachers Make a Difference?" Substantive papers, nearly all of them involving re-analysis or further analysis of the survey data, were presented by economists, including Levin and Hanushek, and educational psychologists, including Mayeske. The difference in orientation to the same data was clear. One economist, Michaelson, was going on to much more complex and highly specified models—two-stage, simultaneous equation models—and in general the economists were clearly interested in estimating parameters. The educational psychologists were attacking a different question, attempting to infer from the measures of explained variance something about the structure of effects among the various independent variables and pointing out where the principal uncertainties lay. Their overall strategy involved use of regression analysis primarily for gaining initial information that would aid in the design of experiments to resolve the uncertainties. For example, these data show that there is a large area of uncertainty between the teacher's characteristics and the family's characteristics in their effects on academic achievement, though not between either of these and other school characteristics.

I will return later to examine the broader implications for disciplines' relations to policy of these different strategies. I want to turn first, however, to another dimension of difference between disciplines evident from the results of the report and the controversy and further analyses following it.

The result of the report was this: although there was a small relation of various school characteristics to a student's achievement, one set of variables in the school environment did show a substantial relation to a student's performance. This was the backgrounds of students in the school as a whole, in his grade, when his own background was controlled. The more educational strength in the homes of other children in the school—books and magazines in the homes, high average parental education, and other similar measures—the more highly a student performed, whether or not his own family background included these characteristics.

This result derived from several techniques, but principally from a two-level regression analysis with individual student performance as the dependent variable, individual background characteristics as one set of independent variables, and school-aggregate background characteristics as another set of independent variables—along with other school-level variables. It was designed, implemented, and reported by sociologists in the report staff; it was objected to by two of the economist pairs, Bowles and Levin, and Kain and Hanushek—both of whom argued that the effects were less great. It was not examined by the further analysis of statistically oriented educational psychologists in the U.S. Office of Education, for they carried out an analysis at the school level only, which does not allow distinguishing a student's own background from those of the other students in the school.

In this dimension of difference, the difference is clearly between the sociologists and the other disciplines. Such multiple-level analysis with regression methods has had several expositions in the sociological literature in the past several years, but none, so far as I know, in other disciplines.[3] It is a kind of effect which is peculiarly sociological since it stems from other persons in the environment. It is an effect which is difficult to incorporate in an economic model which examines the achievement increments expected to be producd by expenditures on different factors, simply because it cannot be easily related to expenditures. It is an effect that educational psychologists or statisticians would not be likely to look for since it is not generally seen as an educational input by educators, and apart from reorganization of school populations, it is not a variable under their control.

The report was published at a time when such reorganization

3. See James J. Fennessey, "The General Linear Model: A New Perspective on Some Familiar Topics," *American Journal of Sociology*, vol. 74, no. 1 (July, 1968).

of school populations was very much a policy question. As a result, it has turned out that the greatest policy use of the report has focused around this result, in conjunction with the previously mentioned result that most of the formal educational variables which school administrators control, excepting some things about teachers, showed almost no relation to student achievement. The results have been used principally to reinforce the arguments for positive school racial integration, in courts, school boards, and executive agencies. It is clear that here also, just as in the previously discussed disciplinary differences in use of regression analyses, a policy focus has brought to the surface existing differences in the disciplines and has not brought the disciplines together.

To return to the difference in general strategies in use of regression analysis—and presumably other statistical techniques—by the different disciplines, these strategies appear related to broader differences in approach to policy in these disciplines. This difference is well illustrated by the Cain and Watts paper in the *American Sociological Review* and my reply to it in the issue. The economist's approach can be exemplified by a proposal of Cain and Watts. They propose that rather than standardizing raw regression coefficients by a ratio of standard deviations to provide standardized coefficients, one should standardize by dollar costs. Then every regression coefficient would show the effectiveness for student achievement of a dollar expenditure on different school resources. These coefficients, then, could be compared because they would show the administrator just how much achievement would be earned by a dollar spent in each of various ways.

In this, as in other aspects of the economists' work, it is clear that they see their policy role, much more than do other social scientists, as giving quite specific advice about particular "factors of production" in education. The vision implicit in this approach is the development of a large structural model with parameters estimated so that one can describe the direct and indirect effects of all variables. One can also use the model in an attempt to optimize by adjusting input resources to give highest achievement for a given expenditure on education.

The educational psychologist and statistician in their approaches to policy do not differ from the economist on the set of variables or educational resources in question. But they do differ greatly in the assumptions they are willing to make about model specification. It is clear from the approaches taken by statisticians and educational psychologists in this case that they have far less fully developed models than do economists and are far less willing to make prior specification of the model. Indeed, their orientation to policy seems more nearly to assume a state of knowledge prior to that assumed by the economists. Their policy advice seems more nearly to be in the specification of the causal model in respect to what factors seem to be important, how they are related to one another, and where areas of indeterminacy lie. They clearly do not see their policy role in the same parameter estimation and optimization way that characterizes the economists.

The sociologists, as evidenced by this case, differ on one dimension from both the economists and the educational psychologists and statisticians, and on the other dimension appear closer to the educational psychologists than to the statisticians. They differ from the other disciplines in the range of variables they are interested in and willing to incorporate in their models. They are more eclectic than the others, with a particular sensitivity to variables that are part of the social environment—as in this case. In their overall strategy in the use of regression analysis, they appear close to the educational psychologists and statisticians, assuming a state of knowledge prior to that assumed by the economists. Their policy advice is more likely than that of economists to be in qualitative terms, even when based on quantitative data analysis, as in the present case.

We may now return to the broader question of integration of the social sciences through policy analysis. This extended example I have given does not offer much hope or promise toward such integration. The social sciences involved continued to look at the problem through their own sets of spectacles and to make very different assumptions about what policy advice should consist of. Perhaps the most promising element suggested by the example is the fact that the policy question, studied by persons from these different disciplines, forced a confrontation and an explication of the differences, perhaps leading to greater comparability of approach in the future. However, I suspect that this is too optimistic a view. The forces internal to each discipline appear sufficiently strong and different in the various disciplines so that they constitute powerful constraints upon integration. There is little indication that such internal forces in the various disciplines will diminish in the future.

Commentary on Coleman's Paper

By Robert Bierstedt

AS ONE who is wholly innocent of statistics, who would not recognize a regression coefficient—raw or cooked—if I bumped into one in the street, and who prefers to hide in the recesses of nineteenth-century social thought where only Quetelet and Le Play disturb my non-quantitative reveries, I obviously have no equipment to bring to bear upon the details of Coleman's paper. Let me say that I am impressed by it, as I am by all of Coleman's work. Surely no one in sociology has had so remarkable an effect upon recent social policy. One would have to go back to Ogburn's *Recent Social Trends,* produced in the Hoover administration— yes, Virginia, there was a Hoover administration—to find anything of comparable significance, and even then the comparability can be questioned. The Coleman Report[1] itself is a prime and important example of the beneficent relationship that can obtain between social science and social policy, even if such reports in general do not contribute to the architectonic of sociological theory and even if, in addition, their recommendations are ignored by those charged with the responsibility of making policy decisions.

The Coleman Report has other distinctions which are relevant to our conference. It does not raise the tiresome issue of *Wertfreiheit* which has plagued the social sciences for so long. Stated simply, and with only this incidental reference to Max Weber's famous essay, John Dewey thought it possible to find a scientific basis for policy, whereas Bertrand Russell, on the contrary, maintained that normative judgments not only are outside the realm of science, they are equally far outside the realm of knowledge. Everyone now knows the distinction between categorical and normative judgments, and James Coleman, while adhering strictly to the canons of objectivity in his research, does not hesitate to express his own opinions when called upon to testify before con-

1. Which, because of his regard for his co-workers, Coleman would modestly prefer to call by some other name.

gressional committees. It is a commendable thing and one that merits our favorable attention.

Finally, with respect to Coleman's paper itself, I have no way of disputing his suggestion that those who agreed or disagreed with his procedures did so, not only and not so much as individuals, but rather as people operating in the framework of their own disciplines, whether sociology, statistics, economics, or educational psychology. His case for this conclusion, although not, as he says, conclusive, is nevertheless convincing, and I see no reason not to accept it. Do we then have in the Coleman paper a contribution to the integration of the social sciences—although this was no part, of course, of its purpose? I think we must accept Coleman's own tentative conclusion that we do not. Differences in perspective, in approach, in method, and even in the use and interpretation of specific statistical techniques are there for us all to see. We are thus reduced to the inference that no one discipline, even on purely technical matters, could prevail. Coleman's paper thus raises an embarrassing and difficult problem in the sociology of knowledge, and it may be one that we do not currently have the resources to resolve.

In this situation we can, perhaps, confront the issue of the integration of the social sciences through policy analysis in a broader and bolder perspective. It would be an aid to integration, for example, if we had fewer disciplines to integrate. Let us see whether any of them—or how many of them—are dispensable. We might say, for a start, that anthropology is an easy candidate for dismissal. Ethnography is only a polite word for beachcombing, and anthropology itself, of which ethnography is a subdivision, is only a kind of rural sociology. In saying this, of course, we have to ignore certain studies of urbanization in West Africa, notably those of Kenneth Little, and also those poignant glimpses of urban poverty brought to our attention by the tape recorder of Oscar Lewis. In any event, anthropology is hardly distinguishable from sociology except, perhaps, that its practitioners prefer to study the primitive medicine man rather than, say, the Wall Street lawyer.

Sociology is also an attractive candidate for abandonment. Such a step would please W. G. Runciman, the young Englishman who has recently argued that sociology is neither a fit nor dignified subject for inquiry and that the discipline—if such it is—cannot sustain an autonomous existence. In a polemical essay, Runciman contends not only that there are no clothes on the emperor but that there is, indeed, no emperor. He swears that sociology cannot be distinguished from either anthropology or history, that its explanations, if any, are "parasitic" on the laws of other sciences, especially psychology, that the search for sociological theories is "misconceived," that there are no laws of social systems and cannot be, and that "sociology" is a residual term attached to research "which is either too sweeping or too incoherent to be called anything else." [2] So much, in his opinion, for sociology.

Having thus subtracted anthropology and sociology from our modes of inquiry, we have left political science, economics, and possibly, psychology. Political science, of course, is a subdivision of sociology in the sense that it deals with one of society's institutions rather than with all of them. If sociology can be abandoned, so also, *a fortiori*, can political science. As Talcott Parsons has argued, in language somewhat similar to Runciman's, there is no such thing as political science in any of the senses in which we are ordinarily inclined to use the word "science." We can thus dispense with it also except, of course, as it indulges in descriptive accounts of various governments and of governmental activities, in which respects it becomes a part of history.

The next question concerns economics, which is surely the most successful of the social sciences. What do we do with it? Here, I think, the answer is easy. Three quarters of it we consign to mathematics, where it takes its place as an applied part of that discipline, and the fourth quarter—the degree to which *homo sapiens* is not *homo economicus*—is consigned to sociology. which we have already abolished.

And finally, psychology. Psychology as currently perpetrated upon us is the study of the Norwegian white rat and the American college sophomore. Half of it is physiology and the other half, again, is sociology.

In this parlous situation only one solution remains—namely, to awaken the philosophers from their semantic slumbers and to demand that they get on with their own proper job, which is the integration and synthesis of the inquiries and conclusions of the

2. *Sociology in its Place* (Cambridge: The University Press, 1970).

separate social sciences into some kind of *Weltanschauung* or, more precisely perhaps, *Gesellschaftanschauung,* which would give us some total notion of the nature and characteristics of human societies. Then we could surrender our tasks and stand in line at the Parthenon, ready to celebrate the virtues of Athena.

Unfortunately, the situation is not so simple. Philosophy may not be able to re-assert her ancient sway as an integrating discipline. Certainly we find no such function in its contemporary practice. We find instead an inquiry caught on the treadmill of an eternal dialectic, dwelling on the meaning of its own analyses and indulging in "the systematic misuse of a terminology specifically invented for that purpose"—an observation that could apply equally well to certain kinds of contemporary sociological theory. It does not seem likely, in short, that we can appeal to Balliol or to Brasenose for a way out of our difficulties.

Let us, therefore, ignore these preposterous suggestions and approach our problem from an entirely different—and presumably more serious—direction. One of the dusty controversies in sociology is whether it is a general social science or a special social science. Is sociology a general kind of inquiry into society, conceived of abstractly as a set or system of social relationships, or is it a special kind of inquiry directed to the study of those phenomena, such as crime, recreation, or the family, for example, which are left over, so to speak, after the concerns of other special social sciences, like political science and economics, have been subtracted? Is "the social" a special category like the religious, the political, and the economic, or is it a general category that includes the others? This question can be illuminated by a paradigm taken, with modifications, from Sorokin: [3]

Phenomena	*Variables*
Economic	a,b,c,d,e,f
Political	a,b,c,g,h,i
Religious	a,b,c,j,k,l
Legal	a,b,c,m,n,o
Social	?

3. P. A. Sorokin, *Society, Culture, and Personality* (New York and London: Harper and Brothers, 1947), p. 7.

The question is whether there is a separate category of the social, parallel with and distinct from the categories of economic, political, religious, and so on, which then becomes the proper sphere of sociological inquiry, or whether sociology is concerned instead with the a, b, c's that all the others have in common.

The first alternative would make of sociology a special social science, like economics or jurisprudence, for example, although precisely what "the social" might mean in this sense is not altogether clear. It might mean only what Simmel referred to as relations of "polite acquaintance," a study of sociability (*Gesellig-heit*), and in that case we would have a rather trivial discipline. The second alternative would make of sociology a general social science, one operating perhaps on a more abstract level and surely a more significant one, but one also that might invite an indictment of imperialism. There may be no satisfactory answer to this question. If we take the second view, however, we might argue that it then becomes the responsibility of sociology to perform the integrating function to which this conference is addressed. I confess to some prejudice in favor of this view, but I am also appalled by the magnitude of the task. I would note, in addition, that efforts dedicated to this enterprise—efforts of writers like Giddings, Tönnies, von Wiese, Sorokin, MacIver, and Parsons—have resulted not in a science, that is, a coordinated set of causal propositions, principles, and laws, but rather in a series of taxonomies. As one who has also engaged in this exercise, I should like to defend its importance. It is an essential prolegomenon to the construction of any kind of scientific theory. But this is not the place to do it. I want only to make the point that taxonomy is an enterprise that can have something to do with integration.

But let us become more serious still and attend to the role of policy analysis in the integration of the social sciences. This role, I suspect, is a minimal one. We have been inundated by reports of special governmental commissions, both in this country and in England, all dealing with policy. The Coleman Report and the Wolfenden Report are outstanding examples of their kind. There is no evidence, however, that they have contributed to the integration of the social sciences. Some of them, like the reports just mentioned, have had a considerable impact; others, no matter how distinguished the contributors or how cogent the recommendations, are destined to languish in an unread file. Some, in fact, can be found after three weeks only in the wastebasket. Political considerations affect them all—especially, as an example, the recent Report of the Commission on Obscenity and Pornography. This one, the Kerner Report on Civil Disorders, the document entitled *Toward a Social Report,* and the Young Report, *Knowledge into Action*—to mention only four—all involved the cooperation of many social scientists, and all of them are first-rate accomplishments. But I think we have to concede that they have had little influence upon policy and none at all on the integration of the social sciences.

It may be said that the members of these commissions, representing as they do different disciplines, would learn from one another. They undoubtedly do. I have recently served on such a commission whose members were several political scientists, an economist, a psychologist, a foundation executive, directors of research in both public and private organizations, a dean of engineering, a professor in a graduate school of business, and a sociologist. We emerged from the experience with, I am sure, a high regard for one another. But there is no scintilla of suspicion, on my part at least, that our labors will have any effect on the management of research in the social and behavioral sciences in the Department of Defense—which we were commissioned to review—or that any of our recommendations could help to integrate the social sciences. As a matter of honest fact, some of our recommendations were also political. We urged the Department of Defense to get out of foreign-area research altogether and suggested that such research be funded in a much more broadly based governmental agency.

Whether or not this report will suffer the silent fate of so many others, I have no way of knowing; but whatever its design and whatever its influence, it cannot do much for the social sciences. Its message moves in one direction only—from the social science community to the government and not from the government to the social science community. I think that this is generally the case and that we cannot, in consequence, hope that policy analysis can contribute to the integration of the social sciences. It is possible, of course, that this view is unduly pessimistic and that cooperative work in such new fields as social indicators will be able to induce some degree of conceptual compatibility. But the skepticism remains.

Finally, a more basic question arises—the question whether, in fact, we need to strive for integration. I mentioned above that sociology, conceived of as a general social science, might accept this responsibility. The truth is that sociology is not itself an integrated discipline. Its practitioners range from those who regard it as a positivistic philosophy of history to those who regard it as an instrument for social criticism. (I mention only one spectrum of variegated opinions.) If we cannot integrate our own discipline, it seems unlikely that we could do the job for the other social sciences as well. It may be, in fact, that integration is not a desideratum to be commended. It may be, indeed, that there is a plurality of social worlds and that it is desirable to see them through the lenses of different conceptual schemes.

Commentary on Coleman's Paper

By Andrew Hacker

DESPITE the sequence in the phrasing of our topic, I am not entirely clear whether our chief purpose is to embark, yet again, on an attempt to integrate the various social science disciplines, or if our principal concern is to make ourselves more useful as policy analysts than we have hitherto been.

I am moved to ask this question if only because the paper on which I was asked to comment focuses on a body of research, the Coleman Report, which is itself not a little schizophrenic on these two goals. For while that report purports to provide illumination for policy-makers on how they may more effectively deploy their resources, the very manner in which that research was conducted induces the suspicion that it was also made to serve as an exercise in sociological scholarship and a testing-ground for certain disciplinary techniques. Indeed, the criticisms of that report, or at least those cited in the paper before us, dwell less on public questions of effective education and more on the private dialectics of social science.

Is our first interest, then, to aid our country in confronting its social problems, with the corollary that we may achieve a rapprochement among the social sciences in the course of carrying out this commitment? Or is our highest priority to ourselves, to the hope that we may be able to integrate our disciplines by using a new focus—which this time happens to be policy analysis? Suppose, for example, that policy analysis does not prove to be a useful vehicle for integrating the social sciences. Does that mean that we return to our drawing boards and abandon the public domain? Or, alternatively, suppose that we find we can make ourselves useful only if we offer insights which are non-scientific. In that latter event, should we shelve our private preoccupations in a time of stress and devote our sophistication and good sense to advising on matters of policy? It is much too easy to proclaim that these goals are not mutually exclusive. My own feeling is that they are, and not the least reason for this conclusion stems from Professor Coleman's experience—both in preparing his report and in replying to his critics.

Professor Coleman's approach to our subject, then, serves as a good illustration of some of the things I have been suggesting. To be quite honest, I feel rather short-changed by his paper, for while it purports to concern itself with sociology—his assignment for this conference—it is, in fact, about a very small slice of sociology: regression analysis. His argument, as I follow it, is that sociologists, economists, statisticians, and educational psychologists have varying emphases in their approaches to and uses of regression analysis. Moreover, regression analysts from different disciplines are apparently quite far apart in their methodological assumptions. He thus concludes that regression analysis cannot be counted on as an instrument for disciplinary integration.

But what intrigues me most is that nowhere does Coleman tell us whether an economic regression analyst tends to find different reasons for schoolchildren's success or failure than does a sociological regression analyst. His own approach led him to conclude that the performance of an individual student shows a "substantial relation" to the backgrounds of the other students in his grade. If this is what sociological regression analysis has found, what has the regression analysis of, for example, educational psychology concluded? The fact that so few of those involved in this debate actually talk about education—the policy question in this instance—is instructive.[1] From what Coleman tells us, it would appear that the divergences are not about policy,

1. After reading the criticisms of the Coleman Report written by Glen Cain and Harold Watts—a rejoinder financed by War on Poverty money— I am persuaded that while those authors are very expert on the intricacies of regression analysis, they evidence no expertise whatsoever in substantive matters of elementary and junior high school education. If Coleman is concerned over the plight of poor youngsters, his critics see nothing untoward in exempting themselves from the dirty business of first studying slum schools. They feel it quite sufficient to one-up Coleman's statistics. In other words, all their professions to the contrary, they don't really care a damn about inadequate education. Their world is one of beta-coefficients, F-ratios, and Iso-chunks. And just because they draw on Coleman's data, rather than some other source, does not transform them into policy analysts.

or even implications for policy, but rather over preferences for organizing discipline-based perceptions of those pieces of reality each field elects for its emphasis.   In short, I am not persuaded that Coleman's paper has anything much to say about or do with policy analysis.   Indeed, it may emerge that his report is less an aid for policy than an exercise elaborating an area of its author's academic interest.

To be sure, due to the report we now have data demonstrating that erecting new schools and increasing salaries will not necessarily raise student achievement levels.   While I do not think that Coleman is proposing that we benignly neglect antediluvian buildings or freeze pay scales, what does interest me are the suggestions he offers in his role as a social scientist.   The challenge is to achieve a more successful school experience for groups of children whose potential achievement levels are not being fulfilled under current educational arrangements.   The major policy proposal emerging from the report, according to Coleman, calls for efforts "to reduce the social and racial homogeneity of the school environment." And as a matter of practicality, he goes on, what will be needed are policies "which do not seek to improve the education of Negroes and other educationally disadvantaged at the expense of those who are educationally advantaged."

Speaking not so much as a social scientist, but as a parent who donated his upper-middle class daughter to an inner-city slum school for six elementary years, I can testify that classrooms having even forty percent of their pupils from less literate households simply cannot keep pace with parallel grades in better-off areas.   Youngsters in a fifth grade where a third of the pupils each come from the upper-middle, the intermediate, and the welfare classes—if indeed there are more than a handful of such elementary schools—do not learn as much as those in a school where everyone comes from homes in the $25,000–$35,000 bracket. Upper-middle class parents know this full well.   And because they want their ten-year-olds to get into Yale or Cornell or Johns Hopkins seven years hence, they congregate in the Great Necks, the Scarsdales, and similar suburbs where their college-intended offspring will not be dragged down by children from less achievement-oriented households.   Thus, if we are to talk of policy, we need expert advice on how to induce prosperous parents to send their own children to less prepossessing school surroundings in order to assist the education of less fortunate children. That, after all, is the kind of counsel that policy-makers want and need. Such intelligence would be particularly helpful in the community I know best, where the Hackers seemed to be the only one of 1500 faculty families prepared to risk its child's contamination.

We can all agree with the Coleman Report's findings that if there are two or three poor children in a classroom comprised mainly of better-off youngsters, then those two or three children will do better than were they in a school containing only low-income students. Moreover, at least some liberal parents would probably consent to some selective bussing that would bring a few poor pupils out to their districts each morning. But the populations of our metropolitan areas are now such that these showcase ratios of twenty-two upper-middle class children with three low-income youngsters mixed in would hardly begin to absorb anything like the millions of poor boys and girls who need to be aided by exposure to offspring of more advantaged families.

If I have spent so much space on this example, it is only because Professor Coleman himself raised the subject. And I still do not feel that I know whether or not sociology can assist policy-makers in this area. Moreover, if I said that I felt short-changed by his paper, it is also because he does not even raise the question of whether the difficulties of disciplinary integration faced by regression analysis are also inherent in the many other methods employed by his discipline. In short, I would like to hear from the James Coleman who wrote *Union Democracy, Community Conflict,* and *The Adolescent Society.* For on those occasions he was a wide-ranging sociologist and not simply a regression analyst. After reading the paper we have before us, I must conclude that sociology as a discipline has not yet been heard from. Surely the fact that we do not have an interdisciplinary consensus on the use and interpretation of regression analysis does not, by itself, justify the conclusion that sociologists and economists and others cannot reach a scientific concurrence by other means. I am not persuaded that the disagreements Coleman tells us about need deter the emergence of an integrated social science. In my own view, there are much better reasons why such a synthesis is not going to occur, and I will turn to these momentarily.

At this point, my own exposition may be aided by referring to the two other papers before us. I am especially entranced by Professor Lane's enthusiasm over the promise for policy analysis inherent in an integrated social science. He tells us, for instance, that Robert McNamara's use of program planning budgets gave the Pentagon "new management tools" which, among other things, served to "improve performance" in the Defense Department. Considering that the chief assignment of that agency has been to show some success in Southeast Asia, I wonder whether this is the best example—unless, of course, one wants to argue that an operation can be a success even though the patient died. Undeterred, Lane goes on to quote, apparently approvingly, the proposal that "behavioral and social scientists with appropriate training should play a greater role in social and foreign policy making," and that public funds be provided for "rotating professorships in the social and behavioral sciences to 'advise members of Congress and the staffs of congressional committees'."

Persons such as ourselves have, I would gather from Lane, the competence to create coherent analyses for such policy questions as: Is it better to save lives through a disease-control program or to improve functional literacy of the disadvantaged? We are equipped, he suggests, to set up equations showing "how much defense risk one should take in order to improve the quality of life in a country." And, indeed, we can be called upon to establish the quantums of "better health" and "greater economic security" and "increasing enjoyment of the arts" which combine best to promote the pursuit of happiness.

I will only remark that I wonder why none of the hesitations that occurred to Professor Lindblom did not arise in Lane's mind, for Lindblom advises us that "enriched policy analysis . . . ought not to be confused with social science," whereas Lane's paper does little more than uncritically compound this confusion. The reason may be that Lane, unlike Lindblom, fails to consider the possible limits of man's ability to systematize his knowledge of himself and social reality. Optimism and enthusiasm are one thing; making promises on which one cannot deliver is another. When Lane concludes that "what policy analysis requires is good causal theory," I can only murmur, "Yes, of course. Quite so. But haven't I heard that before?"

My own position—and problem—is that I simply cannot envisage the creation of an integrated social science, through policy analysis or any other available means. I have made these assumptions clear on a number of occasions, not least in a paper prepared for this Academy almost a decade ago. I hope I will be forgiven for introducing some of those reflections once again, in a somewhat amended form.

Scholars always have and always will differ in their descriptions of the world they see. What must be abandoned is the hope that social analysis can be either objective or scientific or, indeed, integrated. "Objectivity," Karl Popper wrote, "is closely bound up with the social aspect of scientific method, with the fact that science and scientific objectivity do not and cannot result from the attempts of an individual scientist to be 'objective,' but from the cooperation of many scientists." There may be cooperation among social scientists from various disciplines in the sense that they share and criticize one another's research; however, this communication need not produce an agreed-upon body of knowledge. In fact, controversy rather than consensus is the rule on all questions of method and substance transcending the commonplace.

And I am afraid that I am forced to part company with Professor Lindblom also in my conviction that this is the way things are always going to be. When he writes that it is "premature" to expect an all-embracing structure of social science knowledge; when he says that "it will be a long time" before we can see things as part of an architectonic whole; when he doubts that social science has yet captured enough pieces to infer the design of a grand structure—I am, for all his skepticism, still struck with the hopes he holds out for what may take place in the years ahead.[2]

Pleas for more time assume that our current approaches to integration are but babes in arms, creatures with unfathomed potentialities if only they can be nurtured to adulthood. The sup-

2. Lindblom does say, parenthetically, that integration may be "possibly forever impossible of achievement." I would only add that I am less agnostic on this score than he is.

position is that the passage of time will somehow bring not only more refined techniques, but ultimately an enhanced and integrated understanding of the human condition. Yet those who ask for time never really examine just what it is that their request implies. Will there be a greater consensus among scholars on perceived realities in 1990 than there is now? The evidence, if such it can be called, is that so long as scholars are affected by differing interests and spring from varying backgrounds, disagreements over perceptions will persist. There is little reason to believe that policy analysis or any other attempt at integration will lead to a consensus within or among disciplines. Thus, the demand for more time carries with it an unarticulated theory concerning the progress of human knowledge. It assumes that somehow, and contrary to all past experience, students of society will begin to agree on some major propositions about the world they are studying. Just what breed of men and women these scholars of the future will be, devoid of entrenched interests and personal obstinacy, is difficult for me to imagine.

I am not saying that we are stupid. It is simply that there are limits to our intelligence. To believe that we can understand ourselves and our society is a presumption, and I use that double-edged word designedly. There is no law of nature which says that beings such as ourselves must have the capacity to comprehend the world—or anything apart from a small fraction of it—in which we happen to reside. I am not making a case for obscurantism, or for foregoing further study. I am only asking, at this very late date, for some humility: for an end to pretensions and self-deluding promises. They are bad for scholarship, bad for citizenship, and bad for character.

I would like to expand on another remark of Professor Lindblom's, here too relating what he said to our own situation. He pondered, on at least two occasions, on "the effect . . . on personality and culture" which arises from "life in a milieu of exchange relationships." I will hazard a few words on these effects as they apply to the academic personality and the culture of research—at least in the social sciences.

I have no idea who proposed to the Academy that it organize a conference on this topic. However, I might speculate on some of the motives and motivations underlying such a decision. For the past two decades, academic and institutionalized social science has been receiving support from the larger society. By "support" I mean not only money, but also a measure of deference and an immunity from too sharp a scrutiny of what social scientists actually did. These were good years—generous salaries, extensive travel, release from undergraduate teaching, full-time secretaries, and stipends for our disciples. We were free to do what we wanted to do, to pursue paths of our own choosing, and our aspirations were unquestionably underwritten by foundations, government agencies, and even internal university money. All we had to do was to tell the National Science Foundation, the Office of Naval Research, the National Institutes of Health, the Office of Education, or even NASA that we were creating and accumulating new knowledge, and an account was quickly opened in our name.

Not the least consequence of this largesse was to persuade us that our labors were systematic, significant, even seminal. In other words, we began to take ourselves and our outpourings very seriously. I suppose that those years were the worst possible time to expect that we might question our own assumptions, to perhaps even conclude that many if not most of our premises were misguided or ill-conceived. In other words, we had done well in the "exchange relationship" with our benefactors. So well, in fact, that whatever we produced, they unquestionably assumed to be a worthwhile return on their investment. However it would be idle to believe that such an environment would not have an effect on our own personalities and the culture in which research is conducted. Or are we prepared to protest that we are the only ones immune to such subtle pressures?

Integration is hardly a new goal. We have been talking about integrating, synthesizing, and coordinating the social sciences for quite some time. This is hardly the first conference on this topic. What is new is the introduction of policy analysis as a proposed vehicle for achieving this end. This seems a very shrewd move, for "policy" connotes doing something purposive about the social disruptions and dislocations of our time. "Policy" means mustering resources to ameliorate poverty, pollution, prejudice, crime, congestion, and all the other conditions we find disagreeable, and "policy analysis" suggests that the introduction of systematic and experienced intelligence can provide assistance in devising optimal and effective methods for combatting social pathologies.

But why "policy analysis"? Why should we desert mathematical models, structural-functional matrixes, sample surveys, and all the other foci we once thought might bring the social sciences together? The answer, of course, is that fickle foundations and budget-cut bureaus are no longer willing to fund pure and purposeless research of the sort we have hitherto been doing. "Policy," on the other hand, is very much in vogue. So why not profess an interest in this area, using it as a screen behind which to get on with our customary concerns? For grants are now available for studying alcoholism, drug addiction, judicial administration, and a whole host of other problems. If we earnest a commitment in these and similar areas, we may yet save our students' stipends, our computer rentals, our summer salaries, and our semesters off from teaching. Our first test in the "policy" arena will be to see whether we can persuade policy-makers that social scientists have something to offer in the realm of public policy. I have a hunch that this may not be so easy an enterprise, particularly in light of the comments of a Democrat who has counselled the incumbent Republican administration:

Social science is at its weakest, at its worst, when it offers theories of individual or collective behavior which raises the possibility, by controlling certain inputs, of bringing mass behavioral change. No such knowledge now exists. Evidence is fragmented, contradictory, incomplete. Enough snake oil has been sold in this Republic to warrant the expectation that public officials will begin reading labels.

Commentary on Coleman's Paper

By Charles C. Hughes

MY COMMENTS are less directed at than prompted by Dr. Coleman's paper. Let me explain. As an anthropologist, I do not operate in the same ball park as Dr. Coleman—or, if in the same ballpark, perhaps I play a different game. I cannot, therefore, engage with him in discussion of the specific methodological questions and issues that comprise much of his thoughtful paper. By the same token, I will leave the economists alone; for, except for some of my colleagues who have that special interest and training, "multiple regression" might rather be taken to mean an aberrant evolutionary process than the analytic tool it is in the hands of these practitioners.

I do, however, follow the gist of Coleman's argument as he develops what appears to be the unspoken difference between the basic conceptual stance or frame of reference taken by the economists, on the one hand, and the sociologists and other members of the study team on the other. It seems to me he is talking about the same kind of structural and philosophic problem that separates a number of the social or behavioral sciences from each other; that is, despite the widespread diffusion of concepts, research techniques, research setting, data, and even appropriate problems from one behavioral science discipline to another in the last couple of decades, there still remain varying cores of assumptions about the nature and kind of relevant variables that will enter into the research process, and it is at the level of these implicit models that the differences lie. When I talk about diffusion of concept and research technique across disciplinary boundaries, I am talking, for example, about such things as the concept of self, self-image, alienation, or the ubiquitous identity; about concepts of social system, social organization, role, and institution; about the use of structured questionnaire surveys, or even to some extent participant-observation—a time-honored anthropological technique raised to the level of an art in the hands of an Erving Goffman; of studies in mental health, or those of a cross-cultural nature, and many more. I am not, of course, asserting that there has been such widespread diffusion of concept and method that homogeneity prevails; certainly we are far from that. But I am asserting that the language, the idiom, is tending to look much more similar than it used to, even though the thought lying behind that idiom may still differ considerably; and what especially differs is not necessarily the particular ideas or thoughts that are included so much as the pattern or configuration—the model—of which they are the elements. Such models —when the behavioral and social sciences are viewed with some perspective—are simply not cut from the same plane of thought and apprehension of events, nor are they equal in scope and magnitude so far as included domains of inquiry are concerned. They are not simply different arrangements of essentially the same elements; rather, they are each a congeries or syndrome of partially similar, partially overlapping, and partially different elements and assumptions.

Let me illustrate part of what I mean by referring to the fields of the sister disciplines of anthropology and sociology. These are often taken as equivalent—or at least so close in basic orientation and purpose that they can be lumped together in a single university department so that a course in one can serve as an introduction to a course in the other. Indeed, at face value many of the concepts used in both fields—and many of the specific kinds of problems investigated—are much the same. There is, consequently, reason for thinking of a close affinity, especially when those problems are in the area of social life, society, social process, institutions, groups, and the like.

But what, then, of much of what else goes on in anthropology; for example, problems in human evolution, anatomical structure, linguistic patterns, cultural diversity, archeological remains, the rise and fall of civilization, man's clothing and cosmetic habits, his mental productions, his ways of building a house and locating it with reference to the rising sun or resident kinsmen? How do these all fit together, and how can they be reconciled or integrated with a science of human social life?

Perhaps the essential point, pure and simple, is that they cannot, for they all conform to and derive from a different model, a different conception of the domain of relevance for legitimate, anthropological problems; and the activities of anthropologists are informed by this largely implicit configuration of assumptions about the primary object of study. In this case it is man—everything about him that can be known. Ambitious, to be sure, and certainly overly immodest, but there it is. Perhaps one can say that for sociologists—or at least for many that I have known—the comparable point of entry into the welter of behavioral processes and the final anchoring point for conceptualizations is the interactional level of human behavior, the level of the social fact, an apprehension so firmly established by Durkheim. Note that this is not directly contradictory of many of the problems and/or concepts dealt with by anthropologists, but it starts from a different paradigm and only in part overlaps with concerns of the other discipline. Perhaps another way of putting it is that the primary problems of one discipline may be derivative issues of the other. For sociology the primary issue is the social level of human existence and its multiple ramifications and implications, while for anthropology the primary issue is man's existence as an animal form, which includes the development and structure of social life.

What this discussion implies is that there is no isomorphism between any given social science and a distinctive area of problematic concerns in the real world; rather, when used by their adherents functionally rather than tribalistically, disciplines are heuristic devices for understanding and attacking given problems. And in respect to the richness, variety, and bewildering permutations of the data to which the behavioral and social sciences are addressing themselves—human behavior in time, space, and circumstance—it is far too early to curtail such wide-ranging approaches. Pushed to the extreme, it is not quite the "Let a thousand flowers bloom," but that is the spirit which, in my view, should continue to inform the behavioral sciences for some time to come. And what, then, of integration? What form or forms does it take under such circumstances? What, indeed, is meant by the term when used with reference to this conference, and is there any implicit assertion being made that there should be integration? These, too, are questions prompted and stimulated by Dr. Coleman's paper.

If by "integration" is meant uniformity, then in terms of the discussion above I clearly think there will not be any such integration very soon—nor should there be. In this I am in agreement with Dr. Coleman, who takes a fairly pessimistic viewpoint regarding that outcome. But one need not necessarily put a negative evaluation on such an outcome; instead, taking another model of integration, different from that of uniformity, let us think of complementarity among elements, rather than similarity; of—again with thanks to Durkheim—"organic solidarity" as contrasted to "mechanical solidarity." Anthony Wallace, in another context, has spoken of a dichotomy which also expresses the thought being put forth here: the "replication of uniformity" as against the "organization of diversity." I suggest, given the great diversity in behavioral science problems, frames of reference, skills, differential knowledge, and so forth, that the latter model be guiltlessly accepted as the basis for viable coordination of action—in other words, a confederation rather than a totalitarian government.

Where, then, does policy analysis fit into this discussion? I suppose, if I am to be consistent with what I said earlier, my stand must be that, insofar as policy analysis represents an attempt to respond creatively to real problems in the human world, there is considerable potential for it serving as the arena in which interdisciplinary cooperation and cross-fertilizing—to that extent integration—may occur. But not in every instance. Obviously, much depends upon the particular issues at hand, the particular disciplines, and especially the particular personalities who are thus thrown together. In my own interdisciplinary research experience, structural compatibilities are by no means consistently translated into personality congruencies; many other factors supervene in this process—factors having to do with perceived stress, working style, competitiveness, and so on. But sometimes the urgency and importance of the given problem being subjected to consideration and analysis by the several social sciences may create the atmosphere in which the petty territorialities are overlooked, and a productive outcome is achieved for those working on the problem. This may well occur even though the specific policy recommendations emanating from the interdisciplinary analysis are rejected—a good case in point being the research team of social scientists during World War II who worked on the analysis of Japanese morale and made strong recommendations against dropping the atomic bomb on Hiroshima. As we all know, that policy recommendation was not accepted. Was the enterpise therefore a failure? In view of the many subsequent instances of interdisciplinary activities and orientations on the part of, for example, Alexander and Dorothea Leighton, Clyde Kluckhohn, Morris Opler, Ruth Benedict, and the others, it would be hard to say the effort was unproductive.

Conference Discussion III

CHARLESWORTH: Good morning. Some people are missing. McCord I haven't heard from. I assume he will be here. Tom Schelling has two meetings this week. Two days here and two days in Washington, so he gave us one day and he will take one day down there. I regret that he won't be with us. He is a good contributor. We all are, but I am sorry to lose him.

We will follow our well-established custom of asking our writers of commentaries to speak on behalf of their points of view. Of course, we will recognize that it is regrettable that Coleman isn't here and that it isn't feasible to name a surrogate to present his point of view. So I would like to suggest as a procedural point that the people who do the speaking pretend that they know how Coleman would react to what they are about to say, and then say it.

BIERSTEDT: I'm a little sorry, as Andy Hacker is, that Jim wrote the kind of paper he did. I think Andy's indictment has some merit to it, namely, that Coleman was discussing only a very small part of sociology and not really addressing himself to the question of the conference, except perhaps incidentally.

Certainly his paper threw me for a loss, as I remarked at the beginning of mine, since I know nothing whatever about statistics. I rather imagine I am the last person in the world ever to get a Ph.D. in sociology without any training whatever in statistics. I am so unqualified to talk about regression coefficients that I had to indulge instead in some dim witticisms about the social sciences in general.

Jim's paper though, insofar as I understand its general tenor, says that when it comes to a complicated statistical technique like regression coefficients, people in different disciplines—namely, economics, statistics, sociology, and educational psychology—are inclined to use different kinds of coefficients. Some of them use raw coefficients, some of them use standardized coefficients, and so on.

I see this as a fascinating problem in the sociology of knowledge. Even what might be supposed to be a purely mechanical technique or tactic in statistics can be susceptible to different use and different application by people in different fields and with different kinds of training. If Jim were here I would like to ask him with what kind of technique this difference becomes discernible. I take it that people would not use the multiplication table differently if they came from different disciplines or that they would not expect square roots to be differently used. However, if we take Jim's word for it, when working with regression coefficients they do do things differently. What about coefficients of correlation? Are there different kinds of coefficients of correlation? Are there some that would be used in some circumstances and some in others?

In other words, I can imagine a spectrum here from, let's say, the multiplication table to Jim's regression coefficients and wonder at what point these differences begin to appear. I think that's a significant question, and I'm not sure that Jim gave us an answer to it. Nor did he give us an answer, as Andy points out in his paper, to another rather substantial question; that is, whether the conclusions of the people in these four fields on the substance of the Coleman Report were different. We know only that the techniques were different. We don't know whether they arrived at different conclusions. So this is the basic problem, it seems to me—or at least this is the basic problem that Jim's paper presents to me.

I think, if I may, I should like to defend him a little bit against another of Andy's indictments, namely, that he seemed to be more interested in regression coefficients as a statistical technique than he was in the education of the children. I think that is probably not altogether fair.

HACKER: I wrote that sentence very carefully. I didn't say "more than." I said "perhaps as much as."

BIERSTEDT: Well, let me see if I can defend Jim against even so mild an indictment.

It seems to me that one kind of response that he got to his paper was a methodological response in the technical journals, and he was simply taking this opportunity to answer some of his methodological critics. Jim has certainly testified often before congressional committees, and he has certainly exhibited, to me at least, a more than satisfactory interest in the subject involved, namely, the education of the children.

Well, from that point on I was reduced to sheer speculation, and I asked myself the question that has frequently occurred in sociology—the degree to which it is a general social science and the degree, on the contrary, to which it is a special social science. Many have taken the view that it is a special social science and that only by developing our own rather narrowly defined area of inquiry can we make any progress within the field. Other sociologists, Sorokin for example, have maintained on the contrary that it doesn't make sense to set up a separate category of the social and that sociology has to be more of a general social science, dealing with those kinds of variables that are common to all kinds of social inquiry from economics to jurisprudence. It also has to take into consideration those variables which somehow escape inquiries in the separate disciplines. An example might be Max Weber's attempt to trace the relationships between the Protestant Ethic and the rise of capitalism, a problem that belongs neither to religion as such, nor to economics as such.

Now, I don't know what the answer is here. My own preference is to perceive sociology as more of a kind of general inquiry. If that is the case, then I do think that we should assume some responsibility for the kind of integration that we have been talking about in this conference—some responsibility for making the effort if the effort seems to be a desirable one. I hope that if we do make that effort we can make it without any kind of disciplinary imperialism, which is the thing I am always inclined to distrust, as probably all the rest of us are too.

Finally, in my own paper I asked a question as to whether engagement in policy or policy analysis or even policy recommendations does help at all in the integration of the social sciences. Here I came to the skeptical conclusion that it does not. This is a conclusion that I reached on the basis of my own experience of having served on a National Science Foundation Committee quite recently. This was a committee that attempted to study the kind of involvement that the Department of Defense had in the social sciences, especially in behavioral research, and to determine whether its involvement was right as well as to make recommendations for changes if we thought changes were desirable. This we did.   We had a heterogeneous group of social scientists, including even the dean of a school of engineering.

Although we worked together in great harmony and, I think, with great respect for one another, I am unable to see that this kind of work contributed very much, if anything, to the integration of the social sciences.   Nor, as a matter of fact, am I very sanguine about the possibility that it will contribute to any changes of policy within the Department of Defense.   I suspect that it will be one of those reports that simply remains unread for the most part.   Therefore, on the matter of the conference itself, I can't be very hopeful, and I can't be very optimistic that policy research can contribute to the integration of the social sciences.

HACKER: Just a few remarks.   When I was given Coleman's paper to read, I dusted off the Coleman Report and reread it.   I think that now I have a measure of what that report is about in a way that I didn't when I first skimmed it.   Then I read the various studies and critiques of this report that Coleman alluded to in his paper.

To begin with I was made rather angry by the first critique. Here were two professors who were content to confine themselves to a technical argument over the proper use of regression analysis. I also noticed that their research had been funded by the Office of Economic Opportunity (OEO).   Now I got just furious at this.   The OEO is supposed to be doing something about children who have lead paint poisoning or about setting up clinics in Appalachia, and here are two professors getting two-ninths of their salary from "poverty" money for criticizing Coleman's statistics.   This is immoral.   The policy analysis that many of us want to get into is simply a way of financing that summer cottage or raising our incomes up to the thirty thousands.   These two critics of Coleman wouldn't know a school from a fallout shelter if they saw one.   In fact, they weren't even writing about education.   They were simply playing their own game and getting paid for it.

It bothers me because it's bad for character.   It's corrupt. It leads to self-delusions.   It can also be bad for the country, as it has been in the case of the predecessors of policy analysts, the systems analysts who were helping us in Southeast Asia by telling us how to bomb hamlets. What makes this even more difficult is that we are not even sure that they were successful in their mission. We didn't win in Vietnam. So, you know, you are caught two ways here. You can either say they were successful, and therefore they were evil; or that they were unsuccessful, which means they weren't really evil but were trying to be evil and didn't succeed.

I've been doing a little book this last year on New York City, and I decided to start out by seeing what our new urban "experts" could tell us. I read, for example, a book by Jay Forrester at Massachusettts Institute of Technology called *Urban Dynamics*. He built a city in a computer. He set up a beautiful model. One of the proposals that came out of his model was to ship the poor out of cities. The mind begins to reel here. This is a policy suggestion coming out of Massachusetts Institute of Technology. So my general inclination is that I don't want to offer my services. I think I will do more harm than good, both to the republic and to myself.

Another matter here which is in the Coleman Report ties into something that Ed Lindblom said regarding the whole notion of the inherent conservatism in policy analysis. We all know the chief finding in the Coleman Report. But why wasn't it that class size had some effect on the performance by students? If there is one thing that has come out in research on schools, it is that the smaller the number of kids in a class, especially when you get down to twelve or ten, the better the kids are going to do. But this didn't come out in the Coleman Report, and I wonder why.

MacRae: That's not an undisputed finding, I think. A lot of research is on Coleman's side.

Lane: A lot of research says it depends on age and——

Hacker: Right, but we are talking about the first through sixth grades. The reason I mention this is that I then looked much further into Coleman's data. What he did was simply ask each of the schools how many teachers and pupils were there and divide to get an average class size for each school. What he got, of course, was the normal range of public school class size, which is usually twenty-two to thirty-two.

My point is that we do know that if you get the teacher-student ratio down to one to ten, or one to twelve, or one to eight, then you can, with this individual attention, bring students along very nicely. Now, the "conservative" element here is that Coleman worked only with prevailing pupil-teacher ratios. It may well be that one of the answers for disadvantaged children is to have classes of eight, but that proposal couldn't come out of the Coleman Report because none of the data concerned classes that small which could be used as a point of comparison.

TAX: That was irrelevant to his conclusions because they dealt with the mix in the group. There could be eight kids, all——

HACKER: That's what I meant when I said that his finding was based on a status quo. What I'm saying is that it may well be, even in an all black school, if you have teacher-pupil ratios of one to eight, then those kids would come out just as well as they do in Scarsdale.

TAX: I don't think you would, even with one to one.

HACKER: I think you would.

TAX: A middle-class teacher of another culture is still only one, and as far as the child is concerned, a large proportion of his social contacts outside the school and inside the school would still be people of his own culture. The problem here is getting enough of a mix in order for another culture to be transmitted. You would not expect in a school that a single person representing middle-class culture would have much effect on a community of another culture. We have a number of universal generalizations about acculturation, and we could have predicted Coleman's conclusions simply on the basis that this was a cross-cultural situation with one teacher trying to pass on a culture to—no matter whether eight or thirty—children of another culture in a school in which all were of that other culture except for the teacher.

HACKER: I'm sorry, I disagree with you completely. To begin with, we are talking about young children, and even a white, middle-class teacher can have quite a substantial effect on a group of small black kids. There is a tremendous difference between a one-to-thirty and a one-to-eight teacher-student ratio. This is a fact. But that kind of fact has only happened in a few experimental situations and couldn't be included in the Coleman Report because it wasn't part of his data.

MCCORD: Aren't you in a way contradicting yourself? You began by saying you were not satisfied with being engaged in this policy analysis, and then you point out this one very specific point which is a disagreement between you and Sol Tax. It is obviously researchable and would have to reckon with policy implications which it would be very valuable to try out. It would be possible to set up a whole series of experiments and test it as a policy. Is it worthwhile to have a middle-class teacher dealing with eight kids or not? What I am saying is that you are advocating, in your last statement, one type of policy research.

HACKER: But not as a social scientist. I just wonder how many of the things we propose to do in this policy area are in our "scientist" roles.

TAX: My thought is that this is a generalization. Some people can probably make a lot of money and not be corrupted, and some people without money can be corrupted just because they are working for somebody else.

HACKER: No, you can't make a lot of money and not be corrupted. There is no exception. (Laughter)

My last point is: No, Virginia, we're not going to integrate the social sciences. What I would say here is that the reason why we have various social science disciplines is that they are about all that we can manage. None of us is smart enough to do more than master a part of the forest, and we've each chosen a part of the forest that is manageable for us. We just don't have it in us, either collectively or individually, to put together more than a certain number of data about the reality that makes up the world. In other words, it is no accident that we persist in our disciplines. That's about all we have the brains for.

There will come along, as there does every so often, a Marx or a Freud. But their kind of insight isn't made in committees or from conferences. None of us is Marx or Freud, and we can't turn ourselves into their equivalents by sitting around and putting our small bits and pieces together in different ways.

MCCORD: I take slight issue with your point. I agree that with the information explosion it is just too much for mortals to handle. I do question whether the particular way that the disciplines have been sliced up historically is necessarily the best way.

At Syracuse, an excellent program in the social sciences exists. The requirements for this program are that the students have to take three years in a discipline plus the equivalent of about a year in two other fields. A typical combination might be political science as a major and some economics and sociology on the side. Now, the point I am making about this program is that it has an institutional arrangement which allows tremendous flexibility. All the person has to do is to be able to get four advisors to agree that he's got a focus that has something to do with social science, and then he can follow his own route. It allows for the kind of program that Tom Schelling has talked about. He mentioned a combination of law and neurology as being useful. I agree. The Syracuse program provides an institutional agreement whereby students who want to make an unusual mix of the social sciences and humanities are allowed to do so, and the kind of people Syracuse has turned out are, of course, extraordinary.

TAX: I'm shocked at us. We are like the shoemaker and his shoes. We are willing to talk about the social sciences as though we were old-time Mississippians talking about the races as being unmixable because you can see they are not mixing since Negroes like Negroes and whites like whites, each to his own group, and so on. This appeared to be true, until someone asked *why* and discovered that there were laws and regulations keeping them apart.

The analogy would be too bitter if, when you say that we don't have the capacity to understand two disciplines, I respond that that's why disciplines remain apart. I have the same capacity to learn half political science and half anthropology as I have to learn all anthropology or all political science, so it is unlikely that the reason why the disciplines are different is that human capacity to understand is limited. The same capacity can be used in innumerable ways; thus, you can't use status quo as the reason why it should be that way, which sounded like the argument that you were making.

HACKER: What I was offering was one of a dozen possible explanations as to why we keep on with the disciplines. There are a dozen other reasons. But one of them is that this arrangement is manageable for little-minded people.

TAX: But because the same little mind can do a lot of different things, you were picking one group of things to be a variable independent of the problem that we are talking about. If we say you've got to master the whole of a given discipline before you can do anything in another discipline or we won't feed you, we mean the minimum requirement for professional status is all that a person can handle of one discipline, and we are in a circular argument. The disciplines necessarily have to remain as they are because that is the way we have arranged them.

HACKER: I don't disagree. If you want to cut it another way and have a discipline called anthronomics and another one called ecopolitics—both manageable for the same size minds as the previous two—I'd say splendid. However, you are going to find it difficult to move from the current ones we have to the new ones that you have suggested——

TAX: That is our problem. How would we do that?

HACKER: Oh, the usual way—set up a still another faculty committee.

TAX: We ought to spend our time—we've lost most of it now —but we ought to spend our time thinking and talking about what there is to do. If we were to accept the model that there are no disciplines anymore—those lines are erased because the Supreme Court has said that you can't segregate anymore—how would we begin to remake the world? In relation both to the disciplines and to policy?

HACKER: Let me give you again a personal example here. I teach courses in sex. It's about all I can manage at this point. I am very expert on the subject, and as a result there are a lot of other things I am not expert on, like arms controls. But don't ask me what disciplines sex involves because it involves all of them or none of them, depending on how you want to do it.

MCCORD: That's a good example. You're a sexologist.

HUGHES: My comments will be fairly brief, I think, for two reasons. One is that Andy Hacker is obviously a hard act to follow, and the other, that he has set some things in motion which I think we will want to get back into.

I find it difficult to tie into Coleman's paper. It is not the kind of sociology that I was trained in or have worked with, and so I have to address the question more broadly. I think that there were issues raised by Coleman's paper and by our discussions of yesterday and today that get us back to the primary subject of this conference, and we can spend some more time with these basic issues. For example, we seemed to be arguing against the point that integration is even desirable, much less possible. That seems to be a central kind of theme.

It is as if we are conceiving of integration as a uniform, homogeneous kind of act or pattern. But surely there are varying meanings of this term and varying expressions of it. For example, does it mean simply that two persons from different social sciences are able to understand the language of each other, and if so, to that extent achieve some minimal level of integration? You can cite instances, of course, in which people from the social sciences are not even speaking the same kind of language and, to that extent, are in no way integrated.

But that is only one point on a continuum of integration. Other points might well be the fruitful use of the same kinds of concepts as operationally defined in terms of a given problem area. This, I think, is what implicitly we have been conceiving of as the kind of integration wanted by those who think it may be desirable—a complementarity or perhaps use of the same kind of concepts in problem areas where disciplinary boundaries are hard to draw or unnecessary. What I am suggesting is that we could, I think, have spent more time in talking about what, in effect, we mean by integration and not assume that everybody does, in fact, know what it is.

I have another comment on the question of integration as related to policy analysis. If we are looking at Coleman's paper as an example, I think we would have to agree that taking a social science problem with applied implications, such as this one, as the focus makes it clear that there has been little integration in any viable sense between sociology and economics. There are still worlds of difference, basic frames of reference here, that divide the representatives of these two disciplines. So it does raise the question of whether policy analysis is the way to go if we are hoping to achieve integration. Perhaps it is not, or at least not in all instances.

But why should we worry about this in any case? If, indeed, it does come about, I see it as surely an evolutionary kind of a thing, a process. We are a little immodest, I think, when we assemble people from our own and other disciplines, here or in other groups like this, to say we will this day, here and now, integrate the social sciences or even begin the process of integration of the social sciences. This is something bigger than all—or both of us—as the saying has it. Integration will occur when conditions warrant, and I think that it will go on.

If you take a little bit of history into account, it has gone on. What is really only a hundred years ago or so, there were not the things we are today calling sociology, anthropology, or psychology. They were "moral philosophy" or something else. Only much more recently has social psychology become a "discipline"— whatever "discipline" may mean.   So I think it is a process of the growth of knowledge, and then the assigning of areas of that knowledge to different units of social organization in universities and elsewhere.

In the long run I am not at all concerned, really, about whether there will be integration, meaning by that conjoint activities tied down to the behavioral process level. I think this will go on when the problem demands it and when, in the process of looking for an outcome, it is shown to be fruitful and profitable. So I think maybe we should stand back a little farther from our present scene and our present concerns, as indeed Sol Tax was suggesting yesterday, and look at us from as much of a distance as we can.

Another comment is sparked by something that was just going on between Sol Tax and Andy Hacker. We can see a great deal of disciplinary redundancy in our activities. I am impressed by this in some of the current activities that I am involved in, which have to do with trying to build into the medical school curriculum a behavioral science dimension. One thing we have to face very clearly is the question of talking about the fields of anthropology, sociology, psychology, and economics not only separately, but also in something of a coordinated, comprehensive, and—especially— selective way.

Do we expect medical students to learn everything about each one of these fields? Is that what we mean by behavioral science dimension? The answer is obviously no because, in effect, in each of these fields we don't really expect every graduate student to master everything about that particular field.   The field represents a corporate social process, and he has selected certain emphases within that. Regarding the medical students, we are being forced to the hard question and issue of saying what is most salient, of establishing priorities among concepts, facts, and techniques relevant to an understanding of social man in a medical, health, and disease context. And such a task-imposed selectivity underscores the wide areas of congruence that do exist among behavioral science fields.

For me, I think this process, begun fairly early in my professional activities, has continued to be one of trying to sort out and establish priorities of knowledge in relation to action as well as knowledge in relation to problems, knowing that these problems are continually changing and that knowledge and disciplines are really "holding companies" or resource pools from which one draws when appropriate. My own preference in regard to the possibilities of integration, therefore, is to tie it in to some kind of problem focus. Policy analysis may be one of these foci. Sometimes such problems are forced on us by the society at large, or else they arise endogenously, so to speak, from the discipline itself; but in both cases we focus on problems and then assemble resources and bring these to bear when appropriate.

Finally, it seems to me that in this third session of our conference we are beginning to touch again on very familiar themes, and maybe we can wrap them up in the next hour and a half. I am very pessimistic about doing that, but one we have touched on is the general question of the relationship between science, or intellectual academic pursuits, and society. We keep coming back to that as a motif but never spell it out clearly, and we are obviously all in considerable turmoil about it in this day and age of universities being attacked from the right and left and in-between on the basis of their irrelevance. Tied in with this is the whole issue of pure as against applied research, which also seems to trouble many people.

I think I am not as troubled by it as are some of my colleagues. I don't see it as any kind of insuperable dichotomy. In fact, in relation to one issue that came up yesterday—and it is also touched on in Easton's paper; that is, that we should establish institutes that really do work in the community in order to buy back our moral standing in society—some illustrative points can be made.   I am now at a university which, with a number of others in the country, prides itself on operating in terms of the "land grant philosophy."   It is not a philosophy, of course, in any sophisticated sense, but rather a value commitment regarding the uses of knowledge.   It is rooted in the Morrill Act, which asserts that knowledge should be useful for something, such as growing more crops or bigger pigs.   And that, surely, is a worth-while goal of human action.

The idea of the uses of knowledge bothered me at first in going from Ivy League training to my present position, but then I realized that, perhaps thinking in an anthropological vein, we wouldn't even be here without the neolithic revolution having oc-curred; therefore, why should I be so standoffish at this stage? So I can live very comfortably with that kind of activity and use of knowledge under university auspices.   Yet I think, at the same time, there has to be what we commented on yesterday—the academy or the university giving the place and time for reflection on some of these issues because otherwise it won't happen.   It is a more efficient way of trying to advance our understanding of the world than leaving it all to the practical men and/or the adminis-trators who, for the most part—and having been one I can suggest this—don't have time to raise their eyes from the memo pad in front of them and think about larger conceptual issues.   There just is not time during the day.

So I defend the place of the university both as the conceptual-izing area as well as its being broad enough to encompass action units that will feed back and forth between practical issues and the development of concepts and theory.

KARIEL: I'd like to reinforce what I've been selectively hear-ing and, at the same time, resist what I see as a kind of skepticism about the possibilities and problems of integrated social science research.   I would be a little bit less skeptical and a little less humble about what we might be able to do, and at the same time plead for a measure of modesty and, if you like, humility in our operation.

It seems to me that an excess of knowledge, or an excess of sophistication about the techniques that are suitable for distinc-tive social science disciplines, techniques that we think are often demanded as if they had some objective existence, keeps us from recognizing the promise of an integrated or concerted effort, not to analyze policy, but in fact to proceed—I guess I hear myself paraphrasing Marx—to make policy; that is, to make it in a self-reflective fashion, in a self-conscious way, not to philosophize, but to commence action. Perhaps not with Marx, but with Dewey, I would regard action as integrative. It integrates a diverse number of interests, styles, disciplines, and social science languages. It seems to me that it is only Dave Easton who has explicitly intimated this particular possibility in his paper, arguing for, if you recall, small-scale innovations—what R. B. Ling has called microrevolutions.

HACKER: But he's a poet.

KARIEL: Poetry, then, is his form of action.

Easton is arguing explicitly for experimental probes, university based. He is arguing for pilot studies, which is a nice, modest term. I would have no reservations at all about pilot studies and then about encouraging pilot studies to expand until the world is permeated by pilot studies. That would be, I think, all right. We would thereby fuse policy analysis and political action or policy-making. As all pragmatists hope, we would fuse theory and practice, or give life, indeed give validity, to theory or to a purely analytical mode of combining those two. I think this has been vaguely suggested by a number of things we have said, and it pulls us back, I think, to a pragmatic posture.

MACRAE: I would like to come back at this time to Jim Coleman's paper in a different way. I think that Coleman undersold what he accomplished in his report. I don't know whether he would defend himself, but I want, in a way, to defend him. Having looked at the Coleman Report, having thought about it just a little bit, and having tried to read some of the secondary literature, I feel it has had a tremendous impact. So the question that I think needs to be explained is: Why did Jim Coleman feel so pessimistic about its impact?

First of all, what has been done and what hasn't been done? Some of you might know more than I do about these points, but the most conspicuous thing to me is that it has stirred up a very interesting, interdisciplinary debate. The very fact that people in different disciplines have responded to the Coleman Report, used its data, and made use of its interpretations, even though criticizing them, is, I think, a very important, prospective long-run contribution to social science. Economists, sociologists, and educators have talked with one another about the same data, which is really rare. The fact that the report and data are in the public domain and the interpretations not simply given confidentially to statesman furnishes, I think, a very interesting model which applied social science (policy science) can gain from.

So I think that there has been a great success, but the reason that Coleman doesn't see it as a success is that he is taking a short-run view. He put so much work into this—it was a monumental work of research administration—I think he hoped it would have effects directly on education in the short run. These were stymied by a lot of groups—some disciplinary, some vested interests, and the like—and for this reason he feels a sense of failure. I don't regard this as a failure, however, because I think one has to regard the impact of something like this in terms of both the present generation and future generations.

Now, in the present generation people like us are set in their ways, more or less than we are, and represent these disciplinary reactions that he is talking about. But I think the next generation, particularly in a field where disciplinary disputes are resolvable with statistics and quantitative analysis, is very likely to synthesize these different approaches. With new studies, new approaches, new analyses, I think the future generations of social scientists are more likely to achieve synthesis in the kind of areas that Coleman is working in than almost any other areas that I know of.

One thing that Coleman objects to, however, the economic structural model where one considers factor costs and productivities, is, I think, conceivably a very useful way of proceeding, and I wish there were a highly technically oriented economist here to argue for this point of view. Another plug that I want to put in is for the value of the economist's approach, although perhaps Ed Lindblom will do this, if he wishes, more eloquently than I.

So the point that I would make is that there are short-run obstacles but long-run gains in the creation of an interdisciplinary literature and, possibly, the training of younger scholars who will move into this field as policy researchers in a way that the older generation can't quite do, straying across disciplines in a way

that Coleman and his adversaries don't quite do.   In this connection the question that Harold Guetzkow raised earlier of how one
is hired in these areas has to do with the future of interdisciplinary
integration in terms of careers.   Would a young man who is
capable of doing interdisciplinary work in arms control or in education go to work for two years with no prospect of tenure in an
applied organization, or would he opt for the tenured positions
that are securely within the grasp of the existing disciplines?
The question of the relative importance of these avenues of personnel flow, possibly in a contracting academic market, may be
one of the most crucial factors affecting the future integration of
the social sciences for policy purposes in the next generation.

McCORD: I'd like to pick up your point on the younger
scholars.   As Ed Lindblom and others pointed out, what we are
apparently doing within the disciplines in graduate schools is
crushing imagination, broadness, and creativity.   I agree with
Sol Tax that what we've got to think of are ways in which the
young scholar can be encouraged in institutional ways, whether it
is policy analysis or some other path, to blossom and to go into
other fields, which will, as you point out, require all sorts of things
such as changing tenure rules, departmental boundaries, and rewards within the field.

I think your last point about the curtailment of the market
for Ph.D.'s is probably well taken.   We haven't really touched
on it, but according to the last figures I saw, we are going to have
about a thirty-three percent unemployment rate of Ph.D.'s by
1975, which in effect is going to push people into government or
some kind of policy analysis whether we wish it or not.

BIERSTEDT: I don't know if it will have that consequence.
What could happen is that the Ph.D.'s we have will move down
on the prestige scale or the stratification scale of colleges and universities so that after a while, if the unemployment rate is going
to be as high as you suggest, we will have Ph.D.'s in junior and
community colleges.   I think that is a more likely outcome.

HACKER: It is like all the Jewish boys who became dentists
and pharmacists in the '20s and '30s.   They should have been
doctors.

TAX: It is interesting to consider the history of interdisciplinary versus disciplinary development in social sciences in

these past twenty or thirty years. I think there was a stronger movement toward interdisciplinary things twenty years ago; then with the great growth of government fellowships and other funds defined in terms of disciplines, it was the disciplinary groups which had money, students, and fellowships. Definitions and boundaries were fixed pretty much by government.

I recall, as president of the American Anthropological Association a dozen years ago, talking to the National Science Foundation (NSF) where anthropology was already in the research division but not in the education part. It happened to be a strategic moment to get anthropology—not just physical anthropology, but the whole of anthropology—accepted in the NSF programs for science education, the first of the social sciences to be so accepted. Then at once we had pressed on us all the programs that chemistry, physics, or biology had, and we soon had our visiting lecture program and a curriculum development project. Because the discipline was accepted, we had sudden great growth. The social sciences thus came in as disciplines; fellowships were awarded to students within disciplines, and disciplinary Ph.D.'s were paid for. With the money being allocated in this fashion, the growth of the disciplines and the retreat into disciplinary fortresses followed.

Now the money is gone, and we have an overproduction of Ph.D.'s. It is a perfect time for a sudden great movement again toward interdisciplinary work. At the same time our students want to be "relevant," and there are problems in the world that people are interested in. We happen to have come together at a moment when, even if we hadn't come together, the time would have been right for change in both of the directions to which this conference is oriented. Interdisciplinary policy orientations now have a great chance of success.

CHARLESWORTH: I haven't said anything substantive at this conference. I'm not going to harangue you at length on any ideas that I have, but I am impressed with the tendency in American disciplines for young Ph.D. candidates to get into more and more remote corners in order to become scientific. I was wondering what some of you, particularly Bob Bierstedt, might think about this idea.

Let me preface it by saying that at the end of World War II there was a movement in Washington to integrate the armed forces. Now this could be done by creating an umbrella department, which is what they did do, or it could be done by expanding an existing department; for example, it was talked about expanding the Navy Department. It already had an air force, and a land force, so you needed only expand those things and abolish the air force and the army. Now, we are aware of the movement toward conglomerates in American commerce and industry. I guess most of us don't know as much about that as we ought to to make a generalization, but from the information that I get, it is quite extensive. These organizations, presumably quite diverse, are being pulled together, and apparently the thing is working beautifully or the process would certainly be slowed down or even arrested.

I believe one of the things Franklin Giddings said was that sociology is generic and political science, for example, is a specific. So you just throw one of the specifics into the generic pot, and it makes more sense. I was wondering what you people would think about something like this. A complaisant university administration meets with a committee of the sociology department and says, "Gentlemen, you are going to take over the social sciences. Start offering courses. Offer a course in city government."

"There is already a course in city government."

"Well, offer one of your own—the sociological aspects of city government, and so on. Just start offering courses which will duplicate all the courses that are given in the social science departments."

I really believe that there is something to be said for this, practically and from the standpoint of substance. Does any one of you care to comment on it?

BIERSTEDT: That's a pretty costly proposition, isn't it Jim? You are duplicating efforts. It reminds me of the Japanese spy who was sent to Washington during World War II to find out where we were carrying on a particular kind of activity, and his mission turned out to be a total failure because he reported back that we were doing the same thing all over the place.

LINDBLOM: Let me ask you: Would the sociology department alone do this, or would all the departments?

CHARLESWORTH: No, just the sociology department. Or, if you don't like the sociology department, some other department.

Now, if Bob's department would offer a course in city government and it was a better course than is presently being offered by the political science department, it would thrive—and that would be the end of the other course, and we would have integration, at least to that extent.

BIERSTEDT: Well, you'd have administrative integration perhaps, if your experiment was successful, but you wouldn't necessarily have any conceptual integration.

CHARLESWORTH: Presumably, this course would be taught by a sociologist.

LINDBLOM: I think Mr. Bierstedt put his finger on the point. There is a big difference between administrative integration and intellectual or conceptual integration. You don't get the latter by administrative integration. I think if a sociology department were asked—invited to expand—to do a course on monetary theory, they'd hire an economist to do it.

CHARLESWORTH: That isn't what I am talking about. They would hire a sociologist.

HACKER: To talk of policy analysis is to talk in melioristic terms. There is a school of thought represented by Edward Banfield which says that we are not going to make things better except in a very small margin and that amelioration will often take place by accident rather than by design. Those who propose our entering the policy area have a different idea. Personally, I am closer to Banfield than I am to them. My own concern is to understand, not to engage in therapy—at least not in my role as a scientist.

I was interested in Ed Lindblom's comments on therapy. I did my Ph.D. thesis many years ago on "The Politics of Psychotherapy" and I learned quite a bit about how psychiatry works. Take a patient, John Jones, who has a backache for which they can't find an organic cause. If you have an authoritative and charismatic therapist, he can be a Freudian or an Adlerian or, in another culture, a witch doctor. The doctrine itself isn't important, for no matter what explanation is given to the patient, if the therapist is charismatic, the backache will disappear. In other words, science and therapy don't have that much connection.

KARIEL: I just don't see why efforts to understand are necessarily amelioristic.

HACKER: I didn't say that. I said efforts to understand are efforts to understand.

KARIEL: Yes, but understanding isn't likely to be had unless one proceeds to change the situation or act upon some environment.

HACKER: How so? When Banfield studies a city, he doesn't act upon it.

KARIEL: We can't tell yet whether he has acted upon it. It would depend on his ability to find readers.

CHARLESWORTH: If someone understands something but is not going to do anything about it, isn't he like a monk in a monastery rather than a parish priest?

HACKER: We are in a tertiary stage economy, and we can afford lots of monks.

KARIEL: I want to come back to my point. I think we are underestimating the activistic impact of work such as Banfield's. The impact may not be immediate, and it may be exclusively, for all I know, on Banfield himself. Still, I would doubt this, as it has not only been able to change him but has also been able to change those who have read him sympathetically so that, having read Banfield, they view the world around them in a slightly different way. Of course, if Banfield had more dimensions, more men would have been changed; and more being changed, more would act upon themselves and upon others in a different and presumably enlarged fashion.

HACKER: My favorite work of fiction, Henry, is a book entitled *Books that Changed the World*.

KARIEL: Well, I'm not as masochistic. I think——

HACKER: I'm not being masochistic. I ordered the wine last night.

KARIEL: Well, that's compensation. (Laughter)

BIERSTEDT: Would you go so far, Andy, as to be similarly skeptical of the proposition that there are ideas that change the world?

HACKER: There are sentiments that change the world. We tend to emphasize the influence of Rousseau or John Locke or Karl Marx because we are expert in Marx, Locke, and Rousseau.

There are influential ideas, but they are not ideas in the scholarly sense. They are thoughts in ordinary people's heads.

BIERSTEDT: What about Einstein's ideas that led to nuclear fission?

HACKER: That realm is obviously clear. I am talking about the social realm. Suppose there never had been a Marx. The history of the last century would still have been much the same. Look at all the revolutions we have had that never had a Marx. Genghis Khan did not have a Marx.

BIERSTEDT: That was force. We are talking about ideas.

HACKER: There were ideas behind Genghis Khan, but they didn't come from books.

KARIEL: Isn't it true, Andy, that the world has acquired a different meaning, if not a different concrete structure, as a consequence of Marx's metaphors, Freud's metaphors, and so forth?

HACKER: I am aware that Marx has given a vocabulary to all sorts of people.

KARIEL: What do you think does change the world? Certainly ideas have a place in it, and books have a place, and science has a place.

HACKER: At a certain point in history, men of affairs began to quote Locke, which gave us an excuse to make links between the bookwriters and the people who quoted them. The chief reason we remember Marx is that men of affairs quoted Marx. There have been all sorts of cultures that have undergone fantastic changes with no books behind them.

TAX: We happen to have books as one of the mechanisms by which we can communicate in a larger society. In places where there are no books, things also happen, but on a smaller scale.

HACKER: Take Agnewism or hardhatism. What books?

KARIEL: That is not a fair question because I would regard those as different forms of action. Books are one form of action, and Agnewism is another form of action.

LINDBLOM: Gentlemen, I find this interesting, but I think we are digressing, and I would like to make another try for some momentum and continuity on our main business. I expect to fail in that attempt, but I can't restrain myself from trying.

We have at this point, it seems to me, come to expressed agreement on some very crude conclusions, such as that integration of the social sciences—and of the social sciences with other sciences too—is a good thing in its place, though we differ on what its place is, what the desirable form of integration is, and whether it should be pushed very hard. All of us believe that some form or other of integration is desirable at some times for some purposes. And we, of course, all believe that policy analysis is inescapable and desirable. Again, we have discovered disagreement on how much of a priority to give it and what form it should take. We also see the reciprocal relationship between policy analysis and integration, each serving the other. Which of these causal relationships of mutual support we choose to emphasize is, again, a point of some disagreement.

Now, is there any point in making one last desperate effort to push in a sustained way on the remaining disagreements? One possibility occurs to me. I assume that all of us have been talking about the need for integration and its relation to policy analysis in the light of what we have in our heads as a picture of what is wrong or inadequate about social science. Although yesterday I couldn't induce any of you to round out a statement of what questions we want to answer that we haven't yet answered in social science, it might still be possible here this morning to try for some explicit statement of what is wrong with social science.

Consequently, what I am suggesting—and I would like to get the suggestion into the record even if it isn't picked up—is the possibility that we could push our inquiries concerning desirable forms of integration and a desirable relation of policy analysis to integration by making explicit to ourselves and each other a diagnosis of what is inadequate about social science. We could then consider explicitly the implications of each identified inadequacy for integration and policy analysis.

By inadequacies in social science I would mean some such list as I will now offer. It represents a hasty diagnosis, and I'd be happy if my list would encourage others of you to try your hands at a list here and now, and then to indicate the implication of your list for integration and for policy analysis.

I would put down as a first serious inadequacy in social science the inadequateness of its tools. I can't help but be impressed with how much of the distinctive character of economics is not in the content of its theory but in its excellent analytic tools.

Sometimes they are very simple, such as the concept of the demand schedule, which can be applied to unravel, for example, many complexities in the analysis of values that philosophers and many other social scientists still stumble over because they can't conceive of values arranged as schedules rather than as priority lists. Or there is the concept of the multiplier, or the notion of a margin. These are central to economic analysis and are tremendously powerful, although simple, little notions. So, one of the inadequacies of social science is that such modest tools for analysis are not widely distributed, and that our young social scientists are not systematically trained in the use of them.

Secondly, it seems to me that social science is crippled by its passion for nomothetic propositions. This is an uncritical ambition for the social sciences.

KARIEL: What does nomothetic mean?

LINDBLOM: Propositions true of all times and all places. Classical propositions aping the ambitions of the natural sciences with their mechanistic explanations. It seems to me that this represents an impossible ideal.

When I make these two points—this is a footnote here—I am sympathizing with a great deal that Mr. Guetzkow was saying in his paper, and I think he would agree with both of these propositions.

If we are on the wrong track in such a heavy-handed and uncritical pursuit of nomothetic propositions, then I think my third point follows: we lack a strategy or a discriminating sense of what kind of propositions are feasible for social science and therefore what kind of propositions are worth getting, considering their value and their feasibility. We have not taken seriously the problem of creating new designs and new strategies for the social sciences that pull away abruptly, sharply, self-consciously, from aping the methods of the physical sciences.

McCORD: In existing social sciences, under your third point, can you think of a successful example or illustration of some kind of strategy which has worked? Or are you just saying that we have to develop it?

LINDBLOM: I think the social sciences are in so early a part of their infancy that I can't give you a good example. I can suggest what an example might look like, however. In my own work on decision-making, I have tried to show that there is a possible strategy (to which I have given the name of disjointed incrementalism) that contrasts sharply with conventional notions of decision-making. It seems to me that there must be possibilities of developing similar strategies for problem-solving in academic, scientific, and scholarly work—strategies that are as distinct from conventional notions of nomothetic science as my disjointed incrementalism is from the older conventional notions of rational decision-making.

My fourth and last listed inadequacy in social science is that social science is insufficiently ambitious. Does this point seem to contradict my earlier point that we are overly ambitious in trying to pursue nomothetic propositions? I think not. That is a careless, clumsy, uncritical ambition. If we were to develop a strategy science appropriate to social science, however, we could greatly step up our ambitions to do significant work.

The implications of these four inadequacies for integration is this: I don't see that integration is a high priority method of coping with these four inadequacies. As for policy analysis, I don't see any obvious connection between it and the four inadequacies.

Tax: To take off from what you say to a slightly different conclusion, one easy thing for me to do as an anthropologist is to discover and adapt to my kind of problems the tools that economists have found useful. The test would be whether with your tools I can make new propositions that are not nomothetic and that I can see are useful. If we also select problems which people beyond ourselves think useful for society, we might have what we are after. Perhaps interdisciplinary work for policy analysis is a matter of who sits in a room. If I should invite you to a meeting of anthropologists to explain the rules that you have and that we've been stupid for not knowing about, we might suggest ways to use them and test the suggestions against you.

I can give you an example of this. Once, at Columbia University, Ralph Linton and a group of anthropologists sat with Abram Kardiner who said, "You give me the data on your primitive tribes and I'll tell you how to use Freudian analysis or psychoanalytic technique in order to discover what the basic personality structure is of the people that you are studying as opposed to the people in Western society." From a joint seminary, then, the whole interdisciplinary area of personality and culture burgeoned, and people went off in the field with such tools as the Rorschach and Thematic Apperception Tests and the notion of the basic personality structure.   Something like this could happen in no time at all if you would give us the demand schedule—the notion of what it is and why you think we might use it—and let us try to think of how we could apply it.   We would have a new tool to play with—and we can get students interested in a new tool anytime.

Then, almost suddenly we would begin to collect data that would be different.   Whether or not we call our borrowing of the demand schedule or your visiting us "interdisciplinary" things is a matter of semantics.   What does it matter where we get a new tool, whether we steal it from you or get it honestly?   If we can find it useful, good.

Now, if around that table we had not only you and some anthropologists, but also some policy people seeking something relevant in anthropology, economics, or the problems we talk about, and we get steered a little in their direction, we would have put all these things together and speeded up the evolution.   We would have thrown something constructive into the historical process that is going on anyway and helped it along.

BIERSTEDT: Just for fun I'd like to argue the reverse of some of Ed Lindblom's most stimulating points—to disagree with the first three and agree only with the fourth.

He says that one of the problems that we have in social science is a lack of adequate tools.   I think a case can be made, in sociology at least, for just the reverse.   Frequently we spend so much time improving the versatility of our tools that we are not paying sufficient attention to the subject matter to which they are applied. One of the criticisms of Coleman's paper today was that he is too much interested in regression coefficients, or at least as much interested in regression coefficients as he is in education.   It was the nineteenth-century German logician Lotze who expressed this best, I think, when he said that the constant whetting of an axe is apt to become a bit tedious if it isn't proposed to cut anything with it.   I think that we have sometimes done this.

I have myself had occasion to remark that the significance of our results in sociology tends to vary inversely with the precision of the methods employed.   As Robert Redfield put it in a very brilliant paper some years ago called "The Art of Social Science," we have learned to do very well a number of things that simply aren't worth doing.   We can do market research very well.   We can find out whether housewives want to buy cereals in red boxes or white boxes or blue boxes—that kind of thing.   But what do we know about the sociology of war?   Practically nothing.   We have a tendency in sociology, it seems to me, to ask only the questions for which methods have been developed, rather than to ask important questions and then try to develop the methods for answering them.   In other words, the methods have become the independent variable and the subject has become the dependent variable.   I'd like to turn the thing around.

I don't entirely disagree with Ed Lindblom——

LINDBLOM: May I object—to show that there is something in common between us?   You were just saying we are, in a sense, trapped by our tools.   We do what our tools permit us to do.

That means exactly what I said; we need better tools.

TAX: But the fusion would make a great difference because one can go on developing a tool way beyond its original function. One takes a new look at it in its primitive state and sees how he can change and use it.

BIERSTEDT: It's like the correlation coefficient to the fifteenth decimal point, or something of that kind.   That is what I had in mind.

HACKER: Suppose I put it to you that we can and should discourse on the causes of war, although the odds are great that our discourse will be not scientific.   Would it satisfy you if we gave more of our efforts to subjects you consider important, even though we ended up being more speculative than scientific?

BIERSTEDT: Very much so, although I would be disinclined to accept the dichotomy which I think is at the basis of your observation.   I would use all of the scientific resources that have been developed since the industrial revolution in sociology, at least all kinds of techniques, and try to invent new ones, as Ed Lindblom suggests.   But I would say that this would not exhaust the resources of scholarship in sociology.

I conceive of sociology, myself, as a humanistic discipline, not only a scientific one.   I would judge your essayistic approach in terms of the cogency of the argument. Let me give you a very important illustration, that is, Max Weber's thesis. I submit to you that no one knows whether it is true or false. We judge it in terms of its cogency. I, myself, happen to regard it as a remarkably cogent piece of reasoning, but I don't know whether or not it is true.

HACKER: A good beginning might be to encourage from graduate students more seminar papers which are simply essays rather than precise studies of minutia.

BIERSTEDT: Exactly. Exactly. I would certainly approve of that.

KARIEL: Don't call the others more precise, but differently precise.

BIERSTEDT: All right.

Ed says we have a passion for nomothetic propositions. But this is the way we have been brought up. We have all learned about the Southwestern School of neo-Kantianism, Rickert, Dilthey, and others, and this, we thought, was one of the things that was happening when Auguste Comte first invented the word "sociology." This, then, must be the goal. This must be our aspiration. We must have something such as Avogadro's law on the diffusion of gases, or Newton's law of gravitation, or even Gresham's law, or something of that kind, and it has been one of our greatest disappointments, as I mentioned yesterday, that we haven't achieved any of these yet except certain propositions that are so trivial——

LINDBLOM: Such an ideal is inappropriate for the study of man who is a learning animal. One thing you can be sure of is that every time the United States goes to war it fundamentally changes the causal explanation of how it could ever possibly get into another one.

BIERSTEDT: There is a certain difficulty there, with that point of view, and you raised it yourself. If we don't seek nomothetic propositions, then what kind should we seek?

LINDBLOM: That's what we need the new strategy for. I don't have the answer.

BIERSTEDT: And if the only alternative is a set of idiosyncratic propositions, then we are doing history, as you said. When we go into one war there is a change in the causal situation with respect to a succeeding war, and then we are writing history rather than doing science. I might have no objection to that.

LINDBLOM: The fact that you and I can't think now of a suitable alternative doesn't mean that there isn't any alternative. It means that we haven't been very wide awake, we haven't been looking. That is a real challenge to me.

BIERSTEDT: Yes, but the point I am making now is that logically there may be no alternative to the nomothetic proposition except an idiosyncratic one, and in that case we would be writing history.

LINDBLOM: As I understand it, the natural scientists are now breaking away from nomothetic propositions in principle, and they are finding some organic propositions that we might be interested in.

BIERSTEDT: Well, one final observation. I want to say that then we are insufficiently ambitious. I would like to see the social sciences attend to important problems, serious problems. I mentioned the problem of war, the problem of revolution. Whether or not we have any methods that are currently adequate for application to those subjects, I would like us to enlarge our vision in the social sciences.

GUETZKOW: May I suggest three ways in which our methods might be broadened to develop a capability to encompass such problems as those involved in revolution and war? First, let's drop our structures enthroning parsimony. Then, let's get down to the development of social sciences as a cumulative enterprise, abandoning dilettantism. Finally, let us admit we no longer can work alone—that by and large our efforts can be accelerated through the organization of ourselves into teams.

Gradually we can drop interest in precision for its own sake, as we cease to ape the physical sciences. So perhaps we are ready to drop the imperatives of parsimony. Of course, elegant, simple models are useful, but if they fail to predict with adequacy, neither the elitist nor the professional will be greatly disturbed by our willingness to add an extra parameter here or there. The sensitivities of those focusing on the esthetics of their models will be offended, but those who are integrating the social sciences with policy analysis will rest content, believing that the next round in the integration of the model will yield another step toward parsimony unobtainable at the moment.

Could it just be that we fail to be authoritative in our work because of the snobbery of the social science elite and the contempt with which policy analysts regard the playboys occupying the academic fun houses? The social scientists are trapped in their career schemes—they seldom can take the time to study the work of their colleagues, let alone build upon it, for fear of being labeled pedestrian. One gets promoted for brilliant ideas, but how often do our colleagues receive career rewards for integrations of the literature—for replication of studies? The policy analysts who are attempting to get on with the work find the contentiousness of the supersocial scientists a tedious exercise in ego-building, seldom conducive to the construction of integrated knowledge.

I would not "dispromote" members of Lindblom's elite. It's my hope that the structure of the disciplines and professions will soon be organized so as to reduce penalization of those concerned with integration.

BIERSTEDT: But we live in a culture that places so high a premium on originality.

GUETZKOW: Right. That's why I hit innovation in my comments on Professor Lindblom's essay. It's not always originality; it's often just "newness." And many times newness is a mere shift in jargon.

One of the reasons it is so difficult to be cumulative is that our bibliographic systems are lamentably antiquated. We have very few "data banks" for our facts. There are hardly any "theory banks" as yet in existence. We seldom use computers to retrieve more than concepts; we shuffle along with such pitiful devices as KWIC and KWOC (Key Words In Context and Key Words Out of Context). As information explodes, our human memories become even more inadequate to cope with the scholarly tasks we face.

My third addition to the Bierstedt list is the emphasis the social scientists place upon individualism, contrasting with the alacrity with which policy scientists take to working with teams. There's a narcissism which permeates the ethos of the super-elite, which is even evidenced in descriptions of the social sciences by

as balanced and humble a person as Professor Lindblom.   Yet if
we are to encompass large parts of the social scientists as we integrate them for problem-solving with the professionals, it seems
to me we cannot help but work through teams.   Such groups, it
would seem, might provide nets through which integrations of
policy and science can occur, when such rough Bierstedtian problems as revolution and war are tackled.

Andy says the elitists and professionals cannot do it, that we
possess little more than common sense.   But has he appraised
the products of brilliant talkers against the integrated teams,
working without the constraints of parsimony, building cumula-
tively?   Is he willing to grant teams tenure so they can consolidate their efforts?   Is he willing to assess the cumulative contributions made in eclectic terminology against the verbal flashes
which fit neatly between hard covers for the requirements involved
in a promotion?   Is he willing to study computer programs which
exhibit models without parsimony—or does the faculty committee crave products for quips as it seeks "fun" in intellectual life?

Instead of viewing the problems involved in the "Integration
of the Social Sciences through Policy Analysis" as insolvable just
because we—a conference composed largely of super-elitists—
were asked to address the "wrong" problem, why can't we tackle
sometime in the months ahead with a goodly number of professional analysts another formulation, namely, "Integrating Social
Science *with* Policy Analysis"?   After all, we have only our
preconceptions to lose!

KARIEL: I am still on Ed's quest for some candidates for his
list.   I can't help but note that we are talking about a wealth of
different things.   We are talking about tools.   We are also talking about concepts and models.

I want to use an additional term here because I think that the
kind of tools that Ed Lindblom is asking for are metaphors.
They are techniques for holding or grabbing, as if somebody said,
"Here, experience *this*," and managed it somehow, as metaphors
of course do.   Think of the notions that were originally intro-
duced; for example, the notion of "margin," which, of course, is
a metaphor derived from the larger context.   Or "disjointed incrementalism," whose metaphorical base is well disguised by the

difficulty of articulating the term. You know the terms. Another was "demand schedule," and so forth. Well, the question you are really raising is, What are the appropriate metaphors for social science? And I think it is really impossible to say, or for us to sit down here and to think, as poets do, of new metaphors. Within our various disciplines we systematically discriminate against metaphorical inventiveness. The system of education, and I don't mean just graduate education, but all the gradations that constitute the totality of our curriculum, is such as to make it really very, very difficult to carve out time in space within which to become metaphorically inventive. We are so fully driven to become absorbed by our own language that we are unaware of its metaphorical basis.

Now, I would think that the way out of this kind of predicament, if you conceive it as such, is to become conscious of the metaphorical basis of our respective disciplines. First of all we must become aware of the metaphors that direct our work—such metaphors as "body politic," which is, after all, still a useful tool insofar as it enables us to talk of the head of state and to be reminded of the fact that we do not discuss, say, sexual organs or erotic zones of the body politic. (Laughter) Once we become more aware of the metaphorical character of the respective disciplines, of our tools for holding experiences, I think it may be possible to become more free to invent new ones or to promote such inventiveness.

That brings up the question I raised much earlier, which I think ought to be put on the agenda for a social science; that is, What are the conditions for creativity? We do know something about these conditions, but we are reluctant to implement that knowledge, partially because the implementation of such knowledge is not likely to be elite-serving. So we restrain ourselves for the benefit of prevailing balances of interest.

LANE: I want to deal less with ideas and more with institutions and implementation, so let me talk a little bit about that. This is to implement, then, whatever agreement we have, if any, on both the policy analysis question and the integration of the social sciences.

Gradually it dawned on me that in talking about ideas we are often talking about the holders of ideas, that is to say, manpower. So a recurring theme that has come up here is, Who is going to do what, and what are the career lines? This is a point that Sol Tax made along with McCord and some others. This also implies allocation of time, which came out when Schelling was talking about my suggestion for careers and for allocation of manpower. He said that the same person can do two different things at different times, so some systematic thinking about allocation of time and people is important.

I just observed on the policy analysis question that the pressure for placing our Ph.D.'s is making us much more interested in government careers. Very few political scientists go into government, but now we are concerned about it. We have to place them, and because of this we have to find a new advantage in governmental careers. I noticed in the National Register between 1968 and 1970 there was a very small number of political scientists going into goverment, that is to say, not Federal government, but state and local. However, this small number represents a doubling for that two years. So my guess is that by looking at careers, people, and allocation of time, we will have another way of grappling with some portions of this.

The question of communications has come up. It is an enormously important thing—the interstructure really of a discipline or a set of disciplines. We need better cross uses of abstracting services and bibliographic tools, data archives, and theory archives, so that information generated by one discipline is available to another, or perhaps better still, joint bibliographical tools, abstracting services, and journals for the intersections that we decide upon for two or more social sciences. This deserves some attention. The initiation, creation, and marketing of journals is an interesting thing, and it turns out that the marketplace is often dysfunctional for the way in which ideas should be communicated.

There isn't that much to be said about education except that we have talked about several kinds of things. One is the joint course. Another is the program. Another is the degree. Harvard has given a degree in political economy for some time. With the new policy institutes my guess is that there will be some joint degrees. They need to be carefully devised, which isn't easy to do. This, of course, is also related to the careers question. The proliferation of these institutes is interesting. Much less research, I think, will go on now in departments and much more in institutes, partly for the reason that individualized research is too small for the magnitude of the problems and partly because the institute is a device for facilitating team research, particularly interdisciplinary research.

This brings me to the fourth element here. I have talked about manpower, communications, and education. The fourth is resources, which really is different now when we have such major resources as the National Science Foundation and the National Institute of Mental Health. Here I think that Sol Tax's argument earlier that now the National Science Foundation is interested in interdisciplinary research—they haven't done it very well, but they have set up programs, and this is not generated out of nothing—reflects the same kinds of interests that have produced this conference.

The National Institute of Mental Health is now concerned with new programs, those combining training and research. These were two separate divisions, and now they want to combine them. They are also a source of educational programs, including fellowships and post-doctoral fellowships.

McCORD: It seems to me there are two institutional arrangements that already exist, one of which seems to be an enormous success. The other one I don't know enough about to say whether it is successful. I am thinking, on the one hand, of the "think tank" at Stanford which, without actually using team research, at least is an institutional way of bringing together some forty diverse people who, in the process of their association, not only have a delightful life but experience a stimulating exchange of ideas. There are unexpected combinations that occur.

The other institutional arrangement I was thinking of is the Santa Cruz College system, which, as I understand it, has created separate colleges of 250 students organized around some central theme, so that one college is more or less devoted to biology, another one is more or less devoted to the study of poverty, and so on. This system doesn't exclude the students from gaining any knowledge of literature or other subjects, but it does serve as a focus for the students and faculties at each college, which, in effect, forces them to integrate various fields.

CHARLESWORTH: Gentlemen, on behalf of the Academy, I want to thank you for your trouble in coming here, for the time devoted to the preparation of your papers, and for the earnestness of your participation. I anticipate, on the basis of previous experience with monographs, that this one will have a wide impact. I anticipate that it will be widely discussed in class and used as reading matter and will, in the end, have fully justified our work here in making this conference a success.

WITHDRAWN
COLLEGE OF ST. THOMAS LIBRARY
Libraries

SEP 2 2 1977	DATE DUE		
	RESERVE		
		Dr. Porter	
		MAY 2 1 1985	

198759

The American Academy of Political and Social Science

3937 Chestnut Street   Philadelphia, Pennsylvania 19104

Board of Directors

NORMAN D. PALMER
HOWARD C. PETERSEN
WALTER M. PHILLIPS
PAUL R. ANDERSON
KARL R. BOPP
ELMER B. STAATS

MARVIN E. WOLFGANG
LEE BENSON
A. LEON HIGGINBOTHAM, JR.
RICHARD D. LAMBERT
R. JEAN BROWNLEE
COVEY T. OLIVER

Officers

President
MARVIN E. WOLFGANG

JAMES C. CHARLESWORTH, *President Emeritus*

Vice-Presidents
RICHARD D. LAMBERT, *First Vice-President*

JOSEPH S. CLARK   CLARK KERR

STEPHEN B. SWEENEY, *First Vice-President Emeritus*

Secretary	Treasurer	Counsel
NORMAN D. PALMER	HOWARD C. PETERSEN	HENRY W. SAWYER, III

Editors, THE ANNALS

RICHARD D. LAMBERT, *Editor*   ALAN W. HESTON, *Assistant Editor*

THORSTEN SELLIN, *Editor Emeritus*

Business Manager
INGEBORG HESSLER

Origin and Purpose. The Academy was organized December 14, 1889, to promote the progress of political and social science, especially through publications and meetings. The Academy does not take sides in controverted questions, but seeks to gather and present reliable information to assist the public in forming an intelligent and accurate judgment.

Meetings. The Academy holds an annual meeting in the spring extending over two full days.

Publications. THE ANNALS is the bimonthly publication of The Academy. Each issue contains articles on some prominent social or political problem, written at the invitation of the editors. Also, monographs are published from time to time, numbers of which are distributed to pertinent professional organizations. These volumes constitute important reference works on the topics with which they deal, and they are extensively cited by authorities throughout the United States and abroad. The papers presented at the meetings of The Academy are included in THE ANNALS.

Membership. Each member of The Academy receives THE ANNALS and may attend the meetings of The Academy. Annual dues are $12.00 (for clothbound copies $16.00 per year). A life membership is $500. All payments are to be made in United States dollars.

Libraries and other institutions may receive THE ANNALS paperbound at a cost of $12.00 per year, or clothbound at $16.00 per year.

Single copies of THE ANNALS may be obtained by nonmembers of The Academy for $3.00 ($4.00 clothbound) and by members for $2.50 ($3.50 clothbound). A discount to members of 5 per cent is allowed on orders for 10 to 24 copies of any one issue, and of 10 per cent on orders for 25 or more copies. These discounts apply only when orders are placed directly with The Academy and not through agencies. The price to all bookstores and to all dealers is $3.00 per copy less 20 per cent, with no quantity discount. It is urged that payment be sent with each order. This will save the buyer the transportation charge and save The Academy the cost of carrying accounts and sending statements. Monographs may be purchased for $2.00, with proportionate discounts.

All correspondence concerning The Academy or THE ANNALS should be addressed to the Academy offices, 3937 Chestnut Street, Philadelphia, Pa. 19104.